Video Game Design

by Alexia Mandeville

A Wiley Brand

Video Game Design For Dummies®

Published by: **John Wiley & Sons, Inc.**, 111 River Street, Hoboken, NJ 07030-5774, www.wiley.com

Contents at a Glance

Table of Contents

Introduction

Making a video game may seem like magic, but it's just a series of practical processes, resourcefulness, and tech skills that lead to an end result: a published game.

This book is meant to reduce any confusion or ambiguity you may have around game design and provide the practical steps to making a game.

About This Book

If you're curious about how games are made, this book will help demystify the role of a game designer. Drawing from my experience on both large and small teams, I focus on examples from my smaller projects, which are especially relevant for hobbyists and indie developers creating their own games, rather than those working within massive 100-person teams.

This book is packed with tips, real-world examples, and practical advice, making it perfect for beginners, indie creators, or anyone who's ever wondered how to make a game and about the work that goes into it.

I organize the content into seven parts:

Part 1: Getting Started with Game Design. I cover what game design is, why it matters, and how to structure your design workflow. Then I explore some paths to becoming a game designer, what skills you'll need for game design, and how to get there.

Part 2: Exploring Game Design Elements. Here I cover some of the most widely used tools for making games (including many free or low-cost ones) and some tips for managing your project. Then I get into the meat of it, including game mechanics, game systems, story, art, and user experience.

Part 3: Balancing Your Game. I cover what balancing a game means, as well as how to do so, including some processes for playtesting and collecting feedback.

Part 4: Designing Your Own Game. Here's the fun part! All the steps you need to bring your own game to life starting from a concept. This book wouldn't be complete without covering how to finish your game as well, one of the notoriously hard parts of the project.

Part 5: Publishing and Marketing Your Game. After you've made a game, it's important to know how to find people to play your game. This part covers the top places where you can distribute your game and provides some tips and tricks I've learned from distributing my own games and games I've worked on.

Part 6: The Part of Tens. You can get into game design in many ways. This part includes ten game designers and their own paths to working on games, to provide examples of different routes you can take in the industry. I also provide a list of resources, including community websites, tools, videos, and more.

Glossary. I cover some of the terms I use in this book and common terms you may find in the business of making games.

I'm excited to provide you with this info in the *For Dummies* series because making a game has quite a few parts, and it can be pretty technically complex. As a game designer you may need a wide variety of skills. This For Dummies book provides a modular, easy-to-reference guide for making games, with many examples of my processes with the thought process behind them. The idea of making a game can be daunting, but learning about it shouldn't be!

Foolish Assumptions

If you're reading this book, I assume that you're a hobbyist, student, beginner, or maybe even an indie looking to find more information on how other games came to be from another indie developer. I expect readers to be interested in the technical knowledge of making games, but maybe not technically proficient just yet. You may be dabbling in a side project and need some more support. A lot of this book is about the systems engineering that goes into design, but not actual programming engineering or coding.

Icons Used in This Book

Throughout this book, icons in the margins highlight certain types of valuable information that call out for your attention. Here are the icons you'll encounter and a brief description of each.

TIP

Marks tips and shortcuts that you can use to make your design process easier.

REMEMBER

Highlights information that's especially important for you to know.

TECHNICAL STUFF

Denotes bits of information that are more technical in nature but which can generally help deepen your understanding of a topic.

WARNING

Tells you to watch out! It marks important information that may save you headaches and heartache down the line.

Beyond the Book

In addition to the abundance of information and guidance related to video game design that I provide in this book, you can find even more help and information online. Check out this book's online Cheat Sheet: Just go to www.dummies.com and search for "Video Game Design For Dummies Cheat Sheet."

1

Getting Started with Game Design

Dig into (just a little) history behind game development and how it became more and more accessible to many different people throughout the years.

Learn what game design is and what it looks like. Understand the importance of game design in creating games that players love to play.

Explore the phases of the game design process, what it means to be a game designer, and how to be intentional in your designs.

Discover how to become a game designer and develop a designer's mind and the tools and skills you'll need to do so.

IN THIS CHAPTER

» Learning what game design is

» Thinking like a game designer

» Overviewing how game design became more accessible

» Leaning into the fun

» Making your first game

Chapter **1**

Introducing the Art of Game Design

'm so excited for you to dive into this book, break down the mysteries of game design, and maybe even start working on your own game. Maybe you're just getting started or maybe you're already deep into a project. Either way, this chapter can help you understand what game design really is, how it's evolved, and how you can use it to design your games.

Discovering What Game Design Is

When I think back to all the work I've done on games and the work I see my colleagues doing, it's clear that being a game designer means wearing a lot of hats. Sure, most jobs require a mix of skills, but a game designer is kind of like the general manager in construction. You need to know a little bit about a lot of different things. And the things you need to know differ from genre to genre. Because every genre has its unique elements, many game designers specialize in one area, like level design or progression, and build their expertise from there.

Game design is making a thousand little decisions that add up to one amazing experience, like the following:

>> Tweaking how many items drop from a chest

>> Deciding why some items are rare and making them feel special and hard to get

>> Designing levels that guide players without them realizing they're being guided

>> Balancing abilities so that no one character or strategy dominates the game

>> Writing lore that makes players care about the world and its characters

>> Mapping out progression systems that keep players coming back for "just one more level"

>> Deciding how fast a character runs and how high they jump

>> Choosing the perfect sound effect for picking up a coin

>> Testing and re-testing mechanics until they feel "just right"

>> Creating tutorials that teach without boring or frustrating players

>> Ensuring that the game is accessible so everyone can play and enjoy it

>> Crafting choices that make players stop and think about the consequences

REMEMBER

When someone takes on the role of a game designer, they are responsible for orchestrating all these decisions, building frameworks to guide them, and crafting systems that streamline the decision-making process. See Chapter 4 for more about what it takes to become a game designer.

Looking at a Brief History of Game Design

I frame this section around notable moments in history when game design and development became more accessible and how these changes shaped the way we make and play games, working back from today. I stick to the last 30ish years or so, just because the internet became mainstream and available in many U.S. households in that time frame. Ever since then, games have been growing at an exponential rate.

As of 2025, it's incredibly simple to get started in game design. You can download game engines like Unity, Unreal Engine, or Godot for free access resources like free asset libraries, and learn new skills through platforms like YouTube.

Software like Blender (a free tool for 3-D modeling) or Procreate (for digital art) allows creators to produce their own assets, and platforms like Itch.io let anyone publish games for free, often within minutes. And once you publish a game, social media lets you promote it to people who may want to play it. The barriers to entry for game design today are time, practice, and dedication rather than expensive tools or access to industry secrets and publishers.

The result is an explosion of creativity and people who publish games:

>> More than 89,000 games were published on Steam as of January 2025.

>> Thousands of genres and user-generated tags describe a diverse array of experiences, from "frog detective mysteries" to "farming horror simulators."

The democratization of tools and knowledge enables everyone to shape the industry, instead of a select few dictating what games are. Just like you can take many different paths to make a game, you also can define what a game is in many different ways. At the time that I'm writing this, the industry is having a difficult time. Many companies are doing layoffs, and larger projects are having trouble getting funded. But making games on your own and sending them off into the world has never been more accessible.

Time to go back in time, starting with 2016:

>> **2016:** *Pokémon GO* was released, which was a global hit. This game took advantage of what mobile phones have to offer like most other games hadn't: portability to explore the world and their camera. Ingress, the game made by Niantic prior to *Pokémon GO,* has done this as well, but adding in Pokémon was lightning in a bottle for Niantic. For me, *Pokémon GO* inspired me to focus my graduate work on augmented reality (AR) and map-based mobile gaming. I eventually got to work with some of the people who made the first version of *Pokémon GO* when I designed *Peridot* at Niantic, a fortunate time in my career.

>> **2014:** Facebook (now Meta) acquired Oculus, making VR a mainstream focus for tech and gaming. This acquisition has since really changed the VR landscape! For example, I was in a Target the other day and walked past an aisle end cap holding new Quests for sale. You never would have seen that in 2014. Alongside their hardware efforts, tools like Horizon Worlds and other accessible VR platforms are making it easier for smaller teams to experiment with VR and AR game design with a built-in audience.

>> **2013:** The launch of the PS4 and Xbox One gave indie developers easier access to console publishing thanks to digital storefronts like the PlayStation Store and Xbox Live Arcade. However, to this day, some friction exists in publishing

on consoles due to factors such as platform-specific certification processes, higher development costs for console-ready builds, and strict licensing agreements. Additionally, console publishers often require developers to secure development kits, which can be expensive or difficult for people to access.

>> **2010s:** Kickstarter, a crowdsourcing platform for new products, took off. This enabled board game designers and video game designers to post their game online and get some funding to work on their game. Big games like *Cards Against Humanity* came from Kickstarter. And it wasn't until 2012 that Oculus launched its first Kickstarter for the Oculus Rift, sparking widespread interest in virtual reality (VR) gaming.

>> **2009:** People became more aware that a small team or even a solo developer could release something that could become huge when they saw *Minecraft*. The developer, Notch, became a great example of a solo developer who achieved global success with a release on the internet.

>> **2007:** The launch of the iPhone and the App Store introduced a new era of mobile gaming. It wasn't until 2009 that some mobile games become phenomena like *Angry Birds* and *Fruit Ninja*. Mobile phones also introduced the free-to-play (F2P) model, allowing developers to monetize games through in-app purchases and ads, which is now big business.

Also in 2007, Facebook opened its platform to developers, leading to the rise of social games like *FarmVille* (2009) and *Mafia Wars* by Zynga. These games pioneered new ways of engaging players through social mechanics and microtransactions.

>> **2003:** Valve did something really big and launched Steam. This made it easier for indies to release their games alongside all the larger studios out there. Back in those days, there were way fewer games being published on Steam. A year after release in 2004, only 65 games were published. But, obviously, that took off between then and now!

>> **1990s:** Last, but certainly not least, the internet became accessible to lots of households in the United States. Dial-up became the standard for home internet connections, using telephone lines to connect to the internet. This enabled games to be created and shared with people outside of your household without a publisher. Dial-up began to decline in the 2000s with broadband internet, but I'll never forget all the times my friends were over at my house playing some game we found on the internet, hogging the phone line from my parents.

Trekking back to today, top genres of games include open-world role playing games like *The Witcher* and cozy games like *Stardew Valley.* There's been a rise in more niche genres in the last few years such as narrative-driven indie games like *Disco Elysium,* and experimental puzzle games like *Gorogoa.*

In the future, and with technology like AI and social platforms progressing, we can look forward to more dynamic gameplay, more cross-platform experiences, and better tools to empower both game creators and players/streamers.

TIP

You can learn a lot from the history of games and game development. I like to work on the beginning bits of a game and get it off the ground, so understanding how other teams started and what games looked like in the early part of their life has helped me set expectations for development and scope. Games like *World of Warcraft* (WoW) may be huge now, but when they first launched, they all had design problems (like loot that spawns on a world basis instead of on a player-to-player basis). The trick is that these problems aren't game blocking enough to keep players from progressing and enjoying the core of the gameplay.

Leaning Into the Fun

Plenty of frameworks are available for deciding what goes into a piece of software or a game, but I'm about to say the quiet part out loud: Frameworks aren't always the best way to create a truly fun game. I think the reason that many hit indie games these days were made by smaller or solo teams is that smaller teams have less red tape, which fosters creativity. A lot of the biggest hits were initially made by small teams. *Take Grand Theft Auto* for example; the initial team that worked on the first playable version was made up of 11ish people.

Instead of designing with strict rules or setting up red tape for yourself, making fun the priority should be your guiding principle when deciding which features to include. For every feature or concept you're considering, ask yourself:

>> **Does it fit the game?** Does it align with the theme or the core principles you've established? If not, shelve that feature or concept for later use (we call that "throwing it in the backlog" in the industry).

>> **Is the team (or are you) excited about it?** If the energy and excitement are there, it's likely worth exploring. Developers who are excited about something will put their heart into the design and implementation.

I almost added, "Do we have the skills to make it?" But here's the thing — many great games were made by people who didn't have the skills when they started.

They learned as they went, driven by their excitement. Sometimes, the best features come from diving into the unknown because you're genuinely thrilled about making them happen.

TIP

For every milestone I hit in my designs, I like to take a step back and assess where I can trim extra features to focus the game's design and what the most fun part of the game is and why.

Preparing to Think Systematically

A game designer is holding a lot of interconnected information in their mind. They need an understanding of how the game's systems (the rules, data, and calculations that make the game tick) work on their own and how they interact with each other. If you want to know more about game systems, check out Chapter 7. Every mechanic, feature, and interaction is part of a web of cause and effect, connected by feedback loops that shape the player's experience.

Here's what a game designer should think about when making a game (learn more about what a game designer does in Chapter 4):

>> The core loop and how all the other systems on top of it feed into it to make it rewarding to repeat over and over again

>> How systems can be broken down into smaller, more manageable systems

>> How variables impact the systems so that the systems are fair, challenging, and enjoyable

>> Designing systems for emergent gameplay and unexpected behaviors

>> Creating feedback for player's actions using visual, auditory, or gameplay cues to let players know how their actions impact the gameplay

Systems that you may end up having to design may include

>> Balancing resources so that players don't have a million old boots and not enough wood for what they want to build

>> A procedural system to spawn a new creature with a unique body, tail, and color every time

>> A progression system to level up a character as they complete quests

Diving Into the Game Designer's Mind

As a game designer, I'm often thinking about how to make patterns apparent in gameplay to teach players what to look out for in my games. I'm also thinking about how to lean into the theme and feeling of the game and how to make sure I think of features I have the skills to create. These are the top things that shape the way I design.

To get a sense of this in a practical way, in a branching narrative I published called *Chief Emoji Officer* (see Figure 1-1), my team and I wrote a big story in which players can make choices and explore the outcomes. In the game, players communicate using only emojis to navigate office politics, climb the corporate ladder, and make decisions that shape their career. But this wasn't enough for us and this game, and we needed to think about how to create a core loop and really drive home the satirical mood of the experience.

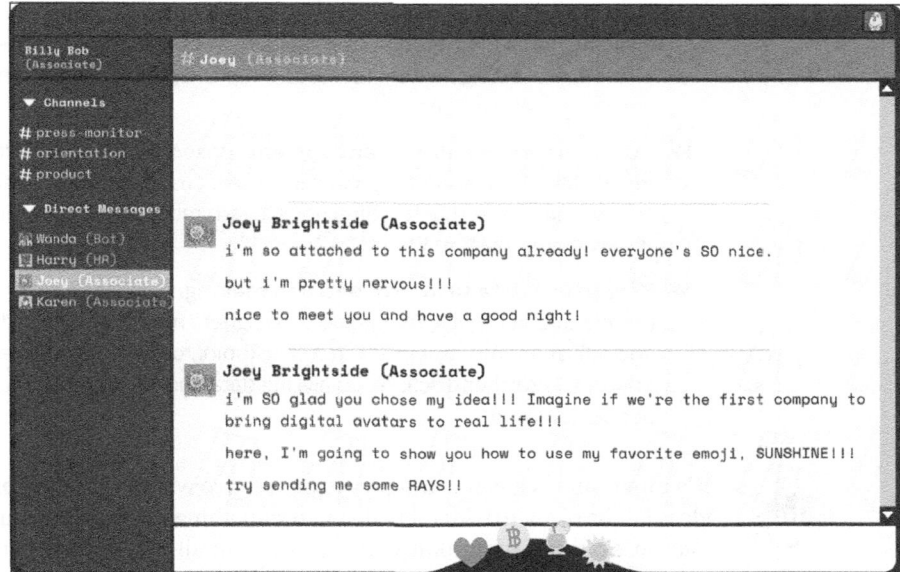

FIGURE 1-1: A screenshot of *Chief Emoji Officer* (the desktop version on Steam).

So, we broke up this story into chapters, which helped us do the following:

>> **Create a pattern for players.** There was a summary and evaluation at the end of every chapter of the choices, kind of like a score.

>> **Increase the parody.** We used a system that was like an employee evaluation, aligning with our corporate satire theme.

>> **Create a sense of progression.** As players moved from chapter to chapter, they discovered more unlockable content.

>> **Write the story more quickly.** We didn't risk an overwrite of each other's work (we worked on separate chapters), resulting in less time to finish a chapter.

Game designers are thinking about everything from the feel of the tap of a button to how a story unfolds to reveal a big twist. My favorite game designers have been analytical, scrappy, and ready to build something to test their ideas.

They're often thinking about

>> **How to prototype an idea to experiment and try it out it quickly.** This may mean that you sketch something on paper, make a spreadsheet to test some game data, or even build something in a game engine. Learn more about prototyping in Chapter 4.

>> **How players will perceive something and how it'll make them feel.** For example, will a bright red button make players feel urgency? Does the sound effect for collecting an item feel satisfying? Chapter 10 covers creating an engaging user experience.

>> **How to improve features and systems based on feedback from playtesting.** If players consistently get lost in a level, designers may tweak the environment to add better directions. Learn more about collecting and reviewing feedback in Chapter 12.

>> **How to use data to inform decision making.** If analytics show that most players quit at Level 5, for example, designers may analyze the difficulty curve and adjust enemy strength, add a checkpoint, or improve tutorial clarity. Chapter 12 further discusses analyzing data and why it's important to decision making.

REMEMBER

It's important as a game designer to be creative while also being practical. Have big ideas but be ready to trim them down to something more realistic and feasible. There may possibly be a compromise to that online-multiplayer game you want to make as your first game and something that you'll be able to complete in a few months.

Constructing Your First Game

I'm excited for you to paw through this book and learn some theory and lots of practical knowledge on how to make games. This book may expose you to some resources you didn't know about before and start you in a direction toward whatever specific niche of game you're interested in making.

This book focuses on smaller teams and solo developers who want to make their first game. I include information from larger teams that I've been on, but I had the most fun and got to experiment the most on a team of two, Bodeville, an independent game studio I cofounded with a friend.

Chapter 3 provides an overview of the game design process, and Chapter 14 takes a deeper dive into that process. If you're at the very beginning of your game-making journey, however, you can take these steps to get started:

1. **Do your research.**

   Check out similar games in the genre you're looking to make. Throughout the book, I often recommend that you research other games, but I dive into it in some detail in Chapter 4, which covers what you need to know to become a game designer.

2. **Make a prototype.**

   This can be in a game engine like Unity, in a spreadsheet, or maybe even using paper on a table. Having a prototype allows you to fully explore the viability of your concepts. Chapter 5 covers tools and software; Chapter 13 covers creating and refining your concept.

3. **Playtest it with your friends or peers.**

   Testing it early will get you quick feedback to let you know what's working and what can be improved. Chapter 12 has details about this very important part of the process.

Maybe you have already started your game design journey and are looking for insight for whatever point you're at. If one of the following points describes you, then check out the corresponding chapter to help you with that phase:

» **You have an idea for a game that you're really excited about and want to flesh out the story:** Story and characters are important! Players will make an emotional connection to your game if you have a great story; check out Chapter 8 for details about developing a story for your game that delivers a unique experience for players.

» **You've already started developing your concept in a game engine and you're almost finished but hitting some roadblocks.** Maybe you're struggling with scope, polish, or final tweaks. Chapter 15 covers strategies for getting to the finish line, prioritizing features, and managing your development process efficiently.

» **You have a game almost finished but need tips on publishing and marketing.** Once the game is built, you need people to play it! Chapter 16 dives into marketing strategies, including how to promote your game and build an audience. For details on publishing options, like self-publishing or working with a publisher, check out Chapter 17.

>> **You have a game concept but don't know what tools to use to get started.** Choosing the right tools can be overwhelming, but Chapter 5 breaks down different game engines, design tools, and software options to help you get started. The most important thing is just to get started!

REMEMBER

Have an open mind! Some things may not turn out like you expected them to, and they may turn out even better if you have an open mind to feedback and iteration.

TIP

When in doubt, make a prototype!

Chapter **2**

Knowing Why Game Design Matters

G ame design is the art of taking a bunch of random features and making them actually work together. Without it, you just have a mess of different features with no real connection. A leaderboard here, some achievements there, maybe a points system thrown in for good measure.

This chapter shows how game design holds everything together. I cover why features need to work with each other (not just exist in the same game), how to make systems feel meaningful, and why understanding what motivates players makes all the difference.

Game Design Is the Glue of Games

Game design as a practice is the art of gluing a bunch of features together to make something cohesive that has meaning. To do this, you'll want to define the rules, mechanics, objectives, and generally why a feature or thing in the game exists.

When a designer (or just anyone dedicated to focusing on design) isn't present in a project, I've seen it turn out the same way every time: A bunch of different features are thrown together that don't work well together. Having been hired as an early/founding designer quite a few times, I've seen it often. But the point of hiring a designer is to have someone to focus on making the mess of features have meaning and exist cohesively and deliver a fantasy to the player. Anyone can do it; it's just about having the dedication to focus on it and the willpower to make hard decisions and cut anything meaningless from the experience.

Game design isn't about how well you can talk about how these things are glued together. *Game design* is the act of designing systems that work together by creating patterns, defining how interactions work, creating charts, and writing out content in spreadsheets, among many other design tasks. The act of designing also means finding the right conceit or fantasy and making sure all the features work within this conceit for the user. The designer's job is to add meaning to all these features so that the user is never taken out of the fantasy or the world you're creating.

Imagine a piece of software that has the following features:

>> A leaderboard to show players who did well

>> Achievements to reward certain actions

>> A points system to measure success

Individually, these may seem like great features, but without a connection between them, they don't add up to much. It's the way these features are connected that makes the software meaningful, useful, and cohesive. Instead of just thinking about each feature in isolation, consider how they work together to create a better experience:

>> Why the leaderboard motivates players to continue playing

>> Why certain actions grant achievements

>> Why players want to score points

Next to consider is what falls within a feature to make it work:

>> Does the leaderboard refresh weekly to give everyone a fair shot, or does it track lifetime scores?

>> Do achievements reward discovery or encourage perfecting a skill?

>> Can players track their points, and how do they understand how they contribute to their position on the leaderboard?

To design how these things work together, you'll need to map out how they work by creating the following:

>> A diagram or chart to define how the leaderboard should behave, like what causes it to refresh

>> A list and categorization of achievements and their content

>> A spreadsheet of how many points players can collect over time and from which actions

There's no one perfect way to glue all the elements of your experience together, and no one will be able to tell you the perfect solution to whatever problem you're facing when you're designing something. It all depends! It depends on the choices you've made as a developer up until whatever problem you're trying to solve. It depends on the elements and constraints that exist within your game and the technology you're using to make it.

Many people have given me feedback on my games over the years, pointed out potential solutions, or said "it would have been great if you added x." But they weren't there when it was made, and they don't know the trade-offs or constraints that were present while it was being designed. Your special concoction of glue is unique to your creation. That's what game design is.

TIP

I say the word *meaningful* often in this book. When I say meaningful, I mean that a thing like a player's choice or a developer's choice can be interpreted, potentially has a pattern, and has an obvious reason for existing. So, for example, imagine you're a developer and you added flying to your game. To make flying meaningful, you'd need to use flying for something in that experience. Maybe to reach a high-up place, skip traffic, or to combat an enemy. Without a reason to fly, you don't need the feature.

Looking at Examples of Game Design

To see how game design acts as the glue that holds games together, I'm highlighting the following games that have features coming together to create a cohesive experience:

>> **Tetris:** The "glue" in *Tetris* is the way speed, spatial reasoning, and scoring interlock to create a satisfying, challenging experience. At first glance, *Tetris* is a straightforward game. The blocks fall, and then you fit them together to clear lines. Blocks fall at an increasing speed, creating pressure. Simple

controls allow for focus on strategy rather than execution. Clearing lines and scoring points are the primary goals, but the real hook is the increasing challenge as the pace picks up.

>> **Dark Souls:** A game known for being difficult, but the challenge is meaningful. The difficulty feels fair because every death teaches players something, making each victory hard-earned and satisfying.

>> **Portal:** *Portal's* glue is between the storytelling and gameplay, where every element serves player's progress and deepens the game world. The portal gun allows players to be creative and "think with portals."

TIP

When I'm stuck trying to make a feature or system work with other systems and have meaning, I typically look at what other games in the genre are doing and "cut the fat." If you've got a bunch of features, try to focus on just one, make it work really well, and remove some of the extra stuff.

Understanding Player Motivations

People play games because they're motivated by the systems and goals they interact with. Maybe it's the thrill of exploration, the satisfaction of achievement, or the joy of mastery. As a designer, part of your role is training players to understand how the game rewards them and when they'll encounter punishment or friction in the gameplay.

TIP

When you're solving problems in game development, it can be easy to lose sight of putting player motivations at the forefront of the design. To keep the proper perspective, step back every now and then and look at how your systems work together to integrate levers used to keep players motivated.

To create a motivating experience, you'll want to include the following:

>> **A long-term goal:** This enables players to know where they're going and have something to look forward to. For example, completing the main storyline in a role-playing game or unlocking a cool item after hours of gameplay.

>> **A short-term goal:** This helps players feel accomplished while progressing toward the bigger picture. For example, finishing a quest, collecting resources, or leveling up a character.

>> **Rewards!** Nothing like a nice treat or a carrot dangle to get you to do something. For example, completing a difficult puzzle may unlock a hidden area or rare item, making the effort feel worthwhile.

>> **Punishment or friction:** A little challenge makes the rewards even sweeter. For example, dying when falling off a platform forces players to think more about what jumps they'll take.

And these concepts aren't just for games! You may notice that your company's career ladder has levels (the paycheck is the short-term goal), and your next promotion is being dangled right in front of you. Friction? Oh, that's just your manager telling you that you're not promoted this half, but you'll get it next time!

Psychological aspects of gaming

In this section, I get a little more cerebral and dive into the psychological principles within the more mechanical concepts that I discuss in the previous sections. Part of your role as a game designer is to *condition* the player. That is, you're training the player how to play your game by rewarding them when they do something right and punishing them when they do something . . . not quite right.

One of the systems in our game Grift punished players for chatting with a non-playable character if they didn't have enough trust points. If they chatted three times, they were blocked by that character. We spent time tweaking how we signaled this to players and ultimately had the character threaten to block the player, when it became a stronger verbal threat with every passing chat. We relied on societal norms (at least in the United States) for this. For example:

1. First chat: "I don't think I trust you enough to tell you about that."

2. Second chat: "You've already asked me that, don't do it again, or else."

3. Third chat: "I'm blocking you, fool."

But maybe if the players had trust with the character and chatted with them, they would get a monetary reward. The concept of this learning process that uses rewards and punishments to change player's behaviors is called *operant conditioning*. It's associated with behavioralists Edward L. Thorndike and B. F. Skinner, who challenged various animals with puzzles or patterns and observed how they learned to overcome the challenge. So, no matter your player's species, this concept plays a huge role in influencing how players interact with your game and what keeps them coming back.

Rewards motivate players by reinforcing actions, making them more likely to repeat behaviors that lead to something beneficial. Different types of rewards include

>> **Extrinsic rewards:** These are tangible incentives like coins, power-ups, new skins, or loot boxes. For example, completing a quest earns gold or a shiny gear upgrade.

>> **Intrinsic rewards:** The satisfaction that comes from personal achievement or mastery. For example, the pride of solving a difficult puzzle or nailing a tricky platforming sequence.

>> **Social rewards:** Recognition or interaction with others, such as leaderboard rankings, community praise, or a belly laugh from a joke that landed better than you would have thought.

Punishment discourages actions or choices that hinder the game flow. They don't necessarily have to feel harsh, but they should encourage learning or better play and can be either positive or negative:

>> **Positive punishments:** Do something wrong, and the game adds something unpleasant to discourage you from doing it again. In *Elden Ring*, attacking a helpful NPC turns them into a deadly enemy.

>> **Negative punishments:** Mess up, and the game takes away something you like. It's a bummer, but it teaches you to play smarter. In *Animal Crossing*, if you neglect your town, your favorite villagers might pack their bags and leave.

REMEMBER

Rewards and punishments are most effective when delivered quickly, with positive or negative reinforcement the player can understand.

TIP

Think about the pace of rewards and punishment when you're designing a game. Give players rewards after every set action (like killing a boss) so they know when it's coming. Throw in some random rewards, too, to keep things surprising. Mix it up!

Although operant conditioning focuses on voluntary, conscious behaviors that are influenced and shaped by their consequences, *respondent conditioning* refers to learning through involuntary, reflexive responses triggered by a stimulus. You don't have to learn these behaviors. This could be something like the following:

>> Pulling your hand back from a hot stove

>> Jerking your leg when the doctor taps on your knee

>> A low health sound making you feel a sense of urgency

>> Responding to the rhythm of a beat game

TIP

A great flow for conditioning players is to show them how to do something, let them try it, reward them for good behaviors, and set them back for poor behaviors.

Types of player motivation

Motivation in games comes in two flavors: intrinsic and extrinsic. One comes from the heart, and the other comes from all the shiny stuff you can collect.

Intrinsic motivation is powered by what the player enjoys or is interested in. Players with intrinsic motivation play because they genuinely enjoy the activity. Intrinsic motivation is about

>> **What drives them:** Interests, values, and that inner spark.

>> **Why they stick around:** The activity itself is the reward, even if they're not making progress.

>> **Example:** A player may keep exploring every nook and cranny of an open-world game just because they're curious, not because they're trying to win.

Extrinsic motivation is powered by outside factors. Players with extrinsic motivation want rewards ($$$), recognition, or a sweet pat on the back for their efforts. Extrinsic motivation is about

>> **What drives them:** The loot, the badges, the leaderboard glory.

>> **Why they keep going:** They want the rewards, achievements, or praise that comes with success.

>> **Example:** Grinding levels in an RPG to get that flaming sword or aiming for 100 percent achievement completion.

TIP

Great games tap into both types of motivation. They give players the freedom to enjoy the experience just for the fun of it, while also dangling some tasty rewards to keep them moving forward.

Creating Meaningful Experiences

Games don't always have to be fun in the traditional sense. They can be engaging by being meaningful. Having meaning is particularly important in a manufactured game because as players, we're trying to find patterns and make predictions. Games are so great because they're in a controlled environment. In a world in which most of the things that happen to us are by chance and out of our control, this can be a nice escape.

Meaning in games can take many forms, such as

>> **Having a lot of choice and agency:** This means players have the freedom to make decisions that impact the game world, their character, or the story. These choices should feel impactful, with clear outcomes or consequences, reminding the player that they have influence in the world.

>> **Making people feel emotion:** They can craft moments that evoke feelings like joy, sadness, fear, or even frustration. Games like *The Last of Us* or *Heavy Rain* come to mind.

>> **Giving players a challenge to overcome:** Maybe the game tests player's skills, creativity, or perseverance. A well-designed challenge engages people and offers a sense of accomplishment when they beat it.

REMEMBER

On the flip side, an experience may not be meaningful because

>> The player doesn't know what the point of the game is, or maybe they are confused.

>> The game lacks agency, like it's too linear or on-rails. The player might feel like their actions don't matter.

>> The mechanics feel stale and static. If the core mechanics are repetitive or haven't evolved, gameplay can feel dull.

>> If the rules, lore, or environment of the game aren't consistent or don't make sense, it can break the player's immersion.

>> The player isn't getting feedback about which actions to take to progress, and they feel lost.

>> Rewards are monotonous, very same-same, or lacking value.

REMEMBER

A meaningful experience comes from intentional design choices. Your player should feel involved, challenged, and emotionally connected to the world and the story.

Creating agency and immersion

Immersion is the feeling of being fully absorbed or lost in a game, in which players forget about the real world and become completely engaged in the game world. Having the power to make choices and affect their environment to feel like they're a part of the story will increase the immersion of an experience.

Some ways to offer more immersion in your designs are as follows:

>> **Offer branching choices that affect the narrative or gameplay.** If I went back and redid *Chief Emoji Officer,* I'd add more branches and choices. This doesn't mean that your game needs to grow wildly in choices, though. Agency or a sense of unlimited choices can be cleverly faked.

In games like *The Walking Dead* by Telltale, for example, many of the choices may seem like they lead to different resolutions, but in the end, they all branch back into the same narrative path. Sometimes, players just want to feel like they had agency.

>> **Allow players to change the world in some meaningful way like unlocking areas or changing the environment.** Civilization does a good job of this because you can discover new areas and build on the newly found land.

>> **Let players control their pace, whether through exploration, decision-making, or customizing their characters.** An example of this is in *Red Dead Redemption,* in which you can do a lot of side quests or explore the desert while you hope you don't get killed by a cougar.

Something to keep in mind when adding lots of choices or agency is that the amount of content you need to make will also increase, and you may need to account for how large your systems or user interface are. For example, if we had added 100 more choices to Chief Emoji Officer, we would have needed to add more written narrative and more unlockable emojis, endings, and more information to the chapter summary. Adding more agency can increase the scope of your game. (I introduce scope in Chapter 3 and discuss it further in Chapter 13.)

Making players feel something

Emotion is a huge part of why players get invested. Whether it's joy, sadness, or fear, create moments that make players care about what's happening.

Some ways to make players feel something are as follows:

>> Craft scenes and narratives that focus on character development or emotional stakes. See Chapter 8 where I discuss creating a compelling narrative and building believable worlds.

>> Use sound and music to set the tone. An intense beat in a fast-paced scene can create a lot of tension.

>> Create dilemmas that make players question their choices and feel invested in the outcome.

Balancing challenge

A well-balanced challenge keeps players engaged. If it's too easy, they'll get bored. If it's too hard, they'll get frustrated. The sweet spot is where players feel challenged but capable of overcoming obstacles with some effort. Different audiences and genres tolerate more friction, so balancing the challenge of your game typically has to do with who you expect to play your game. Someone who plays Dark Souls may have a higher capability for challenge over someone who's expecting *Animal Crossing*.

Some ways to balance challenge are as follows:

>> Start players on simple challenges and gradually introduce harder obstacles as they learn a strategy for beating them.

>> Give players the right tools to succeed but let them experiment and discover how to use them effectively. This also gives players agency to choose their strategy.

>> Provide ways for players to learn from mistakes and keep going without feeling like they're stuck.

This is just a quick overview of balancing your game. See Chapter 11 for an in-depth discussion of this important topic.

Implementing difficulty curves

A *difficulty curve* is how a game's challenge ramps up over time.

The key is to ramp up difficulty slowly so players don't feel overwhelmed. Gradually increasing the challenge helps them build their skills without feeling stuck. Make sure the game gets harder at a pace that feels natural and rewarding.

An example I like to use is the starting area of *World of Warcraft*. A major part of that game is questing, so what do you see when you spawn into the world? One single quest, right nearby. You take that quest, and off you go to collect some old shoes or kill some pigeons in the field. These first quests are meant to be easy so that players learn the patterns of the quest system and start exploring the world. As you quest further, maybe you venture further out and encounter a level 50 that instantly kills you. It's a good thing you can resurrect.

Some ways to design with a difficulty curve are as follows:

>> Introduce basic challenges early on and then slowly layer in complexity, like adding new mechanics or enemies.

>> Make sure the player can easily understand what's expected at each stage and what's coming next.

>> Use feedback loops. Praise players when they succeed and gently guide them when they fail.

TIP

In the early stages of your game, the difficulty should be easier since players are still learning the ropes. Then over time as they play longer and learn more, you can exponentially increase the difficulty so that they have to develop new strategies to overcome the obstacles.

Designing with flow in mind

Flow is that sweet spot where players are totally absorbed in the game, feeling like they're in control and making progress. If you've ever been absorbed into a game for hours on end and it feels like no time has passed, you were in the flow. The last game that made me feel that way was *Factorio*. Seven hours gone in no time, and I've only built part of the factory! To make flow happen, you'll want to balance the challenge with the player's skill level and keep the core actions uninterrupted.

Some ways to design with flow in mind are as follows:

>> Keep the gameplay steady and avoid frustrating slowdowns (like loading screens or excessive tutorials).

>> Design challenges that match the player's skill level, gradually increasing difficulty as they get better.

>> Allow uninterrupted moments in which players can fully focus on the task, with minimal distractions from UI or other elements.

Designing Around Constraints

What makes designs work? Constraints and rules.

I've used tons of game engines like Gamemaker, Phaser, Unity, Unreal Engine, and more to create games. I've been part of more than 15 game jams and organized around 5 for big teams. I've learned that creating is way more fun when you have only a few ways to do something, not a million different choices. Heard of analysis paralysis?

Construct 2 is one of my favorite engines (besides Unity, of course, because I've used it so much). Construct 2 is great because it has a block-based visual scripting tool, making it easy to quickly create things without needing to learn a complicated language. Most of the interactions you can make are simple "if–then" triggers. Nothing fancy, which creates a lot of constraints with the limited system, but the results are quick, efficient, and delightful!

Think of the most complicated software you can; maybe it has a ton of features and a complicated system for designing something. The result? A lot of designers get stuck or just give up because it's daunting and just too much to learn. Alternatively, think of Figma, a design tool that has very few buttons and tools outside of the plug-in community, but designers are able to make a ton with what's there.

I went off on this tangent on design tools because, just like with the product decisions in these design tools, you'll need to make similar decisions around constraints in your game's design. For example, when I was part of a team designing a quest system for a mobile game, we needed to make a choice on how those quests showed up on the user interface. We decided to only show three quests on screen at a time. Because this game was on a mobile device, we needed to have enough space on the screen to display all the info for each quest in a legible size, while also not taking up too much of the screen. This constraint allowed us to uncover some new questions to answer:

>> Does a quest expire over time to allow other quests to pop up?

>> Do quests pop up on-screen immediately after completion of another quest?

>> If we have x types of quests and only y spots, what types of quests can be active at the same time?

In the end, less really is more. Constraints make designing your game easier because they confine the number of problems you'll have to solve to reach a finished product.

Navigating Legal and Ethical Considerations

When it comes to creating games, you need to be aware of both legal and ethical guidelines to make sure you're on the right side of the law. This means dealing with stuff like intellectual property, contracts, privacy laws, and compliance with international standards. You also need to consider implications of game content and ensure that it adheres to age ratings and content guidelines.

The legal landscape for game development can get tricky. For example, when I worked on a global game that collected player data, the team and I had to follow data collection laws from different countries. When you launch a game at scale, you need to start thinking about compliance across countries. Thankfully, the app stores keep you up to date on your documents and raise any updates to laws across countries. You'll just have to keep these up to date once you've launched your game; otherwise, the app stores will make your game unavailable until it's fixed.

Why does all this matter? Because staying legal builds trust. If players know you're handling their data responsibly and sticking to privacy rules, they'll feel safer playing your game. And keeping to age ratings and content guidelines? That keeps you out of hot water with angry parents and regulators.

You don't need to be an expert in this domain, but it's helpful to be aware of the legal implications of your work to protect your creations, avoid litigation, and ensure a fair marketplace for producers and consumers of games.

Understanding laws that protect your work

When you're making games, you want to make sure no one steals your hard work. That's where understanding intellectual property (IP) comes in. Here's the run-down on how to protect what's yours:

>> Copyright law helps safeguard your game's original content, like code, art, music, and more.

>> Patents can protect unique game mechanics or inventions.

>> Trademarks help protect your game's name and branding.

Copyright law helps protect things like your game's code, graphics, music, and story. It stops others from using your content without permission, and it keeps you from accidentally stepping on someone else's toes (and copyrights).

If you're licensing content, like adding a cool song or borrowing art, you need to get the right permissions to avoid a legal mess.

Copyright gives you the exclusive rights to

>> Reproduce your work

>> Distribute it

>> Perform or display it

>> Make spin-offs or sequels

Trademarks are for branding. When you trademark something, you're saying, "This is mine, and no one else can use it to confuse my players or mess with my brand." Make sure to double-check that no one else already has the rights to your game's name, or you could end up in a costly battle. Also check to see whether the domain is available.

Trademarks protect things like

>> Your game's title

>> Character names

>> Logos

>> Catchy slogans ("It's-a me, Mario!")

Patents protect your ideas or inventions. In gaming, this could be a unique game mechanic, a system, or a special way of playing. For example, if you invent a brand-new way to swing a sword in VR, you may be able to patent it.

TIP

Getting a patent is a long and complicated process, so I recommend consulting a legal expert to see if it's worth pursuing for your invention. I've gotten two patents dealing with haptics in augmented reality, and both took around a year to get registered, and that was through a company that had experience creating new inventions.

REMEMBER

Protect your game if you plan on it being a business. Sure, the legal stuff isn't the most fun or maybe even a top priority, but it's the foundation for building a successful game. Always make sure to think about

>> Registering your work (https://www.copyright.gov/): Consider registering your game's title, logo, and any original art or music to protect your intellectual property.

>> Fair use (https://fairuse.stanford.edu/): Understand when you can use others' content (like music or video clips) without violating copyright laws.

Speak with a lawyer about your specific needs when you start getting serious about your game or protecting your property. You may want to start thinking about this if

>> You're going into a partnership with another game dev

>> You're planning on monetizing your game

WARNING

Get agreements in writing! If you're collaborating with others, make sure that you have contracts that outline who owns what and what happens if things go wrong. Because things do go wrong sometimes, and written agreements can make sorting out the mess easier.

TIP

A lawyer can help you create contracts to use when you're working with someone else. My most frequented contract is the "Agreement for Performance of Services by Independent Contractor." You can find templates on the internet for this as well, but I prefer to utilize my lawyer in case I ever need to call for backup, since they're familiar with my legal agreements. In the case you can't find a video game–specific lawyer, a start-up lawyer can be helpful in this department as well.

Learning ethical game design practices

As a game designer, you should think about the impact your game has on players and society and what you want to contribute to the world. Ethical game design involves creating fair, inclusive, and respectful content that doesn't exploit or harm players.

Here are some things to consider:

>> **Fair monetization.** Design in-game purchases and advertising that's balanced and doesn't exploit players with predatory tactics. If you make players pay to complete the core loop, you have just made your game pay-to-win. Not cool.

>> **Player safety:** Prioritize player safety by considering potential issues like addiction, mental health impacts, and age-appropriate content. It can make sense to make players aware of potentially triggering content if you are choosing to include it.

>> **Mindful representation:** Ensure diverse, respectful, and accurate representation of characters and communities in your game.

TIP

If you want to include people from a particular background, take the time to research and consult with people from that background to avoid misrepresentation or cultural appropriation.

>> **No stereotypes:** Avoid perpetuating harmful stereotypes, messages, or discriminatory content in your game narrative and mechanics.

>> **Respectful and accurate:** Ensure diverse, respectful, and accurate representation of characters and communities.

KEEPING UP ON INDUSTRY NEWS

As I mention many times throughout this book, you have to check out other games to see what they're like and to know what players want in a game. Here are a few resources I use to keep up on what's happening in the industry:

- **Mobilegamer.biz:** Great intel on what's happening in mobile

- **Gamedeveloper.com:** Overall place for a variety of different platforms and genres of game development news

- **GDC Vault:** Game Developer's Conference archive of talks on video for you to view

- **Streamers:** I don't have specific examples for this because there's a streamer for every genre and type of game. You can view a lot of videos on demand from YouTube from these streamers.

Chapter **3**

Overviewing the Game Design Process

break up a game's development into phases because each stage comes with its own unique tasks and priorities. This is a common way to segment the work in the game industry. Thinking of development this way helps you plan ahead! What do you want your game to look like at each stage? How many players do you need to test it to get actionable feedback? By answering these questions, you'll have a clearer roadmap to guide your project, and this chapter helps you to start building that roadmap. Additionally, this chapter covers two other important aspects of video game design: setting (and holding yourself to) an intention and managing scope. Doing both well can help you navigate the journey from idea to finished game.

Exploring the Phases of a Game's Design

I start with an overview of the typical phases in game design, in which each phase has its own goals, challenges, and creative opportunities. I go into a lot more detail about the specific tasks you'll want to complete in each phase of a game's development in Chapter 14. But for now, you can get a general sense of what to expect in each phase and which design artifacts you'll want to get out of each.

Think of *design artifacts* as the building blocks of your game — the documents, prototypes, and tools you create to guide development. Examples include

>> **Concept art:** Sketches or illustrations that define the game's style, characters, and environments. You create these in pre-production to nail down the visual direction before making assets.

>> **Storyboards:** A series of images that map out gameplay, cutscenes, or UI interactions. These are super useful in pre-production to plan the player experience before building something.

>> **Prototypes:** Early, rough versions of mechanics or game ideas to test if they're fun before committing. You make these in pre-production and production to experiment and refine gameplay.

>> **Mechanics flowcharts:** Diagrams that show how different game systems work together. These are handy in pre-production and production for making sure everything works together.

>> **Playtesting reports:** Notes from players trying out your game, helping you spot issues and improve things. You collect these throughout production and post-production to fine-tune the experience.

REMEMBER

The following sections highlight the path my dev journey generally takes. Every game's dev journey looks a little different, so don't stress if your process isn't exactly like this. The goal is to keep moving forward and have fun along the way!

Concepting

Everyone's favorite phase, concepting! This is where it all begins. You're dreaming up your game's big idea, sketching mechanics, and figuring out what makes it fun and unique. This is one of the most fun steps of the process — you get to brainstorm, doodle, and get excited about your vision. You also start thinking about your audience and checking out similar games to see what works (and what doesn't).

Your main goal in this phase should be to nail down the core idea of your game. What are the core actions the player is doing? Are they exploring, battling enemies, or trying to find a boss to battle?

The design artifacts you'll want to create are these:

>> **A high-level concept document that summarizes the game:** This can be the start of your game design document (GDD), which is used to document all the design aspects of your game. This is an important document because it helps you organize your thoughts and keep track of design decisions.

>> **Mood boards to set the scene for the experience and help with references and art direction:** Chapter 9 covers developing your own art style.

>> **A definition of the target audience:** Who's playing your game, what genres of games do they like, and what are their motivations for playing? See Chapter 10, in which I discuss understanding your audience and what kind of experience they want from a game.

Pre-production

This is where you turn your ideas into something real. This means figuring out your core gameplay loop, choosing tools and tech, making concept art, and building prototypes to see what sticks. It's also the phase where you plan out your schedule, budget, and testing strategy (because you'll need it sooner than you think). Chapter 5 covers how to choose your tools for game design, and Chapter 13 covers turning your game concept into reality.

The design artifacts you'll want to create are

>> A game design document (GDD).

>> Early prototypes to figure out which ideas work and which aren't as fun as how you imagined them.

>> A production timeline, even if it's rough. Deadlines are good and helpful motivators!

Production

This is where you start implementing your plans. You start building the game, designing levels, making assets, and fixing bugs. Testing is important here to make sure things work, and you'll probably go through stages like alpha, beta, and maybe even a soft launch to polish things up before launch day. There's a lot to get done in production and a lot of momentum to keep up. Chapter 15 covers how to keep up that momentum and finish your game.

The design artifacts you'll want to create are

>> Fully playable prototypes and production-ready code

>> Polished assets that may take quite a few iterations

>> An up-to-date GDD so you can keep track of your ideas, content, and systems

Launch

The big day is here! Your game goes live, and it's all hands on deck. This stage is about promoting your game, getting early reviews, and making sure the game is uploaded and reviewed for distribution. You only have one launch so make as big of a splash as you can! Then there's room to improve from there and grow your audience over time. Depending on the size of the project, you may want to break your release up with smaller, regional launches (*soft launches*, which I cover in Chapter 14) to test different aspects of your game. You may be testing monetization, features, or stability in different markets and then doing a full launch later.

The design artifacts you'll want to create are

>> Marketing materials for the storefront and social media.

>> Gameplay trailers so players know what to expect.

>> A post-launch support plan, even in a rough state. It helps to know when you expect to update and how often so that you can understand how much attention your game will need after launch. We didn't expect to make many updates post-launch on Chief Emoji Officer, but we made quite a few in the first couple of months, and then one a year later.

Chapter 16 is about preparing for launch day and marketing your game. Chapter 17 covers various publishing options (another way to say launching your game): self-publishing versus launching on an established platform like Steam or Itch.io.

Post-production

So now you've launched! But it's not over yet. Now a lot of your effort goes into marketing your game, connecting with your audience, and making updates. Focus on getting reviews and responding to them, making patches and writing patch notes, and getting feedback from your community.

TIP

Make sure to respond to reviews. How engaged a developer is with their players is a consideration in the featuring process on the mobile app stores. The more responsive you are, the better chance you'll have of getting featured by Apple or Google. See Chapter 16 for more about building a community and marketing your game.

Setting Design Intentions

Design can encompass a lot of things: the visual design of a game, the way the information is organized, the composition of all the elements, or the theming of the game. But at the end of the day, design is really about the *intention* behind your work. So even if you're prototyping and trying out new things to see what works, take a step back after you land on some things you like and set your intentions for your path forward.

When you're deep in the creative process, it's easy to get caught up in experimenting and chasing new ideas (which is great!). But at some point, taking a moment to reflect on why you're making what you're making can make a big difference as to whether you finish a game and whether that game is what you envisioned from the outset.

Creating intention in your journey

Think about what excites you in your work. What feels right? What's standing out? When you spot those things, set an intention around them. It doesn't have to be anything complicated, just a simple focus on what you want to build or communicate. Intentionality adds meaning to the creative chaos. It lets you take all those cool ideas floating around and turn them into something that feels whole and cohesive.

I'm going to make a small tangent into yoga for a second because it's seeped into my creative practice. I had already been taking classes here and there, but a handful of years into my career, I started to take yoga more seriously. At first, it was a way to move and de-stress, but the more I practiced, the more it helped my mental state and focus. Yoga isn't just a practice for flexibility or strength; it's about presence. That presence is about connecting your mind and body to be intentional in your actions and thoughts. I found that this same principle applied to my creative work. Instead of rushing into projects or getting caught up in distractions, I started making space to slow down, reflect, and set an intention. Before I dive into designing, writing, or problem-solving, I ask myself a few key questions to center my focus:

>> What are my core values?

>> What purpose does this have? Should players feel something, or am I making something more utilitarian?

>> What goals am I pursuing with this project? Am I learning a new game engine, or do I plan to monetize the game?

>> What will this project look like when it's finished?

With the answers to these questions, you can then create the following artifacts that help you begin to realize the vision for your game:

>> **Razor statements:** Craft a single line that defines the essence of your game. It should be short, impactful, and highlight what makes your game stand out. I talk more about these statements in Chapter 13, which is all about concepting your game idea.

>> **Design pillars:** Break down the main ideas that shape the player's experience. These should be simple but flexible enough to guide every aspect of development. See Chapter 13 for more.

>> **Experience storyboards:** Map out how players will experience your game from start to finish. This can help visualize key moments, player progression, and emotional beats. Chapter 10 covers storyboards.

>> **Style guides:** Define the look and feel of your game. A good style guide ensures consistency in visuals, tone, and overall aesthetics, keeping everyone on the same page. These may be a part of the GDD but are more focused on the details of the content, like the art or writing style. I have more on style guides (specifically art style guides) in Chapter 9.

>> **Mood boards:** Collect images, colors, and references that capture the vibe of your game. Mood boards help establish a visual tone and inspire design decisions.

>> **Personas:** Create profiles of your target players, outlining their interests, motivations, and playstyles.

>> **Prototypes:** Build quick, rough versions of core mechanics or systems. Prototypes let you test ideas early, fail fast, and iterate before committing to full development.

>> **Core gameplay charts:** Map out the main loop of actions that players will repeat.

>> **Interaction diagrams:** Visualize how different systems interact with each other. This can prevent feature creep and highlight dependencies early.

Establishing design pillars

Design pillars are a set of statements that outline the core values of your game. These can be defined for anything you create, like a game or even a company. I've found it useful to establish these for efforts like a company, so that when you start making more than just one game you can keep aligned on the core of what you want all your games to be. For me and my partner's company, we established these pillars to set the tone for our slate of games:

>> To create beautiful worlds, stories, and characters

>> To build fair games and always respect our players

>> To bring more fun to the world

It was important to me to establish these early on in our partnership because we planned on creating three or so games in the year, and I wanted all members on the team to be aligned on what types of games we were making. This allowed us to brainstorm ideas for new games and prioritize the ideas that fit our pillars and cut the rest. For example, we came up with quite a few ideas for games that lacked story, but this is what we set out to do in this effort, tell stories.

To create design pillars, distill the core ideas that will shape your game. They'll serve as guiding principles that keep the project focused and aligned with the original vision. When creating design pillars, ask yourself:

>> What is the heart of the game?

>> How do you want players to feel while playing?

>> What experiences are non-negotiable?

Design pillars should be framed around the player's experience, not just mechanics. For example:

>> **Do:** Unpredictable enemies that challenge the player's strategy every time.

>> **Don't:** Advanced enemy AI.

Defining your pillar by the mechanic is super specific and can steal your focus away from the player's experience and instead focus on the technical side.

TIP

Too many pillars dilute focus. Aim for three to five pillars that clearly capture the essence of your game. Each one should touch on a different aspect, like gameplay, narrative, or art direction. As development progresses, revisit your pillars. If a new feature doesn't align with the pillars but you feel strongly that it should go into the game, reconsider whether that feature fits the game's direction. Let the pillars evolve and don't be too rigid when you're still in the planning and pre-production phases.

Aligning a team's vision

Aligning everyone on a team means that everyone understands the long-term goals of development and is on the same page about how to get there. Even the best ideas can fall apart if the team isn't working toward a shared goal. Every department — design, art, narrative, and programming — needs to move in the same direction. If your team is just you and a couple of friends, the same holds true.

Your challenge here is communication, and you need to start with a clear foundation. This is where your design pillars and razor statement become truly useful. These should be easy to understand and referenced often. Hold a kickoff meeting to present the vision and allow space for questions and feedback. The best way to communicate this stuff is to

>> **Use visuals and prototypes.** Words can only go so far. Use mood boards, concept art, and prototypes to show what the game should feel like. A simple visual can help eliminate misunderstandings and spark new ideas.

>> **Document the ideas.** Create a game design document (GDD) that outlines the game's key pillars, target audience, experience goals, and tone.

>> **Check in with your team.** Aligning everyone isn't a one-and-done thing. Schedule regular sync meetings to check progress and ensure that new features or ideas still fit the original intent. If things start drifting, revisit the pillars and adjust as needed.

>> **Let people take ownership of the vision in their areas.** If artists, designers, and engineers feel connected to the pillars, they're more likely to make decisions that align with the overall game.

>> **Create channels for ongoing feedback like for playtesting, team demos, or casual reviews.** If someone feels like a feature doesn't align with the vision, encourage them to speak up!

TIP

When we made our games at Bodeville, we were just a two- or four-person team, but we always made sure to check in weekly with each other. We didn't bog ourselves down with check-ins, but we made sure to make visual, asynchronous updates on Discord to keep everyone in the know.

REMEMBER

When everyone shares the same vision, the game not only feels more cohesive but also comes together more quickly, with fewer surprises along the way.

Managing Scope

Scope is the overall scope of your game's content, features, and systems — and what these things cost, in terms of both time and money. Scope includes everything you plan to include in your game, from mechanics and art to sound and narrative. Estimating how large a game will be difficult even if you know exactly what features will be included when your game is finished. Being able to estimate how long something will take gets easier with experience, though even the most experienced people are never able to estimate exactly (and certainly not all the time). Stuff happens.

Managing scope means balancing ambition with realism. In the early stages of a project, you'll be excited and dream big, but setting clear, achievable goals helps you achieve what you set out to do. To manage scope effectively, break down the project into manageable chunks and prioritize what truly matters. Always be asking yourself:

>> What's essential for the core experience?

>> What can be cut or saved for future updates?

I dive more deeply into scope in Chapter 13, but here are a few pointers to consider as you start thinking about the scope for your game:

>> Set clear boundaries and focus on what's most important to avoid getting overwhelmed and ensure that the project stays on track.

>> Chat with your team about scope early (and often) to make sure everyone understands what's in and out of scope for each phase of development.

>> Keep it simple. Simplicity doesn't always mean doing less. Simplicity means strictly focusing on what's essential.

>> Avoid scope creep. *Scope creep* is when a project starts growing beyond its original boundaries, usually due to adding new features, ideas, or requests that weren't in the initial plan. To avoid scope creep do the following:

- Set clear milestones and have a well-defined vision using the tools that I mention (see [Aligning a team's vision] earlier in the chapter.)

- Use a prioritization system to list and rank all features and determine what value each brings to the game and its impact on the timeline.

>> Conduct regular check-ins with the team to make sure everyone is doing their part to hold scope. A "just because we can doesn't mean we should" mindset will help resist the temptation to overcomplicate the project.

>> Keep the phrase "trim the fat" or something similar in mind. It's a good reminder to keep focused on the core of the game.

The best way to focus yourself is to identify the key experience you want players to have. What's the main emotion you want them to feel? From there, trim away any unnecessary complexity. This can mean simplifying mechanics, streamlining art direction, or focusing on core gameplay loops. Going back to your intention helps keep things on track, with the bonus of keeping scope in check. The goal is to create a game that's easy to understand and offers a clear path to enjoyment without overwhelming the player with options or details.

TEAM SUPERSCOPE

When I was an undergraduate, a team in my capstone class called themselves Team SuperScope. The team of 15ish were aligned on making a giant scope multiplayer combat game as the first long-term game they'd ever made. They planned a multiplayer, networked, brawl-like experience for the four months we had in the semester. The team's handful of engineers had issues with the networking aspects of the game early on. In the first month of the semester or so, we were tasked to create a vertical slice, a small-scale section of a game that represents the core gameplay, visuals, and mechanics as they would appear in the final product. They found that they had included far too many features, and their vertical slice lacked a lot of what they planned. The team pared down a lot of the gameplay and features to make sure they could complete it in the time we had. I remember that they created something pretty impressive in the end, but they also had demos that didn't work quite right throughout the class, and probably a lot of stress I didn't see. To meet their deadlines with a workable demo, the team had to make big sacrifices. If something isn't core to the experience, doesn't drive the project forward, or maybe even doesn't make the cut for a deadline, be prepared to let it go.

Chapter **4**

Becoming a Game Designer

N ew games are coming out constantly these days and acquiring and playing one is very easy. Before mobile phones, games were a lot less accessible. Just 25 years ago most people were probably using dial up to get access to some rudimentary online games, and most people didn't have a cell phone (especially not a cell phone like how we think of them today).

Imagine how out of reach designing games must have been at that time. Today, it's as easy as ever to pull out your phone to play a game, and almost as easy to start designing one.

Learning What It Takes to Be a Game Designer

Many people think of a game designer as a glamorous position. It's often seen as the main way to get your ideas recognized on a team making a game. But once you start making something, the best ideas don't just come from the designer; they bubble up from the collective creativity of the entire team, including programmers, artists, writers, and sound designers.

I like to think of game designers as the curators of a large pool of ideas. Rather than solely generating concepts, a designer's role is to sift through the pile of suggestions and inspirations brought forward by the team, identifying which ones align best with the project's vision and goals. They must analyze tons of data, feedback, and prototype and know the values of the project and team to understand how to curate those ideas.

TIP

Designers are also tasked with bringing ideas to life. I've known a lot of designers of varying technical ability, but what has been consistently true is that technical ability always gives someone an upper hand in video game creation. Knowing the tools used to make the game is always helpful when it comes to designing the game.

Bringing ideas to life involves crafting the underlying architecture of the game, such as designing game mechanics, user interfaces, and player experiences. In some cases, the game designer may even prototype and implement content, translating abstract ideas into tangible, interactive experiences. Their role is less about dictating a singular idea and more about guiding a creative process that helps the team achieve a north star.

REMEMBER

Game designers are often seen as the glue that holds a team together. The role is inherently multidisciplinary, requiring a wide breadth of knowledge that spans everything from storytelling and psychology to programming and systems design. In many ways, a game designer's job is to connect the dots between different departments, ensuring that each piece of the puzzle fits seamlessly into the overall experience.

Here are a few behaviors I've seen the best game designers have:

>> Adaptability

>> Curiosity

>> Helpfulness

>> Artistic ability

>> Resourcefulness

Throughout my career I've had a variety of roles: pedicabber, phlebotomist, property manager, data analyst, and, of course, game designer. Each of these jobs has taught me something valuable and nurtured my curiosity about the world. As a pedicabber, I learned about human behavior, spontaneity and improv, and being resourceful. As a phlebotomist, I gained experience working in high-stakes environments, where trust is key. My time as a property manager taught me about customer service and automating systems. My time as a data analyst helped me hone my analytical and problem-solving skills, developing an eye for patterns and systems that translates directly into game mechanics and user experiences.

REMEMBER

Though it's not a strict requirement to have a varied background to excel in game design, I believe that an open mind, curiosity, and a willingness to learn new things can give any designer a significant edge. You can't build immersive worlds without first being curious about the one we live in. Additionally, being receptive to feedback is really important in this role. The games we create are for others to enjoy, and being open to critique helps ensure that what you craft resonates with the intended audience. For me, game design is a constant learning process.

Exploring what game designers do

Not every game designer's daily routine will look the same. The day-to-day tasks will vary based on the size of the team, the other team members' skills, and the type of project they're working on. For example:

» **RPG (role playing game) designers** may spend their days deep in spreadsheets, balancing stats and crafting complex branching dialogue systems or mapping out intricate flowcharts for quest structures.

» **Platformer designers** can be focused on sketching level layouts or building and tweaking levels directly in the engine, ensuring that movement and mechanics feel intuitive and fluid.

» **Action-adventure designers** often invest time in storyboarding, shaping the narrative beats, set pieces, and player progression to create an engaging, cohesive experience.

» **FPS (first person shooter) designers** may spend a lot of time *grayboxing* levels, which means creating basic, untextured prototypes to test spatial layouts and gameplay flow. They may even be using spreadsheets to fine-tune weapon balancing and player abilities.

» **Strategy game designers** will likely be neck-deep in spreadsheets and flowcharts as well, balancing resource management, unit stats, and long-term strategies.

» **Puzzle game designers** are probably working directly in-engine, experimenting with different mechanics, testing player solutions, and refining interactions to create that "aha" moment.

In general, a game designer will be

>> Concepting features or systems by making charts to understand how they work and write specifications for how they are built

>> Creating paper or digital prototypes

>> Charting game systems and understanding the data that goes into them by drafting spreadsheets and filling in the content

>> Identifying problems through playtesting and analysis using data dashboards that are hooked up to the game

>> Mapping out the pacing of the story and gameplay beats by storyboarding

>> Working in-engine to add in new systems and content or test out a new feature to make sure it works as intended

Consider this exercise:

Say you have a leveling system in your game that you already designed and implemented. At this point, you probably have a spreadsheet that looks like the one shown in Figure 4-1.

FIGURE 4-1:
Use a spread-
sheet to keep
track of
game details.

			Player Lvl	Player XP	Play Sessions
Sessions Per Day	1		1	0	7
Session Length (minutes)	25		4	351	14
			7	702	21
	XP	Avg Times Per Session	9	1053	28
Quest_type_1	50	1	10	1404	35
Quest_type_2	100	3	10	1755	42

I give further details about system spreadsheets in Chapter 7, but for now here's what this spreadsheet includes at a high level:

>> How often someone plays per day and for how long

>> Anything that adds experience points to the total amount (like quests or tasks) and how often those are completed within one play session

>> Player level, the total experience to get to that level, and how many play sessions it takes to achieve that level

Using this information, you'll be able to validate or invalidate your initial values by testing with a set of players to make adjustments to timing. You'll want to do your due diligence to see how the player behaviors match up with your original intent. You can ask yourself this question:

"How many days does it take a player to reach level ten?"

As a game designer, I've used and seen many different tools to manipulate data to answer problems like this. Depending at which step in the project you're in, you may opt for a tool like Google Sheets/Excel and do this by hand by observing players. Or you may be a bit more sophisticated and have a database set up to collect data from your game against which you can write SQL queries.

TIP

Game designers will need to remember lots of systems and make updates as they encounter problems through playtesting. It's best to have it all recorded in spreadsheets and documents and kept up to date. This will make it easier to know what information is in the game when you're in the thick of development.

Here are some types of tools and technologies you'll end up using as a game designer:

>> Documentation software

>> Game engines

>> 3-D modeling tools

>> User interface and 2-D artwork tools

>> Data storage and reporting software

>> Project management tools

Knowing the top five game design skills

Although there are various types of game designers — such as *systems designers* who focus on creating and balancing game mechanics, or *content designers* who craft the narrative and world-building elements — I consistently rely on certain core skills in my practice as a *generalist game designer*. I've found them essential for helping the team discover the fun in a game, properly scoping the project, prioritizing tasks, and iterating effectively to refine the final product.

The skills you will want to practice include

>> **Data manipulation:** Designers need to understand what problems they are trying to solve and figure out the data to point them toward the solution. This can mean doing market research, defining data to collect, implementing the

collection, or visualizing the data in a way that informs the team about what is happening in the player base. It can also mean creating speculative data structures to model and simulate scenarios to test out the numbers within the game systems and how a player may progress toward their goals.

» **Prioritization and scoping:** The ability to understand scope comes with experience. It's the result of understanding the roles of people on the team, from artists to programmers. Making placeholder art or scripts is the quickest way to create empathy for other teammates and understand the timelines of tasks they may need to complete. Understanding scope is half the battle; being able to curate the team's ideas and convince people that downscoping is the proper way to proceed are also part of the challenge.

Being able to estimate how long it will take to make a feature or asset and cut features that don't support the core or meta loops directly is important so that the team will actually be able to ship the game. A great way to do this is by setting constraints the team can be creative under. These can be technical or objective constraints. For instance, the team can decide that the game needs to run on a certain platform, like an Oculus Quest, or it can mean defining the main strategy and measurable goals around your social features.

» **Decision-making:** Game development is full of choices, from high-level creative decisions to minute technical details. Being decisive and knowing when to pursue a new idea or when to cut a feature is critical for maintaining momentum and focus. The ability to make decisions comes from understanding scope, the team's abilities and strengths, testing ideas, timeline, and the genre and history of the space you're working in.

» **Communication:** Game designers must convey their ideas to the team and outside stakeholders. Often, designers are asked to present to leadership and other team members, so having the confidence and clarity to speak or pitch to outsiders is extremely valuable. Being able to create concise presentations, flowcharts, and documents to drive clarity on the team is essential in these scenarios. There's nothing worse than asking an engineer, for example, to read a ten-page document to implement a feature. Your information needs to be clear and concise but also include enough context for an executive to read it and understand the vision of the experience.

» **Prototyping:** Rapid prototyping is an invaluable skill for testing ideas quickly and cheaply. It allows designers to experiment with different concepts, identify what works and what doesn't, and iterate on the gameplay loop until they find the core "fun" of the game. This is where the ability to use game engines like Unity and Unreal Engine or even animation tools will help you reach conclusions more quickly. You don't need to be a programmer, but understanding some programming concepts, and being able to leverage the engine to convey an idea or test something will help you do your job more effectively.

Making games is fun

We all know that playing games is fun. But making games is also an incredibly fun process. My philosophy is that if the team isn't having fun, it's unlikely they'll create a game that players will find fun. A happy, motivated team is essential to capturing that sense of enjoyment and funneling it into the game itself. That's not to say parts of the process aren't a challenge. For instance, finding and squashing bugs can be a slog (for me, at least)! When making games, you'll be able to learn a little about a lot of different disciplines, from storytelling and art to programming and sound design. You may even find yourself diving deep into the areas you're most passionate about.

Game development requires an experimental mindset and a natural curiosity to explore what works and what doesn't. It's about trying new things, embracing failure as part of the creative process, and iterating until you find the magic that makes your game stand out. Every day brings new challenges and breakthroughs, and there's a constant sense of progress as you see your ideas take shape. You get to see an idea that started off as a rough prototype with placeholder art become something polished, and that's exciting. There's something incredibly satisfying about watching all the hard work, collaboration, and dedication come together into a finished product. When the game is finally ready, you can look back and feel proud of what the team has accomplished together!

Approaching game design as a craft

Game design is an artform, a means of personal expression, and an exercise in constructing systems and rules that players will navigate. It's also a profession, one that demands dedication, creativity, and a willingness to put in the hard work necessary to create engaging experiences. Like any other craft, game design requires consistent practice to refine not only your creative process but also your ability to make informed decisions and implement your ideas effectively.

REMEMBER

Much like sculpting or painting, the more you engage in the process of game design, the more intuitive it becomes. You'll find that with time and experience, you'll be able to make decisions more quickly, overcome creative blocks with ease, and speed up your overall implementation process.

There is no single, correct way to approach game design. Each designer will find their own methods that work best for them, but generally, most processes fall into one of two categories:

>> **Starting with the story:** This approach prioritizes narrative, world-building, and character development. You begin by crafting a compelling story and then shaping the gameplay to support and enhance it.

>> **Starting with the gameplay:** This method focuses on mechanics, interactions, and the core play experience. You begin by creating the rules and systems that drive the game, and the narrative evolves to fit within these mechanics.

REMEMBER

Regardless of which approach you choose, gameplay and story remain two of the most important parts of a game, because they work together to define the world and mechanics within it. You may start by designing one or the other, but at some point, you bounce back and forth between story and mechanics. They tend to help create constraints for each other that then define the game.

To help you master game design as a craft, develop a process that works for you. Here's a simple framework to guide you:

>> **Research the problem you're aiming to solve:** Whether you're designing a puzzle, creating combat mechanics, or developing a story arc, understand the core challenge or experience you want your game to address.

>> **Identify potential solutions:** Based on your research, brainstorm creative solutions to address the challenge. This may include coming up with new mechanics, refining your narrative, or developing innovative systems that enhance player engagement.

>> **Prototype your ideas:** After you've homed in on a concept, start building a prototype to test it. Prototyping allows you to quickly iterate and refine your design based on player feedback and your own observations.

>> **Test, evaluate, and refine:** Game design is an iterative process. After each iteration, gather feedback, evaluate what's working (and what's not), and make the necessary adjustments. The goal is to keep refining until you've created a polished experience that resonates with your audience.

REMEMBER

As you continue to design and build games, this process will start to become second nature. You'll learn to trust your instincts, identify patterns in your work, and find your own creative rhythm. Mastery of anything comes through iteration, reflection, and a commitment to the craft. Don't fret if you aren't a master the first go-around! You've got time to practice; enjoy the journey.

Developing the designer's mind

To think like a game designer is to be analytical, creative, and curious and to take a rigorous approach in your work. Being a designer isn't just about coming up with innovative ideas, though that can be part of it. The more important work is critically assessing those ideas, understanding their impact, and refining them through iteration. It takes commitment and dedication. I've experienced moments in which I've felt like giving up on a project. Maybe the game wasn't coming together the way I envisioned, or it wasn't fun enough, or perhaps I simply didn't feel like putting in the effort needed to push through the challenging and tedious parts.

A very challenging part of designing our text-adventure game, Chief Emoji Officer, was figuring out a game loop and mechanic that built upon my creative partner's prototype. He had been prototyping a Slack-like interface for a month or so, had a high-level storyline, and an end goal of becoming CEO. We came up with a few ideas including typing a reply to a character, submitting a yes or no, or a thumbs up or a thumbs down. We ended up using emojis to make choices and progress through the story. This process was challenging because we had to discuss many ideas, prototype them, test them out, and ultimately make a game-defining decision. It can be very difficult to figure out which way is the correct path to go, and often those decisions can be full of doubt.

REMEMBER

However, those moments of doubt are part of the process. They teach you resilience and the importance of perseverance. The key to developing the designer's mind is to push past these hurdles and remain committed to your vision, even when it feels difficult.

TIP

Embrace the challenges as opportunities to learn and grow, staying curious about what can make the game better, and be willing to experiment until you find solutions that work. This dedication to both the craft and the creative process is what ultimately sets great game designers apart from the rest.

Here are a few questions we kept asking ourselves throughout our design process to improve the core of our game:

>> How does this game stand out from others in the genre?

>> How do we make choices meaningful?

>> How can we make the characters unique from one another?

>> How can we make the storyline and dialogue funnier and more relevant to what's happening in the industry right now?

You'll also likely ask yourself these more general questions over and over as your work on your design:

>> What is the main goal of my game?

>> Why will players want to play this game?

>> What emotions or experiences do I want players to feel?

>> How does this game stand out from others in the genre?

Curating ideas

Game designers are often bombarded with a flood of concepts . . . from their own brain, from their team, from the players, from a stakeholder, and even from their own parents. I am here to tell you right now that every idea doesn't need to go into this one game! You may need to shelve some ideas and keep them in your notes for a later project.

To evaluate an idea, ask yourself some of these questions:

>> Does this idea strengthen the core experience I want to create?

>> Does this idea solve a problem I'm facing in the current design?

>> Can my team realistically implement this within the available time and resources?

>> How do players react to this idea, and does it enhance their experience?

>> Does this idea offer something fresh while still being accessible to players?

>> Does this idea offer sustained value throughout the game?

>> Does this idea fit within the scope, or is it stretching the project too thin?

TIP

It can often be more important to decide to move forward than to endlessly refine or perfect every idea. Staying stuck in decision paralysis can slow down development, drain resources, and lead to a bloated project that loses its original intent. Making choices, even if they're not perfect, allows you to maintain progress. You can always iterate later based on player feedback and playtesting.

REMEMBER

In the excitement of early development, it's easy to become attached to every concept that pops up. It can be that each one is groundbreaking, creative, or even essential. But the truth is, a game can only support so many ideas before it becomes bloated or loses focus. This is where your ability to curate ideas becomes essential!

Finding your design style

Just like with any creative process, developing a style takes time. Finding your voice as a game designer can involve a lot of trial and error, so prepare to make a ton of games! Some of them may be unfinished, some may be small, and some may turn out completely different from how you originally envisioned them, but I assure you, you'll learn from every single one. Every unfinished game, every prototype that doesn't quite work, contributes to your understanding of what vibes with you and what doesn't.

Over the years I've struggled with finding my voice and style and tried to find ways to home in on it. Here's how I've molded my style over time:

>> **Let other games influence you:** I'm not suggesting you directly copy or rip off other games but let them influence you! Don't be afraid to draw inspiration from the games you admire. Your ideas don't have to be totally new. Your unique spin on them is what makes them new!

>> **Play games:** Playing games is an obvious part of finding your style. Play a variety of genres, not just the ones you're familiar with. Explore indie games, AAA titles, mobile games, and everything in between. Pay attention to how different elements like pacing, mechanics, and art styles impact your personal enjoyment.

>> **Analyze games and media:** Go beyond just playing games, and don't just stop at games! Look to other forms of media like films, books, TV shows, and even art galleries to provide inspiration. By deconstructing a range of media, you'll start forming connections of ideas and getting inspired by other people's work.

>> **Curate style boards:** Collect images, color palettes, screenshots from games, concept art, or anything else that inspires you. Over time, you'll start to see patterns and trends emerge that represent your preferences.

TIP

If you make a lot of different projects, you'll eventually see how your personal style develops over time. I like to look back from years ago and see what I was inspired by at that time and how I've progressed over time. Aside from that, keeping documents, vision boards on something like Pinterest (see Figure 4-2), and even artwork and books in your office and house will help you develop your design style.

FIGURE 4-2: Keeping a vision board to collect inspirations can help you develop your style.

Preparing to hear feedback

At some point in my career, I was told "feedback is a gift." Although I now use that phrase in a somewhat tongue-in-cheek way, the truth is that feedback can be useful. It's not always easy to listen to criticism, especially when it feels personal or clashes with your vision, but learning to embrace feedback is necessary for both personal growth and the success of any product you're working on.

I wouldn't have been able to make any of the games I've made without feedback. I often look for feedback very early in the process. It can be helpful to validate your idea or help you understand the best way to execute it.

TIP

To make the most of feedback, focus on the specific, actionable points and don't be afraid to ask for more details if something isn't clear. Accept that feedback is part of the process and helps you get closer to a polished final product. Over time, you'll get better at handling criticism and using it to make your designs even better.

Be sure that you understand where feedback is useful at various stages in the development process. Feedback about the character design while you are blocking out the layout of a level doesn't help the team. Feedback about the core loop when you're polishing the levels of the game is probably too late! Be specific about what you're looking for at each stage of development to help yourself and your team from being distracted. You can read more on this in Chapter 12.

Collaborating with your team

Even if you're a solo designer for the moment, there's a big chance you'll end up working on a team at some point. Because making games takes many different skills to conjure up a final product, designing games is inherently a very collaborative process.

Collaboration is the process of working together with others to achieve a common goal. For games, this means sharing ideas, dividing tasks, and integrating various skills and expertise to create a cohesive final product.

You can expect the following when collaborating on a team:

>> Diverse perspectives that may not match your own

>> Joint decision-making with input from various team members

>> Communication and meetings to discuss progress, address blockers or issues, and plan next steps

>> Giving feedback to and receiving it from your peers

>> Conflict resolution and negotiation when team members have differences in opinions or approaches

>> A support system that provides encouragement and motivation

>> Shared recognition for team achievements

Learning from other designers

One of the best parts of learning from other designers is seeing how they tackle problems and what tools they use to get there. Understanding their approaches and techniques can be inspiring.

Consider discussing the following when engaging with other designers' (or really anyone else's) work:

>> Why they made design choices the way they did

>> What message they were trying to convey through the design

>> What constraints they were working under to achieve the result

>> What goals or intent they were trying to achieve with the work

REMEMBER

There's not always one way to accomplish something. There's also not a "right" way or a "wrong" way to do something; the world isn't that black and white. Someone may have a completely different process from the way you approach work, but they can still accomplish great things. Stay open minded and learn from others.

Analyzing games

Checking out other games can really boost your game design skills. By seeing how different parts of a game work together to make it fun and engaging, you'll pick up new ideas and tricks. Plus, you'll learn what works and what doesn't, helping you avoid potential pitfalls in your own projects.

Here's a fun exercise to help you identify what works (or doesn't) in a game:

1. **Play a game, any game.**

2. **Figure out what makes it enjoyable.**

3. **Pick a feature and dig into the thought process behind it.**

   For example, in that popular multiplayer pirate game where you sail, hunt for treasure, and battle creatures, try to understand how the mechanics and design contribute to the fun.

4. **List what systems this feature includes.**

   For example, how many attacks did it take to take care of the kraken? What abilities worked best on it and why?

5. **List the interactions that encourage a fun aspect of the game.**

   For example, in this pirate game, the players are given a map to be able to plan their route. The designers leaned into collaboration and made the map live across players, meaning that when one player moved the map, the others saw it update in real time.

6. **Think about what you'd improve about the game, and list why.**

Putting Your Ideas on Paper

As a creative, the biggest step is just starting. Sometimes it can be the hardest step you'll have to take. Putting your ideas on paper makes them real and tangible, moving them from your mind into a space where you can begin to shape and refine them. It doesn't have to be perfect. Just getting something down is progress!

When your ideas are in front of you, you'll see connections, spot problems, and develop solutions. You can prune what doesn't work, expand on what excites you, and start to feel the momentum. It's the first spark that can ignite the entire creative process, and from there, each step gets a little easier.

Gathering the tools to get you started

Get the basics together to start thinking through your concept. Grab your sketchpads, design docs, or whatever helps you brainstorm and plan your ideas. Tools are only as effective as how you use them. I once even used Playdoh to prototype a game!

Here are some tools to help you start crafting and prototyping your game:

>> **Google Sheets:** Perfect for organizing ideas, tracking progress, or even simulating game mechanics.

>> **PowerPoint:** Great for wireframing or creating simple interactive mockups.

>> **Paper:** Sometimes the simplest tools are the most powerful. Sketch out levels, characters, or mechanics.

- **Playdoh:** Ideal for quick, hands-on 3-D prototyping or to visualize physical game elements.

- **Twine:** A fantastic free and open-source tool for creating interactive, text-based narratives. See Figure 4-3.

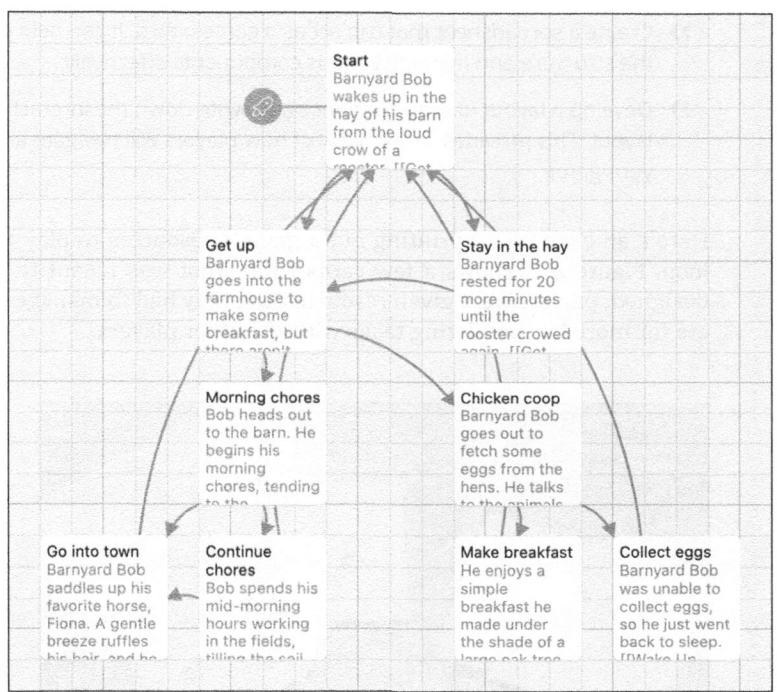

FIGURE 4-3:
Twine is a great tool to help you start planning your game.

- **Google Docs:** Write out storylines, dialogue, or keep track of mechanics in a collaborative document.

- **Cardboard:** Build quick physical models of your game's environment or props.

Designing a game on paper

You can kick off a game project with just some good old-fashioned paper and pen. Start by jotting down your game ideas, mechanics, and features. This helps you organize your thoughts and figure out which concepts work and which don't. However, the biggest challenge is that you can't really answer the key question — Is this fun? — without creating a prototype.

The best ways to get started are

>> Print out items or resources if your type of game allows that.

>> Write a game design document (GDD) (for more on this see Chapter 13). This is a detailed blueprint of your game that includes your game's vision, mechanics, story, and more.

>> Create a spreadsheet that can act as a game board. It can help you visualize the structure and manage various components effectively.

>> Develop a layout of the experience and write down the interactions in the layout. This provides a clear view of how players will navigate and engage with your game.

Here's an example of printing out a game's resources to play through the game loop. Figure 4-4 shows a few cards from what was meant to be a card game I designed; players were given resources and they had to manage them and negotiate for more by completing tasks with the other players.

FIGURE 4-4:
Printing game
pieces in progress
can help you
refine the game.

Figure 4-5 shows an example of designing a game in a spreadsheet. While looking for a new game to make at Bodeville, we tested a new concept in which players battle for resources on a board. We were able to understand whether the metrics and systems were interesting and balanced, and what was missing due to the live, collaborative nature of the document. It's not optimal for some games, but for others it's a great way to create an interactive experience in a document.

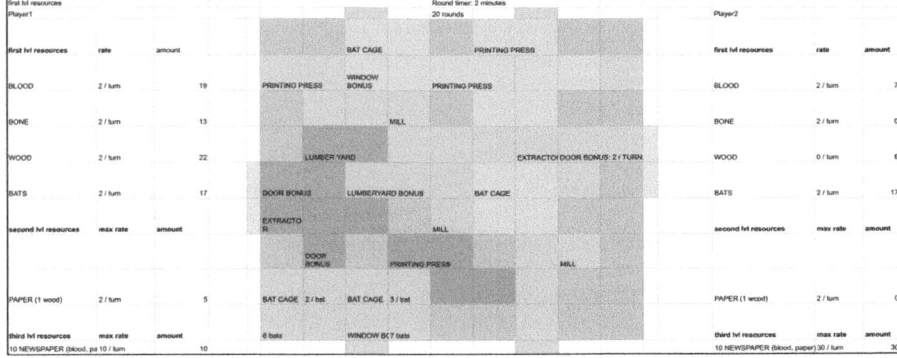

FIGURE 4-5: Spreadsheets can be an unlikely tool to understand what's working (or not) in your game.

Figure 4-6 shows an example of a layout of the experience with the high level of player interactions. It's a top-down view of a map that includes puzzles and points of interest, all made in PowerPoint.

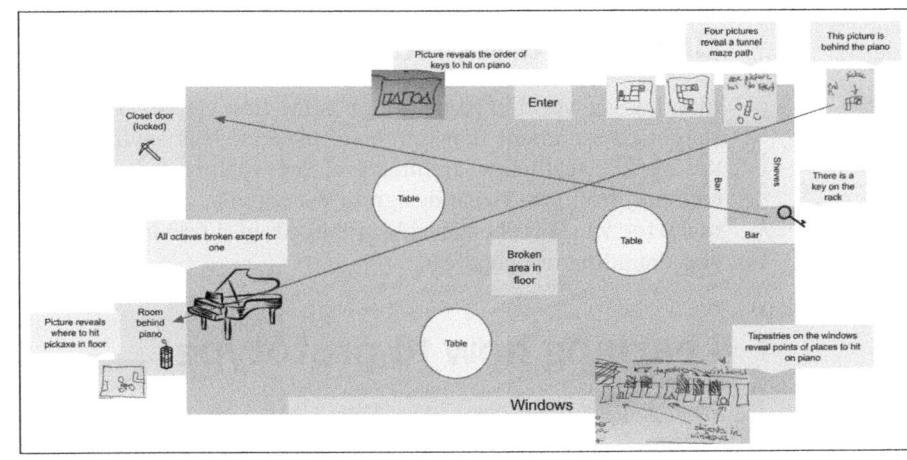

FIGURE 4-6: Yes, you can create a map of your game in PowerPoint.

Designing a system in a spreadsheet

Use spreadsheets to map out game systems, track mechanics, or manage data, as I've done in the spreadsheet shown in Figure 4-7. It's a handy way to keep things organized and see how different parts of your game fit together.

	A	B	C	D	E	F
Scammee Axes						
Determines the liklihood that someone will accept your friend request						
			min	max		
Axis_1_preference			1	10		
Axis_2_preference			1	10		
Axis_3_preference			1	10		
Aesthetic_preference			1	25		
Special_item_preference			Specific item, accessory category			
bio			based on aesthetic preference and what accessory they like			
base_match_rate	match_rate_min	match_rate_max	Deep Question		*Marketing*	*id*
1	0.905	1.275	My parents told me sto		1	scammee_0
0.7723297513	0.6773297513	1.047329751	Can't trust anyone but		2	scammee_1
0.7723297513	0.6773297513	1.047329751	I am very trusting!! You		2	scammee_2
0.7723297513	0.6773297513	1.047329751	Why trust is so importa		2	scammee_3
0.6391511933	0.5441511933	0.9141511933	Have you heard of Gw		3	scammee_4
0.6391511933	0.5441511933	0.9141511933	Is the internet good for		3	scammee_5
0.5446595026	0.4496595026	0.8196595026	People can change, ju		4	scammee_6
0.5446595026	0.4496595026	0.8196595026	I really don't have mar		4	scammee_7
0.5446595026	0.4496595026	0.8196595026	Everyone has the abili		4	scammee_8
0.4713660532	0.3763660532	0.7463660532	I look for love in wheat		5	scammee_9

FIGURE 4-7: Spreadsheets are actually quite versatile when it comes to game design.

Building a world

Imagining a world in game design is the first step to creating a detailed and consistent environment that immerses players. This environment includes defining the world's aesthetics, architecture, lore, history, cultures, and characters. Every element, from the visual design to the sounds, must work together cohesively to make the world feel believable and lived-in. I provide details on storytelling and worldbuilding in Chapter 8.

Learning how to prototype

Prototyping is the process of creating a basic, often simplified version of your game to test ideas and mechanics. It's a great way to explore ideas, test assumptions, and validate concepts without having to invest a ton of time in the idea. Prototypes can range from rough sketches on paper, to Figma screens (see Figure 4-8), to fully interactive digital prototypes (see Figure 4-9), depending on what you're trying to test and the fidelity needed to do so.

FIGURE 4-8:
Use prototypes to
explore and test
your ideas.

When we first started making *Chief Emoji Officer*, we tested out a few different concepts for player input including texting via keyboard and emojis (see Figure 4-10).

FIGURE 4-9:
A fully interactive
digital prototype
can help you
validate
your concepts.

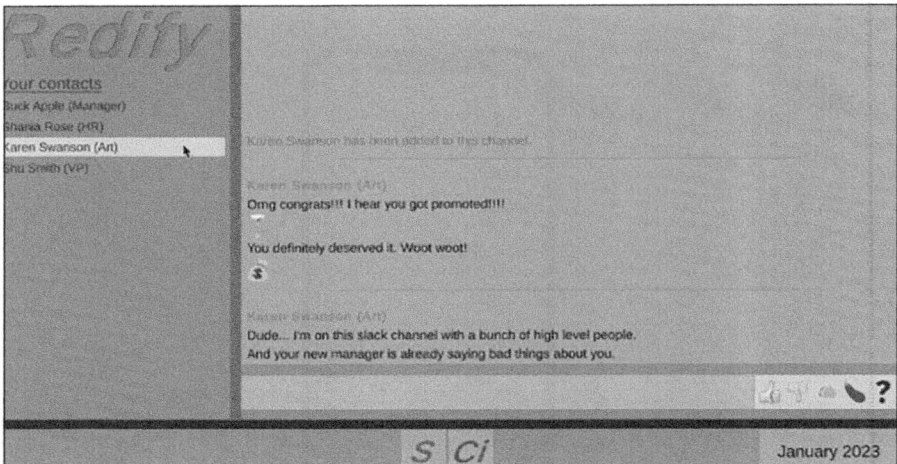

FIGURE 4-10:
Testing player
input for *Chief
Emoji Officer*.

We tested these features well before we had any sort of story, gameplay pattern, or systems in place to evaluate player choices. We're trying to figure out what the most interesting method of input was for players, so we tried the following:

>> **Keyboard input with basic human language responses.** This method was complicated because players can respond with anything. We would have a hard time curating the story and containing all the branches if players had unlimited options.

>> **Thumbs down/thumbs up emojis.** This Boolean choice didn't leave a lot to be interpreted, which felt less fun. If you're just answering yes and no questions, the questions also must be in the format to be answered like that, which led to boring dialogue.

>> **A variety of emojis.** This was the most fun and the input method we went with! It left players room for interpretation; it could be an answer for a lot of different types of dialogue; and we were able as developers to curate the branches, so the writing didn't grow exponentially with exponential branches.

As a designer, you'll spend a lot of time prototyping at various fidelities. You may be coding sometimes, and you may be using paper or various craft supplies other times. Being a game designer means being resourceful to test out your ideas. Here are the top reasons to prototype:

>> **Create smoother communication with prototyping.** Something tangible makes it easier for team members or testers to understand the end goal.

>> **Explore ideas more easily by testing things quickly.** Instead of relying on an engineer or spending effort to code a new feature, you can test it out with a prototype.

>> **Spot design flaws early and understand more about what you're looking to make.** You'll learn a lot by testing out your ideas, such as finding out that the idea you had was too complicated or needs more details for players to understand.

>> **Speed up the design process.** While there's some effort upfront, prototyping can actually speed things up in the long run. It helps you gather feedback, make changes, and validate ideas earlier in the process.

REMEMBER

You don't need to be a skilled engineer to create a game, and some designers don't spend a lot of time in code in the industry. But learning the basics and being able to create your own interactive prototypes will help you sell your ideas to the people you're working with.

Moving from Hobbyist to Industry

You can take quite a few different paths to go from hobbyist to industry, and each one is valid. You can make prototypes and games and publish your own online. You can join an indie or even a larger studio if you've got the portfolio. Or you can attend classes to learn from some experienced folks, network with others, and practice your craft.

My personal journey included going to a large state university as an undergrad in game design and then attending that same school for a Master of Science in modeling and simulation. My first design job was at a small game studio housed within the university that made games for research and training. One of the instructors at the school was the director, and I applied to be an unpaid intern for 10 hours a week. I had saved up money from my previous job in information technology (IT), so that I could focus on school and doing work in the field. I was accepted, and eventually became a paid intern, and then I was offered a full-time position. I stayed there for three years until I moved onto new things, including traveling to South America to do volunteer graphic design work in exchange for a place to stay, and then moving to the Bay Area for a new design job.

Building a portfolio

Most game development jobs require a portfolio to be considered for hiring. A portfolio showcases your skills and creativity, highlights your contributions to a project, and illustrates process and problem-solving. It also serves as a personal branding tool for how you want to be viewed by the world.

A typical game design portfolio is a basic web page including an about page, games/projects, and maybe a resume. Making a portfolio takes time and effort! But a good one can pay off. I recommend including these elements:

>> **A clear headline:** This headline highlights what you want to be known for, like "combat game designer" or "level designer" or "lead game designer."

>> **Engaging visuals:** Show off some of your work or who you are, something like what's shown in Figure 4-11.

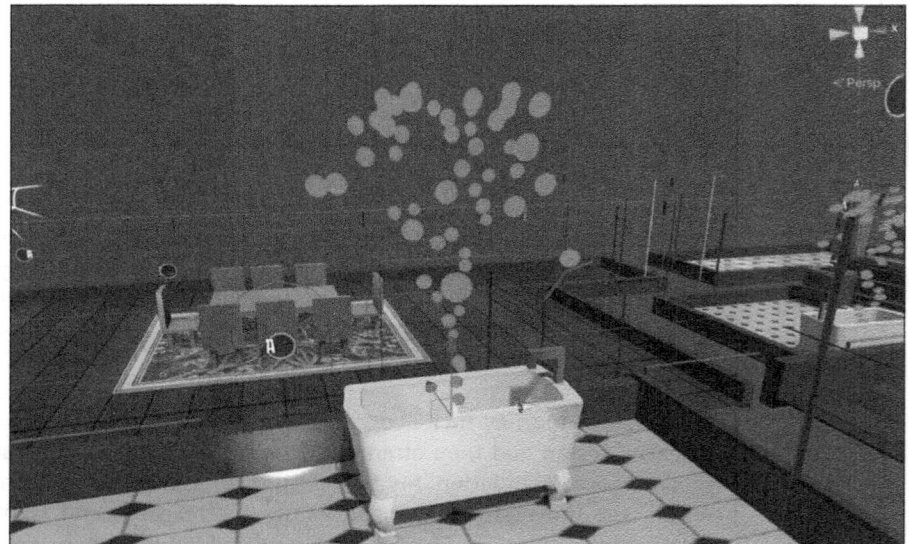

FIGURE 4-11: Include visuals you're proud of to show off your skills in your portfolio.

>> **Your process:** Include detailed information about your design process, goals of the design, outcomes, and any relevant screenshots, videos, gifs, charts, or sketches. Also include tools that were used in the design process. For instance, I worked on the effects for a game I made at Global Game Jam with a few friends. So, I wrote "Visual Effects — I created the water, electricity, spiders, and bubbling ooze FX using Illustrator and particle systems in engine" under that piece's page.

>> **Your contributions:** Contributions can include your specific contributions, especially if you worked with a team. This could be game design, systems design, visual effects, character design, scripting, 3-D art, animation, level design, mission design, narrative design, and so on.

>> **Attributions:** Always make sure to include attributions to content you used that wasn't made by you or was referenced from elsewhere. Maybe you used

Midjourney, or reference images from Pinterest, or references from a specific artist. Always make sure to add a link and information for that original piece of work. It's just good practice.

After you have your layout and menu solidified, you'll need to add those projects! A portfolio piece for a game designer can include visual and prose information about the outcome of the work and the design process you went through to create the work. The goal is to communicate your thoughts about the work and why you created it. This is a story about your 0 to 1 process.

Make sure to only include work you are interested in on your portfolio. It doesn't make sense to include four mobile projects when you don't want to make mobile games. Instead, include one to two mobile games and some other work you're more interested in, even if it's unfinished. You also don't need to include every project you've worked on, just the ones you feel are the most representative of your work.

For instance, I included my recently released mobile games like Chief Emoji Officer in my portfolio and my larger scale work at Niantic and Oculus/Meta because I want to work on story games on a global scale. I didn't include some of my more experimental games, like a Discord text adventure, because I already had narrative games on my portfolio that were more polished.

TIP

Don't forget to include a prominent way to contact you. I'd suggest including LinkedIn, email, and any other social media you use for professional purposes. It would be sad to find out that people wanted to contact you but couldn't find a way to do so.

Joining a game jam

A *game jam* is a supercharged weekend of creativity in which you and a bunch of folks dive into making a game from scratch. You've got anywhere from twenty-four hours to a few days to crank out a game, usually with a fun theme or prompt that gets dropped at the start to spark your imagination.

I have the fondest memories of diving into a game jam with a small group of friends over the weekend. It's a fantastic experience, full of pure creativity and excitement. Imagine a game jam as a hackathon specifically for game developers. There are no high stakes, just a lot of fun and the thrill of seeing your ideas come to life in a ridiculously short amount of time.

Game jams are the ultimate playground for experimenting with wild ideas, meeting other people interested in game development, and practicing your skills. You get to stretch your creative muscles, try out new roles, and maybe even discover hidden talents you didn't know you had.

I highly recommend joining a game jam! Throughout my career, I've participated in more than ten jams ranging from major, widely recognized ones to smaller, internal company jams. And let me tell you, when I joined my first game jam, I had very little idea of what I was doing, and I didn't have much experience.

I've met plenty of people who were hesitant to participate because they felt they didn't have the necessary skills to make a game. But in my experience, game jam communities are incredibly welcoming to newcomers. There's always something valuable you can contribute and learn. I once worked a with newbie who took on multiple duties, including writing the game's manual, crafting all the dialogue, and even creating all the game's sounds! So, even if you're not a programmer or artist, there's still plenty of room for your talents in a game jam. It's all about jumping in, having fun, being willing to contribute, and learning by doing.

Here are some of my favorite game jams to join:

>> **Itch.io Game Jams:** Itch.io is a hub for game creators, offering a variety of game jams throughout the year. From themed challenges to open-ended events, there's always something happening. Itch.io's platform makes it easy to join a jam, upload your game, and connect with a community of enthusiastic developers and players.

>> **Global Game Jam (GGJ):** The Global Game Jam is the largest game jam in the world, bringing together thousands of developers from all corners of the globe. Held annually, GGJ challenges participants to create games around a secret theme revealed at the start of the event. It's a fantastic opportunity to collaborate with local developers or participate online, and to see how different cultures interpret the same theme.

>> **Ludum Dare:** One of the longest-running game jams, Ludum Dare takes place several times a year and is known for its fast-paced 48-hour solo jam (the "Compo") and the more relaxed 72-hour team jam (the "Jam"). It's a great place to push your limits, experiment with new ideas, and get constructive feedback from a passionate community of game developers.

Practicing your craft

You don't need to develop an entire game to keep honing your skills. You can practice and refine your craft in plenty of ways without diving into a full project. For instance, you can work on creating a detailed spreadsheet to track game mechanics or design elements, sketch out a storyboard to map out a narrative or level progression, or build a simple prototype to test core gameplay ideas. Tools like Twine and ChatGPT offer no-code options for experimenting and visualizing concepts, making it easier to bring your ideas to life without a lot of overhead.

TIP

Though these are less hands-on methods, mentoring others or writing about your design processes can also help to hone your expertise. Explaining your ideas and guiding others through their own projects helps solidify your understanding and exposes you to new perspectives.

Acing the design interview

I've had the opportunity to interview numerous candidates from companies like Niantic, Meta, and various smaller start-ups. These interviews reveal a lot about a candidate's potential fit within a team. One of the most critical aspects is demonstrating your ability to communicate effectively. When you join a team, your success hinges on your ability to collaborate seamlessly and contribute meaningfully to the group's goals.

Although many of the candidates I've interviewed have shown great promise, they often fall short in a few key areas: providing specific examples, clearly explaining their contributions, and outlining their process. Here's what you can focus on during an interview to stand out:

>> **Explain how you contributed:** Own your achievements. It's important to be clear about what you specifically brought to the table. Many candidates tend to use "we" to describe team efforts, which can obscure their individual contributions. An interviewer wants to know what you did, how you worked with others, the challenges you overcame, and the strategies you employed. Having research and data to back up your decisions is a big plus, too.

>> **Provide justification for your decisions:** Simply stating that you decided isn't enough. Hiring managers and interviewers are looking for insight into your thought process and rationale. Why did you choose a particular path? Did you use a player type framework, conduct playtesting, or analyze data trends to inform your decisions?

>> **Explain your process:** Showcase how you communicate and iterate with your team. What tools and methodologies did you use to refine your work? Did you employ charts, spreadsheets, or a custom design framework? If you"ve developed numerous puzzles, for instance, did you create a formula or set of guidelines for your designs in order to scale up and create more puzzles easily in a cohesive manner?

>> **Offer concrete examples:** Rather than vaguely stating, "I worked with an engineer," give a detailed account of how you collaborated. For instance, you may say, "I worked closely with an engineer by first providing data to support a proposed change. I then created a mock-up, proactively presented my work, and iterated based on the engineer's feedback and constraints. Afterward, I tested their changes to ensure that everything functioned as expected in the build."

>> **Talk about who you worked with:** This demonstrates your ability to engage with people who have different expertise and perspectives. For example, did you and a producer collaborate to create metrics for prioritizing features? Did you test engineers' changes before they were integrated into the build? How did you work with User Experience Researchers (UXR) to plan player testing?

2

Exploring Game Design Elements

Chapter **5**

Game Design Tools and Software

G ame design involves juggling a lot of different skills and tools. Although it's easy to get excited about the latest software or gadgets, what really matters is how you use them to move your game forward. Choosing the right tool can affect many aspects of your project, including the type of game you create, the resources you have access to (like plug-ins and marketplaces), the cost, and even your career path.

I usually keep the decision about which game engine to use pretty straightforward, but personal factors are definitely involved. Most of my career has been centered around Unity (besides a couple of projects in Unreal Engine), partly because of the companies I've worked for and the opportunities that came my way. Unity has been a go-to for many virtual reality and augmented reality projects because of its robust set of plug-ins and developer kits.

That said, my most recent project, *Garden Walk*, which is available on Android and iOS, was made using Godot. Godot is a cross-platform, free, and open-source game engine that we had never used prior to this project. We decided to dive into a new engine for this smaller project to get a feel for it and try something different. It's been a great way to explore new tools and expand our development skills.

Your choice of game development tools should align with your project's needs and goals, as well as with your personal preferences and maybe even your career aspirations.

Be cautious of getting caught up in shiny new tools or feature sets — what matters most is how effectively you can leverage them to bring your game to life and advance your skills.

Gathering Design Tools

Tools for game development are always changing, with new software and updates popping up all the time. You may want to try out the latest tech, but remember: The core principles of game design don't change. You want tools that work well for you and help you make progress on your game. Instead of chasing every new trend, focus on using the tools you're familiar with that best support your ideas and help you move forward. Here's an overview of some of the types of tools you may encounter (I provide more details about them later in this chapter):

>> **Game engines:** Unity and Unreal Engine are the go-tos for building and testing your game. They let you put your ideas into action and see how they play out. You may even try your hand at Godot, an open-source game engine.

>> **Design software:** For creating and editing art, Photoshop and Illustrator are classics; Figma and FigJam are great for user interface (UI) design and making flowcharts.

>> **Prototyping tools:** Twine is awesome for quickly testing game ideas and story elements. Sometimes, even just sketching on paper or making a spreadsheet can help you figure things out. When you get a clearer direction, take it into a game engine to start making digital prototypes.

>> **Art tools:** Blender, Maya, and ZBrush are powerful for 3-D modeling and animation. For 2-D art, tools like Procreate, or Clip Studio Paint are popular for creating character sprites, backgrounds, and textures.

>> **Project management:** Tools like Trello, Asana or Jira help keep track of tasks and deadlines so that you don't lose track of what needs to be done.

>> **Sound and music:** For creating and tweaking sound effects and music, Audacity, GarageBand, or FL Studio are useful.

>> **Analytics and testing:** Tools like Google Analytic or Firebase help you see how players are interacting with your game and what changes may be needed. For playtesting surveys, Google Forms is my go-to.

Here's a little sneak peek at what tools I'm using right now to make games:

>> Unity for the game engine; `https://unity.com` (see Figure 5-1)

>> Figma for user interfaces and screen mockups; `https://www.figma.com`

>> Procreate on the iPad for 2-D artwork; `https://procreate.com`

>> Blender for 3-D artwork and animations; `https://www.blender.org`

>> Trello to manage my projects; `https://trello.com`

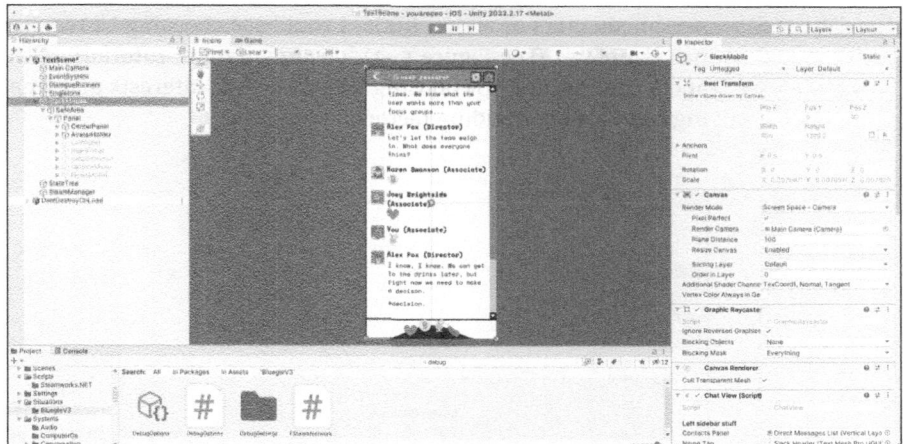

FIGURE 5-1:
Unity allows me to prototype fast and try out new ideas.

Putting pen to paper

I often see people getting caught up in which tools to choose, feeling as though if they make the wrong choice, they could ruin their entire project. Try not to get too bogged down here; getting your pen onto paper is an important step forward. Your first step will be the toughest, but once you take that first step you'll be on your way!

TIP

Putting pen to paper means that you'll be able to try out your ideas faster and understand what works and what doesn't. The best way to do this is to sketch out your ideas, no matter how rough, or start prototyping. Your prototypes don't need to be complicated or even techy. I've prototyped by cutting out cards and even used clay before to get a feel for my ideas.

REMEMBER

You can always change your tools later, or you can complete this project and use a different toolset in the next one. The important thing is to start trying out your ideas.

Picking a game engine

When I started making games, most people around me were using Unity. (Some were even using Flash, but that isn't really a thing anymore.) I picked Unity because we were assigned it in school and the majority of the jobs I was interested in required knowledge of Unity. It was the tool of choice for me at the time (and still is).

A major part of why I went with Unity throughout all these years is because of my interests. I very much enjoy making 2-D games, simulators, virtual reality and augmented reality experiences, and games that can be played on mobile or integrated with social platforms easily. If I were more interested in multiplayer first person shooters or action RPGs, I could see choosing Unreal Engine. Each engine has templates (see Figure 5-2), documentation, tutorials, an asset marketplace, and a community, so choosing based on your interests and what others are making can be a big deciding factor.

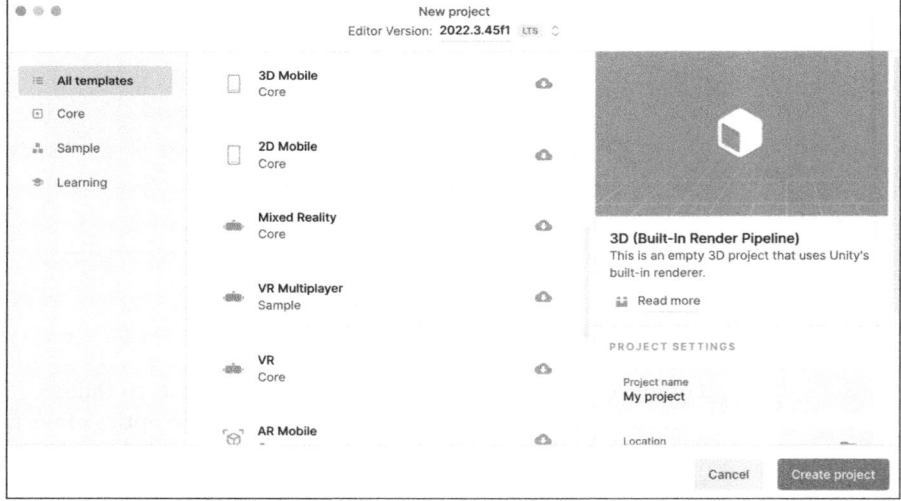

FIGURE 5-2: Unity offers a variety of different templates when creating a new project.

Consider these things when choosing an engine for your game:

>> **Project size:** If you're working on a large-scale project with complex graphics or multiplayer features, Unreal Engine may be a good choice due to its robust rendering capabilities and networking support. For smaller, simpler games, Unity or Godot might be more efficient.

>> **Which platforms the engine supports:** Some engines are better suited for specific platforms. Unity supports a wide variety of platforms, including

mobile, VR, AR, and console, making it a versatile option. Unreal Engine is known for high-end console and PC development. Godot is growing in popularity for 2-D and smaller 3-D projects and supports cross-platform development. I've spent a large part of my career making AR/VR and mobile games with Unity. I know it works well for those things, and I also know I wouldn't choose it for a larger scale web game due to some lacking features and documentation at this time.

» **Available resources:** Look at what's available in terms of plugins, assets, and support. Unity has a huge asset store with thousands of resources, although Unreal also has a good marketplace. Godot, as an open-source engine, is free and has a growing community, but fewer out-of-the-box plug-ins. I do like their shader marketplace, though.

» **Team experience:** If you or your teammates already have experience with a specific engine, that may steer your decision. For our studio Bodeville, we chose to use Unity because we already had a decade of time invested in it. We knew how to do a lot already, and where we could cut corners. A team already familiar with a certain tool will be able to move faster by picking that same one.

» **Cost:** It's free to use all these engines I've listed, but you may want to take a look at their pricing structures. It can start costing you if you choose to sell your game. Godot is completely free, though.

Choosing 3-D tools

When it comes to picking 3-D tools, the two biggest factors are familiarity and price. If you're already comfortable with something, don't mess with success! Stick with what you know and save yourself some headaches.

I've spent a large part of my career in Maya because it's what I learned in school. I'm no 3-D modeler, but using Maya to model and do some animations here and there got me by. When I left the bigger companies to start my own studio, price was the biggest factor for me. I tried to step away from all subscription-based software because I was trying to be friendly to my wallet. I switched from Maya to Blender, which has been fantastic!

If you're just diving into 3-D or want to try something new, check out these options:

» **Blender:** Blender is free and open-source! It does it all, including modeling, animation, rendering. It also has a large community to get help from.

» **Maya:** Maya is subscription-based and is widely used in the industry. It can also do modeling, animation, and rendering. There's also a large community to get help from.

>> **ZBrush:** ZBrush is paid, and it's used for sculpting. ZBrush is also used widely in the industry and has a community associated with it.

>> **Nomad Sculpt:** Nomad Sculpt is a paid sculpting and painting tool built for mobile.

TECHNICAL
STUFF

If you're used to using Maya for 3-D modeling and looking to convert to something more cost effective, Blender has settings to change the key mappings to be "industry compatible." So, you'll be able to use similar mapping to Maya.

Choosing 2-D tools

I use the same considerations for 3-D tools as I do for 2-D tools: familiarity and price. As I said before, if you already know a tool inside and out, stick with it. If not or you want to try something new, here are some options that won't break the bank:

>> **Procreate:** My tool of choice for iPad! Perfect for iPad users who want a smooth, intuitive drawing experience. It's affordable for a one-time fee and has everything you need to create art on the go.

>> **Figma:** This isn't a tool for art *per se*, but I use it for a lot of user interfaces and mock-ups. Known for UI/UX design, Figma is great for creating mock-ups, wireframes, and flowcharts. Its live collaboration features make it a favorite for team projects.

>> **Affinity Designer:** A budget-friendly alternative to Illustrator, Affinity Designer is great for vector art and design work, with a one-time payment instead of a subscription.

>> **Aseprite:** For all things pixel art, Aseprite is the go-to tool. It's affordable, lightweight, and great for animating sprites.

>> **PhotoPea:** PhotoPea is a web-based free alternative to Photoshop.

>> **Gimp:** Gimp is ideal for everything — from artwork, to textures, to UI design. It may not be the industry standard for digital art and design, but it's a whole lot cheaper (free).

TIP

When you're making a game, you'll probably use some combination of these tools to make the user interface, sprites, logos, or painted artwork. Try a combination of a few to figure out your preferred workflow.

Here's a sneak peek at my workflow when it comes to making 2-D games so that you can see how I use these tools:

1. I use Procreate to make icons, buttons, and sprites, which are 2-D images used for making images, effects, and animations in games.

2. I then import the artwork I made in Procreate into Figma.

3. In Figma, I lay out the screens and integrate the artwork into the UI.

4. I also organize all my icons (see Figure 5-3) and imported items in Figma, so that I can share it with my collaborators and keep the artwork organized and standardized in formatting.

5. When I feel good about the artwork in Figma, I export all the assets and import them into Unity for integration into the game.

FIGURE 5-3:
Organizing my icons in Figma.

Becoming familiar with user generated content platforms

User generated content (UGC) platforms like Roblox, Minecraft, and Meta Horizon Worlds are perfect for experimenting and testing ideas without having to build everything from scratch.

UGC platforms are great for experimenting without building from scratch because they require less marketing efforts on your part. The platform already has a community of players and a discovery system for content.

WARNING

UGC platforms are great for easy entry, but you don't own the content as a standalone project. You can't port it to another engine or platform. If that platform ever shuts down, you're out of luck and may have to rebuild everything from the ground up. That said, this is true for many engines and platforms to some degree, though some may make the transition easier than others.

TIP

Many of these platforms have their own way to monetize your creations, making it relatively easy to earn money from your game. Roblox, for example, lets you sell in-game items and experiences, and Minecraft has similar systems through marketplace content.

Learning Project Management

Now for the most fun part of making a game! Kidding aside, managing your project and the tasks within it is one of the most important parts of getting a game done. Every project needs to be managed, but each one may look different. It can be that you use sticky notes, a notepad on your computer, or something a little more robust like project management software.

Managing a project may not be the most glamorous part of development, but good project management keeps you dedicated to the project and ensures that your game gets done.

Knowing that every project needs to be managed

No matter the size of your project, some level of management is always needed. Whether you're keeping track of tasks on sticky notes or using sophisticated project management software, having a system in place is essential. The key is to find what works best for your team and project scale.

I'm going to share a secret with you. I really don't like project management! It takes me away from working on the creative bits of my projects, which I find to be the most fun. I spend time on project management because I know it's for the good of the project, and it helps me keep momentum when I'm feeling lazy or unmotivated. Once all my tasks are laid out for me, it's easy to see what I need to do next.

For smaller projects on which it's only myself and maybe one other person working on a game, I like to keep it simple. I make a high-level plan with milestones and then keep a document with tasks. For any teams involving more than two people, I often use project tracking software like Trello. This way, we can see each other's tasks and where everyone is in the project.

TIP

When tackling a project, break out tasks into smaller chunks. This will make the workload feel more manageable, and it will give you a little boost every time you mark something complete! This approach helps keep your momentum going, especially when you're lacking motivation or feeling overwhelmed.

REMEMBER

Project management is important, but it's not the end-all-be-all of your game. The real goal is to make progress on the actual execution of your ideas. It's easy to get caught up in organizing tasks and perfecting your process, but don't let that slow you down. Keep your focus on moving the game forward! Sometimes it's better to push ahead than spend hours fine-tuning your to-do list.

Planning and scheduling

To plan well, you want to break the project down into smaller, manageable pieces. Set milestones, assign tasks, and create a timeline for each of those smaller pieces. Even a simple to-do list can help you keep an eye on what needs to be done next and what's falling behind. Doing this can make the project feel more organized and increase the chances that you'll finish the work. You have a better chance of staying on task and remembering where you left off if you take a break for a week. Check out Chapter 13 for more details about planning, scheduling, and scoping.

For a project, you'll want to break it down like so:

>> Define your goals.

>> Define your scope: Do you want the project to be big or small?

>> List out all the major tasks.

>> Set your milestones.

>> Assign tasks (assuming you're working with someone else).

>> Use a tracking system like Trello or even just sticky notes if you're feeling spicy.

>> Create a timeline for when you want to hit the milestones and finish the game.

For a better sense of how long all the tasks will take you, you may want to create a schedule. To do this, it's best to write all the tasks down and estimate how long they may take. If you've never made a game before, this exercise is probably moot. Estimating time for something you've never dealt with before can be difficult. Even for someone who's made a game before, it can still be very difficult to make reasonable estimates.

REMEMEER

Humans are poor at estimating theoretical time, and something always pops up to derail the task: a bug that you can't fix, a new tool you need to learn, or a dependency you didn't know about, or you may find you want to redesign the task completely. For scheduling, make sure to factor in buffer time for unexpected hiccups and be realistic about what can be achieved within your timelines.

TIP

Most project management tools will give you a high-level view of all your tasks on a timeline, usually displayed in a Gantt chart, as shown in Figure 5-4. A *Gantt chart* is a visual roadmap for your project. It shows you all the tasks and their deadlines, along with how they overlap and depend on each other so that you can get a sense of the schedule and timing for your project.

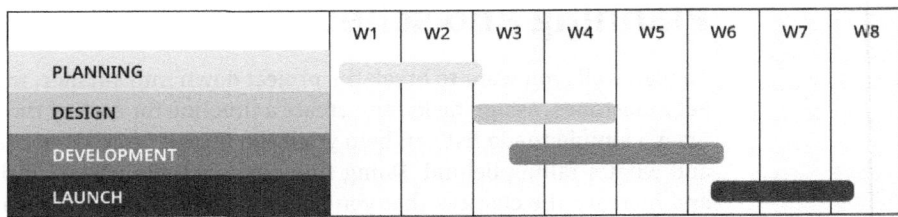

FIGURE 5-4:
Using a project management tool is essential to keeping your game on track.

REMEMBER

A lot of games end up slipping on their schedules. For larger teams and projects, unforeseen challenges can be more disruptive, potentially affecting the overall timeline and team morale. For smaller projects, the impact can be more manageable. Delays are still frustrating, and you'll probably be eager to get your game out when the time comes. But the smaller scale means that you have more flexibility to adapt and make changes without derailing everything.

Using collaboration tools

Tools like Trello, Asana, or even Slack can help you make sure tasks don't get lost in the chaos of development. For smaller teams, a shared Google Doc may be enough because it's a straightforward way to track tasks and progress.

You also need a way to control your source code and keep track of changes to your project. Something like GitHub or Bitbucket are widely used for version control. These platforms let you manage code changes, collaborate with other people, and maintain a history of your project's evolution, making it easier to troubleshoot issues and roll back changes if needed. Nothing worse than completing a bunch of the project and losing your work because your hard drive crashed!

Here are some widely used tools for collaboration:

>> Trello is lightweight and has a lot of powerups to make it even more powerful. The free version allows you to create a few projects, so it can be useful for personal tracking and smaller teams.

>> Asana is also lightweight and has a lot of the same abilities that Trello has. This is also a free limited tool.

>> Jira is widely used in the industry because of its robust reporting capabilities and integrations with source control software. Jira is free for ten users.

>> GitHub is a popular platform for source code management and version control. GitHub is free unless you need advanced collaboration tools. But there's typically no need to pay if you're just doing personal projects.

>> Bitbucket is another source control platform that supports Git and Mercurial. It also integrates well with Jira. Bitbucket is free for up to five users.

After the pandemic and the shift to remote work, tools like Slack or Discord have become essential for keeping in touch. If you need video, both platforms have those capabilities now, or you may use something more standard like Zoom. Zoom is great because it lets you use breakout rooms, which is good to have for brainstorming sessions with larger teams. You can split everyone into smaller groups to tackle different aspects of a project or explore various ideas simultaneously.

TIP

Many of these tools have started integrating artificial intelligence into their features, enabling automation of some more repeatable tasks. I like to use the recording features on Zoom to record transcripts so that I can easily summarize meeting notes or action items. Automation is your friend when it comes to tedious tasks!

Chapter **6**

Getting Into Game Mechanics

A *game mechanic* is a rule or system that defines how a player interacts with a game and how the game responds to those interactions. Game mechanics shape how players interact with the game's world, systems, and challenges. They also define what the players can do in the game world, how they do it, and how that leads to an interesting experience. This chapter takes you through the process of defining game mechanics, provides background into why and how game mechanics affect how players respond to a game, and highlights a few games that use game mechanics well.

Understanding Game Mechanics

As a game designer, when you create a game mechanic, you're defining what the player can do in your game. The agency and choices you give the player define the overall gameplay experience.

Game mechanics have an impact on the following:

>> How much control and choice players have

>> How challenging the gameplay feels

>> The pace of action, strategy, and downtime

>> Replayability and whether players want to come back for more

>> How levels and environments guide movement, exploration, and strategy

REMEMBER

Replayability means that players can return to an experience and enjoy a different experience. It may mean that they can try a different strategy to reach the same goal, or it can mean that they experience different outcomes.

Defining core mechanics

Core mechanics are the backbone of your game. These are the primary things players will do repeatedly as part of your core game loop, like jumping, shooting, or crafting.

Common core mechanics include these actions:

>> Jumping, climbing, and navigating through levels

>> Crafting items or resources to create new tools, weapons, or upgrades

>> Practicing stealth and avoiding detection from enemies

>> Completing puzzles and challenges to overcome obstacles

>> Participating in turn-based combat, in which players take turns making decisions during battles

When coming up with your game's mechanics, other games' mechanics are fair game for inspiration! Some parts of a game can be protected by copyright — like its story, visuals, or music — but the underlying mechanics and systems are not. This means you can explore and adapt existing mechanics to fit your ideas, or even create mashups of mechanics to create something new.

However, if your game becomes successful, you may face legal challenges if it's seen as blatantly copying someone else's work. For example, in 2024, Nintendo sued Palworld over alleged patent infringements, including

>> Aiming and firing items at characters in an open field to trigger combat

>> Capturing creatures in the wild, not just during battles

>> Riding creatures in an open world and seamlessly switching between them

WARNING

When designing mechanics, adding your unique twist can help you avoid potential lawsuits. I wouldn't worry too much about this when you're just starting out. Making clones of games is a good practice for learning how to develop and design games, as long as you're not monetizing them.

Some designers may start with a specific mechanic they want to build from the get-go; some may start with a feeling they want to evoke; and some may start with a story they want to tell. If you're unsure of the mechanic you want to choose for your game, here are considerations to think through:

>> What's the main experience you want players to have? Focus on mechanics that support and enhance that experience.

>> Does it fit the story? If you're making a game that resembles a chat platform, what mechanics best fit that modality?

>> Who are you making the game for? Choose mechanics that match their preferences and skill level.

>> What do other games do? Study other games in your genre. What works well? What feels outdated?

>> Try out mechanics early. Playtest with others to see what feels fun, what needs tweaking, and what doesn't work at all. (See Chapter 12 for more about playtesting.)

>> Will your mechanics keep players interested over time? Or can they play through it only once?

>> Consider how players of different skill levels will play your game. You'll be able to add tutorials or options to make them approachable.

Supporting mechanics

Supporting mechanics are the additional systems or features in a game that complement and enhance the core mechanics. They help create depth, variety, and more engaging player experiences without changing how the core gameplay works. Here's a list of common supporting mechanics:

>> **Quests:** Activities that provide goals and rewards outside the main gameplay like side quests or daily challenges.

- >> **Achievements:** Additional rewards for completing specific challenges or milestones like achievements or badges.

- >> **Social systems:** This can be mechanics that allow players to interact in multiplayer or cooperative modes like team-based mechanics, co-op missions, or player versus player (PvP) modes.

- >> **Progression:** These can be upgrades or unlockables that improve a player's abilities, stats, or tools. Common mechanics can be leveling up, skill trees, or equipment upgrades.

Defining rules

Rules define the boundaries of your game world; they set up challenges, restrictions, and opportunities. Clear, consistent rules help players understand the game while enabling creative problem-solving and strategic thinking.

A mistake I see new designers often make is that they create rules and don't tell the player about them. Work and time are associated with creating the rules and systems, and work and time also are associated with communicating the rules to the player so that they understand the rules and what they're working with.

When I was designing the chat and dialogue systems in the game Grift, my team created rules around how the non-playing characters (NPCs) trust the player when having a chat or conversation with them. Players can either get a reward from chatting with them or risk being reported and being blocked by them. Trust was affected by a variety of factors including match rate and how the player was interacting with the NPC, as shown in Figure 6-1.

In addition to testing these rules in conversation to set the pacing and balancing out the values with the other systems, the team added information to the user interface and dialogue to signal changes or events in the system. We added positive or negative reactions from the characters as players went in a certain direction, a trust meter to the user interface, and text in modals to let the player know about these rules on the backend.

REMEMBER

This system wasn't perfect; we could have simplified it and done more testing. But we spent quite a bit of time on it that took away from other systems we could have been working on. My point is that the more complicated you make your rules, the longer it will take to implement them correctly so that the player knows what the rules are. If players don't know what the rules are, they cannot strategize or move forward, which removes a lot of fun from games, depending on how integral the rules are to the gameplay.

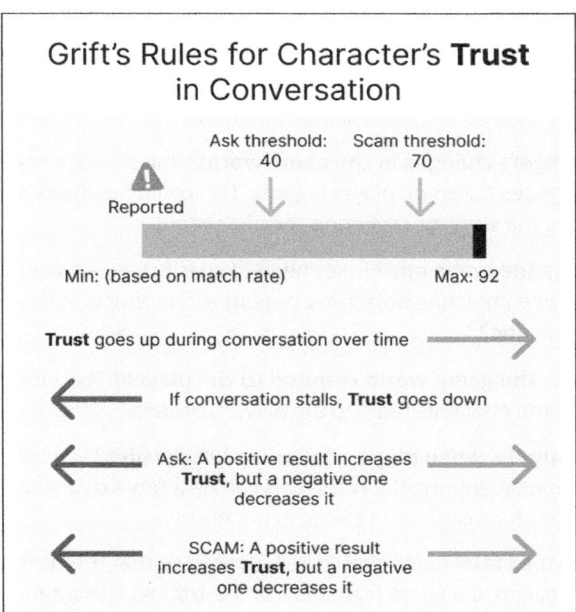

FIGURE 6-1:
An illustration of
how the trust
system works in
Grift: Scam
Tycoon.

Rules set the boundaries of what players can and can't do and govern how the game systems work. They define the conditions for success, failure, and progression within the game. Even if a game doesn't have technical rules to bound a player, it may have the concept of a *magic circle*, a concept used in game design that refers to the imaginary boundary between the real world and the game world. When players step into this circle, they agree to follow the game's rules and temporarily suspend reality to play in the game world. Think of playing hide and seek. When the seeker starts counting, the game world is activated. The others then know it's time to hide!

When you're defining the rules of your game, keep these points in mind:

>> **What's the goal of the game?** Define what players are trying to achieve. Are they trying to score points, defeat enemies, solve puzzles, or complete a story?

>> **What can players do?** Clearly define the actions players can take. This may include movement, interaction with objects, attacking, defending, or any other mechanic that drives gameplay.

>> **What loops are players completing?** Do the actions a player can take lead to the next action and then loop back around? Game loops not only serve the designer's need to make the game replayable, but they also give the player a pattern of play they can understand.

>> **What can't players do?** Rules often come in the form of boundaries that prevent players from performing certain actions. These restrictions help balance the game and guide player behavior.

>> **What triggers changes in the game world?** Rules govern how the game world changes based on player actions. This could be unlocking new areas, advancing the story, or triggering specific events.

>> **How does the game end?** Rules need to specify how a player wins or loses. Is it based on completing objectives, defeating opponents, or surviving a certain amount of time?

>> **How does the game world respond to the player?** This includes defining how in-game elements react to the player's actions.

>> **What happens when players follow or break rules?** Explain the outcomes of following or ignoring the rules. This can be a reward for successful actions or penalties for failure or breaking game norms.

>> **Are the rules fair?** Rules should be balanced so that they provide challenge without making the game feel unfair or frustrating. This often involves tweaking difficulty levels, resource scarcity, or reward frequency.

>> **How will players learn the rules?** Make sure the rules are communicated clearly through tutorials, in-game tips, manuals, or UI elements. Players should easily understand what is expected of them and how the game works.

REMEMBER

For every rule you define, give yourself some time to integrate the communication of that rule through the user interface, story, dialogue, or environment design.

Defining interactions

Interactions shape how players engage with the game world and other characters or objects. The interactions should make players feel as though they can affect the world with their actions and choices. With all choices in games, actions and interactions should feel meaningful. When a player makes a choice, they should not only understand why they are making that choice, but they should see the impact of that choice.

REMEMBER

The top things to think about when designing interactions:

>> **Give players options that actually change something in the game.** What's changed can be the story, gameplay, or world around them. Every interaction should feel like it has a reason to exist.

>> **Make sure that players know what just happened.** Confusion kills the fun.

>> **Start simple and add layers as players learn more about what they're doing in the game.** Start with an interaction that only takes one or two things to learn instead of starting with ten.

Designing patterns for choices can help you scale up your designs as you add more choices and create an expectation with players on what'll happen when they make a choice in your game.

Creating feedback systems

Feedback systems are the way to let players know what track they are taking in your game and what outcomes may come of it. Think of it as your way of saying, *"Good job!"* or *"Try again!"* without pulling them out of the experience. You can give players feedback in a variety of ways like changing the user interface to a different color or updating the dialogue based on a player's actions. And you can be creative with this, too. In Animal Crossing, for example, if you hadn't logged on for a few months, one of the villagers would nag you about how long you'd been gone. Classic.

You can use feedback in more than a few ways in your games:

>> **Visually:** Flashy animations, glowing effects, or color changes are a great way to communicate. Most people notice visuals first over everything else. These can be visual *in-world cues* — like changing the opponent's face in Punch Out as you hit them or the density of the traffic on the streets of Sim City — or visual *interface cues* like a health bar or an on-screen score number.

>> **Auditorily:** A well-timed sound effect or musical cue can make actions feel satisfying and reactive.

>> **Tactilely:** A rumble of an actuator in the controller when a player gets hit or a soft vibration when they find a hidden item can signal that something is happening!

>> **Contextually:** Feedback can come from dialogue, too. It can be the way an NPC reacts to the player.

Feedback is meant to help players learn. If you can add feedback and design a consistent pattern for it, players can recognize the pattern and start to expect it.

Structuring progression systems

Progression systems are how you keep players going in your game. A sense of accomplishment can help people keep moving forward in most things (not just in games). *Progression systems* are made up of similar things throughout a lot of games, like leveling, unlockables, advancement in story or exploration, and milestones. I find that these systems are quite standard, but most of the time you'll be doing a lot of balancing on the system to make sure the pacing is right. Milestones will be spread out in certain ways, and players will level up at different rates as they climb forward.

Here are some things to keep in mind when working on and tuning progression systems:

>> **Pacing:** If the rewards or milestones come too quickly, they lose their meaning, but if they come up too slowly, players might lose interest. Start with smaller, frequent rewards early in the game to hook players.

>> **Variety:** Offer different types of progression, like experience points, collectibles, unlocking new areas, or advancing the story.

>> **Visible progress:** Use progress bars, skill trees, or maps to show players how far they've come.

>> **Growth:** Make the challenges ramp up to match the player's growth.

TIP

Keep the grind to a minimum. No one wants to kill 100 rats just to get a +1 sword.

GRIND VERSUS FUN

Grind is what happens when the game forces someone to do repetitive tasks to progress, like collecting a resource or gaining a better score. Grind isn't always bad — as long as it's balanced with something more fun like player fantasy. The opposite of grind is fun. *Fun* is when the user is deriving value by doing things in a game that empowers them or fulfills a fantasy.

Your goal as a designer is to balance grind and fun so that users feel like they're getting intrinsic value (fantasy) while collecting extrinsic value (resources, score, money). A good example is *Zelda*, which has a hunting mechanic that feels balanced. The challenge of hunting makes you feel like a warrior, but it also allows you to build your skills and gain hearts.

Digging Into How Mechanics Impact Gameplay and Fun

Nintendo is notorious for designing games in which the mechanics feel like a "toy" in the sense that they're tactile and fun to fidget with, and then wrapping progression and story around it. This approach leads to fun because a lot of the mechanics are visceral and have a lot of satisfying feedback. For instance, when Mario throws his hat onto a dinosaur and takes over the dino's body, you have a boomerang-like experience. It's fun to just fiddle with the throwing of the hat. Adding an entire game onto that gives meaning and use to the toy.

Putting player experience first

Always think about the player first. What's going to hook them? What will keep them engaged? If your mechanics enhance immersion and satisfaction, you're on the right track.

You want to step into the player's shoes and understand what they want out of the experience. Many developers may make a game for the cool factor, or because they themselves like a feature, but it may not make sense for the audience of that game. For example, imagine you're tasked with making a game for kids ages 5 to 9. What makes sense for them as a player may not make sense for you as the developer (depending on your age). You can figure out your audience by doing research on the market and talking with your players.

I recently played a prototype of a game that was a twin-stick shooter. The controls were completely different from other twin-sticks I'd been playing, so I had a very difficult time with the controls. The muscle memory from playing those other games kept me from understanding this game's controls. I gave this feedback to the developer, and they said, "I want it to have friction." Their intention is fine, but flow matters. If a player isn't feeling like the experience is smooth and intuitive, they're not going to have fun playing your game. It's important to think about the player and even more importantly the player from the right audience.

Getting a feel for game feel

Game feel is the quality that makes gameplay satisfying and responsive. By tuning animations, controls, and feedback, you can create an experience that feels polished and enjoyable. Think about the last time you played a game where things just felt nice and frictionless. For me, that game was Balatro, a digital card game.

Moving the cards around the screen felt responsive and tactile with the added animations and sounds. That's game feel.

Consider the hierarchy of senses when you're designing an experience. Sight comes first, because the eye is such a specialized organ. Within that, many people notice movement, colors, and patterns above all. Then comes hearing, touch, smell, and taste.

With this hierarchy in mind, you can spend time on the following in order to make a big impact in the feeling and reaction of your game:

>> Add subtle visual or audio cues for player actions.

>> Give weight to movement and physics. Characters should stop and accelerate realistically.

>> Focus on responsiveness. Every input should feel immediate and intentional.

Understanding game balance

Game balance ensures that mechanics, challenges, and rewards are fair and enjoyable. Chapter 11 is dedicated to game balance and helping you get that balance right in your games, but practically speaking, here's what balancing a game means: You start with a certain pacing and metrics in a progression system, and you then spend time testing the system for timing and making adjustments to tune it correctly as you refine your game.

From a player's perspective, game balance is how long it takes you to complete that quest line in World of Warcraft and how long it takes you to level up to get to the epic gear. Some quest lines may feel like they take too long; others feel too short. It's important to balance timing and progression for a right feel for the pacing.

REMEMBER

I'd wager that most designers never got game balance right the first time. It always takes testing and iteration to get it feeling right. Experience helps us designers take a first intelligent stab at the metrics that go into a system.

Exploring Examples of Game Mechanics

Examples are a good way to learn more about game design because the topic can be quite abstract and includes a variety of different skills and topics. With a bunch of games out there to study, I've chosen a few as case studies to point out how each game uses mechanics, rules, and systems. I've purposely chosen three very different games with varying mechanics, styles, and audiences, but they're all indie titles created by teams of one to two people!

Case study #1: Ooblets

Ooblets describes itself as "a farming, creature collection, and town life game" that blends elements of life simulation, creature collecting, and rhythm-based battles. The game's approachable design encourages experimentation and personalization.

The core mechanics in *Ooblets* are

>> **Farming:** Players cultivate and harvest crops to earn income and grow ooblet seeds, which are used to expand their collection of critters. Farming integrates into other systems, such as crafting and town upgrades.

>> **Creature collecting:** Players collect adorable ooblets by winning dance battles, a unique and quirky twist on traditional combat mechanics.

>> **Town life simulation:** Players can interact with the quirky townsfolk, complete tasks, and customize their homes.

The supporting mechanics in *Ooblets* are

>> **Dance battles:** Instead of combat, players participate in turn-based, rhythm-inspired dance battles to resolve conflicts and win ooblet seeds. Players must select ooblets and use their unique dance moves to win battles.

>> **Crafting and customization:** Players craft items to complete tasks, improve their farms, or upgrade their homes.

>> **Exploration and quests:** Players explore different regions to gather resources, discover new ooblets, and unlock story elements. The quests provide direction and rewards while maintaining the game's relaxed pacing.

The rules and interactions in *Ooblets* are

>> **Energy system:** Daily activities like farming and exploring consume energy, encouraging players to plan their actions wisely. Energy can be replenished through food, rest, or other means, creating a light resource-management layer.

>> **Interactivity with the town:** Players build relationships with NPCs by completing tasks and gifting items. Ooblets can be interacted with and leveled up, creating a connection between the player and their creatures.

The feedback systems in *Ooblets* are

>> **Feedback:** Visual and audio cues, such as growing crops or winning dance battles, provide so much delight!

>> **Progression feedback:** Players unlock new ooblets, farming tools, and areas over time, ensuring a steady sense of accomplishment and progression.

The progression systems in *Ooblets* are

>> **Unlockable content:** New ooblets, regions, and upgrades are unlocked as players progress, providing long-term goals.

>> **Meta-progression:** Players can improve their farms, expand their homes, and level up their ooblets, creating a sense of growth and investment in the world.

Ooblets is accessible, deep, and relaxing. The core mechanics are farming, creature collecting, and town life. The supporting systems like dance battles and crafting offer players a mix of creativity, strategy, and charm. *Ooblets* demonstrates how blending genres can create a delightful and immersive experience for a variety of players.

Case study #2: Inscryption

Inscryption describes itself as "an inky black card-based odyssey that blends deck-building roguelike, escape-room-style puzzles, and psychological horror." It combines a card game with escape-room elements and fourth-wall-breaking surprises. *Inscryption* has a great sense of mystery, tension, and discovery that's made it a hit.

The core mechanics in *Inscryption* are

>> **Deckbuilding:** Players build and refine their decks by collecting cards during gameplay, each with unique abilities. This allows for a lot of player strategy to beat challenges and bosses.

>> **Card battles:** Turn-based card battles are played on a grid, with players summoning creatures, attacking opponents, and managing resources. Victory requires both tactical gameplay and long-term strategy as players plan moves and adapt to random elements.

>> **Escape-room exploration:** Outside of card battles, players explore a cabin filled with cryptic puzzles and secrets. Solving puzzles often rewards players with new cards or tools that they can use in their card battles to adjust their strategies.

The supporting mechanics in *Inscryption* are

>> **Resource management:** Players must manage resources like blood and bones to play cards, balancing sacrifices and strategy.

>> **Meta-progression:** Progression persists across runs, with players unlocking new cards, abilities, and story elements. The roguelike structure creates replayability but still rewards experimentation.

>> **Narrative integration:** Story elements unfold through gameplay, with cryptic messages, mysterious NPCs, and evolving environments.

The rules and interactions in *Inscryption* are

>> **Risk and reward:** Players can take risks, such as sacrificing powerful cards for short-term gains, but they have to weigh these decisions carefully.

>> **Player-environment interaction:** Exploration outside card battles involves direct interaction with objects in the environment, often leading to new discoveries.

The feedback systems in *Inscryption* are

>> **Immediate feedback:** Card effects, attacks, and sacrifices are visually and audibly impactful, enhancing clarity and satisfaction. The ominous atmosphere, eerie music, and unsettling visuals provide constant emotional feedback.

>> **Progression feedback:** New cards, mechanics, and story twists are revealed gradually, creating a compelling sense of discovery.

The progression systems in *Inscryption* are

>> **Unlockable content:** Players unlock new cards, items, and abilities with each run, ensuring steady progress even after failure. The game introduces new layers of complexity and narrative as players advance through each act.

>> **Evolving mechanics:** As players progress, the core mechanics shift dramatically, keeping the experience fresh and challenging. These shifts encourage players to explore new playstyles.

Inscryption is a wild ride that blends so many cool elements like card strategy, escape-room puzzles, and a little horror. The deckbuilding and resource management make each playthrough feel different, and the way the story unfolds as you explore really adds to the intrigue. It's a perfect example of how mixing genres and mechanics can lead to something that feels fresh and exciting, even if you're technically just playing a card game.

Case study #3: Thronefall

Thronefall describes itself as "A minimalist game about building and defending your little kingdom." It's a tower defense game that balances strategy and action and allows the player to have a lot of agency of choice. The controls are quite minimalist, and the levels are simple.

The core mechanics in *Thronefall* are

>> **Base building:** Players construct a base around a central castle, choosing from defensive structures like walls, towers, and traps. Players have to decide whether to focus on defense or economy, such as investing in farms or marketplaces for income.

>> **Combat and action gameplay:** Players control a mounted hero who actively participates in battles, dealing damage and rallying defenses.

The supporting mechanics in *Thronefall* are

>> **Resource management:** Gold is earned each night from structures and is used to build or upgrade defenses. Players have to balance spending immediately versus saving for long-term improvements.

>> **Upgrade system:** Between waves, players can upgrade their hero, weapons, or buildings. Upgrades allow for flexible playstyles, such as focusing on ranged attacks, fortifying walls, or increasing income generation.

>> **Wave system:** Enemies attack in waves, with increasing difficulty. Players must anticipate enemy paths and adjust their strategy accordingly.

The rules and interactions in *Thronefall* are

>> **Day/night cycle:** Days are for planning and building, and nights are for defending against waves of enemies.

- » **Player-enemy interaction:** Enemy behavior is predictable but varied, encouraging players to learn patterns and optimize their defenses. The hero's ability to directly engage enemies adds an element of risk-reward, because overextending can leave the base vulnerable.

The feedback systems in *Thronefall* are

- » **Immediate feedback:** Building placements are visually intuitive, with clear indicators for range and effectiveness. Combat actions feel satisfying through impactful animations, sound effects, and damage numbers.
- » **Progression feedback:** After each wave, players are rewarded with gold and unlock options for new upgrades, creating a sense of accomplishment. Enemy types and difficulty gradually evolve, signaling progress and keeping the game challenging.

The progression systems in *Thronefall* are

- » **Scaling difficulty:** Each level introduces tougher enemies and more complex wave patterns, requiring players to adapt their strategies.
- » **Meta-progression:** Unlockable maps and upgrades provide long-term goals and replay value. Players can revisit earlier maps with new strategies to get new achievements.

Thronefall has a good balance between accessibility and depth, offering simple controls that are easy to grasp while providing a variety of upgrades, strategies, and enemy types to challenge players and ensure replayability. *Thronefall* proves that a minimalist yet polished approach can deliver a highly engaging and very replayable experience.

Chapter **7**

Understanding Game Systems

A *game system* is the set of rules that makes a game work. It's how everything in the game fits together, like how you move, what happens when you win or lose, how you level up, and how things change as you play. These rules aren't directly controlled by the player and are behind the scenes to define the game's world and interactions.

A great way to visualize game systems is by making *interactive diagrams* to show how the systems interact with each other. These are charts that show how all the systems work together and what the results are. I go over some tools to make diagrams and charts in Chapter 5.

Core Elements of Game Systems

Game systems are usually full of data and are either stored in the game locally or loaded from a server at runtime. Here's a super simple example of a combat system and the information that may be stored in it:

```
Turn Order: Determined by character's speed (SPD) stat; higher
    speed acts first.
Damage Calculation:
Physical Attack: Damage = (ATK * Power) - DEF
Magic Attack: Damage = (MP * Power) - MR
Status Effects: Track active effects, like burn or stun, and
    their remaining duration.
Victory Condition: Combat ends when one side's team HP is
    reduced to 0.
```

Now, you'll also need to include items that can be used in that combat system, like healing potions or weapons:

```
Weapon Name: Flaming Sword
Weapon Type: Physical
Power: 15
Description: A sword engulfed in flames that increases base
    attack damage. It has a chance to inflict a burn effect on the
    opponent, causing additional damage over time.
Special Effects: Burn Chance: 20% chance to apply a burn to the
    enemy, dealing 5 damage per turn for 3 turns.
```

This can get pretty complicated as you may have hundreds of items. You have to manage that information, keep it updated, make it work with other systems like character or spell systems, and test and balance it out so that nothing is over-powered or is meaningless . . . this is one of the most fun parts of making games (to me at least)!

A common example of a game system component is *leveling*. Say you're catching and collecting creatures while exploring a map. You can battle these creatures with each other, and as they level up, you also level up your player experience, allowing you to unlock new features, items, and maybe even new quests.

Another example of a gameplay system is an *inventory*. Imagine you have a farm you've inherited from your grandpa, and the farm is barren when you arrive. You may need to collect seeds, craft items to water the plants, or collect resources from the world. Your bag may be too small in the beginning, but you can go into the village and buy a bigger one from the shop. These are some of the rules and variables associated with an inventory system.

The main elements of a game system are

>> **What a player can do:** For the farm game, player actions may be farming, fishing, mining, and talking to villagers. These are the main activities that keep the game moving.

>> **Resources:** Things you collect like crops, fish, wood, and minerals. Maybe you use these items to make progress, either by selling them or using them to craft new items.

>> **Stats and variables:** These can be energy, health, money, skill levels (like farming or fishing), or relationships with NPCs (non-playing characters). These variables may improve as you play and help you unlock more things.

>> **Progression:** Progression involves variables that change over time, like leveling up skills, growing crops on a farm, or building friendships with NPCs.

>> **Feedback loops:** These are the rewards you get from progressing through the game, like making money from crops to buy better seeds, or when challenges (like running out of energy) make you plan your gaming strategies better.

TIP

I find that one of the best ways to understand how to structure a game system is to break down game systems from my favorite games and study how they architected them. Creating charts and spreadsheets are a great way to start analyzing your favorite game systems.

Defining the foundation of game systems

When figuring out what to include in your game system, write down the variables you plan to include (like experience points, health, energy, or inventory size) and then focus on how they'll work together to push the player through the game. Think of how these variables will change over time or interact with other game mechanics so that players will feel a sense of accomplishment over time. You can see an example of this in Figure 7-1.

base_match_rate	level	cost	item_name	money_bonus
1	1	0	---	1
0.784661721	2	10	Start a fundraiser	5
0.6586969028	3	100	Run ads on social	6
0.5693234419	4	500	Email 100 influencers	7
0.5	5	1261	Cold pitch in the DMs	8
0.4433586237	6	1464	Lie about your product	8
0.3954690224	7	1630	Farm follows	9
0.3539851629	8	1771	Buy 1000 followers	10
0.3173938055	9	1892	Bait and switch	10
0.284661721	10	2000	Start a newsletter	10
0.2550519488	11	2095	Hop on a trend	11
0.2280203447	12	2182	Make some new hires	11
0.2031536794	13	2261	Pay for press	12
0.1801307434	14	2334	Buy a mailing list	12
0.1586969028	15	2402	Send unsolicited emails	12
0.1386468839	16	2464	Start a podcast	12
0.1198127861	17	2523	Host a webinar	13
0.1020555265	18	2578	Partner with a fake review firm	13
0.08525859978	19	2630	Send subliminal messages	13
0.06932344193	20	2680	Astroturf social media	13
0.0541659252	21	2726	Host a giant party on an island	14

FIGURE 7-1: A spreadsheet showing the progression from level to level and some parameters associated with it.

A good system design defines the following:

>> The core elements or objects in the system

>> How the elements are connected, their relationships, and their inputs and outputs

>> The purpose of the system

When we were designing *Grift*, we knew we wanted to give players a sense of progression by unlocking new accessories as they reached higher levels. They could then use those accessories to add new stats to their bots (the non-playable characters in the game that you create) and make them look cooler and more unique. As players met and chatted with new NPCs, they'd earn experience points and money, which not only helped them level up but also unlocked new accessories they could buy with the currency they accumulated. This system of rewarding playtime and offering new items kept players coming back to see what they could unlock next.

Ask yourself these questions when designing a game system:

>> What are the actions players are doing? Are they farming, collecting, or engaging in combat?

>> What are the main variables (like stats, items or resources, or currencies) within these actions?

>> Which milestones are the player working toward, and will they get a reward when they get to the milestone?

>> When a player makes a choice, what feedback do they get?

>> What friction is there to a player progressing to the next steps? What challenges will they face?

>> How does the system relate to the narrative?

>> What should players feel at each step of the way?

>> How does this system interact with other systems?

TIP

I always push to keep games simple. For every feature or extra thing that you add to a game, it's important to make it meaningful and to think through these questions. Doing this takes time, and it's always been helpful for me to map these things out. You not only need to think about what individual features do on their own, but also how they interact with each other.

Making games work with rules and systems

Just like in real life, rules and systems need constraints for players to feel challenged. Think of going to school — every year you make progress with the end goal of graduating. It can feel really good to finally accomplish that and look back on all the milestones you completed. Sometimes you even get extra rewards at each step of the way.

These rules shape what players can or can't do in the game. A cooldown for an attack may keep you from spamming that option, or a time-limited boss event may make you think more about optimizing your attacks in the time you're given. Strategizing around a game system in this way can lead players to mastering your game. If you give them enough information, they can learn what works and what doesn't along the way.

Here are some examples in action:

>> **Energy systems** in RPGs limit players' actions per turn, forcing players to end for the day or make choices about what they want to do with the energy they have.

>> **Inventory systems** in survival games put caps on how many items players can carry, making players choose between resources to keep and discard. It makes you think about immediate need and long-term survival.

>> **Cooldowns** in action games prevent continuous use of powerful abilities, encouraging players to find the right timing and combination of skills.

>> **Morality systems** record players' choices, changing the outcome of a story. This can mean the difference in an ending, giving choices way more meaning.

>> **Crafting systems** let players combine items to make new ones. It encourages exploration to find new resources and gives purpose to the items.

Using system design principles

Game design principles are useful to refer to when designing any part of a game. You'll have specific ones for your game based on the genre or gameplay. The following are generally recommended for game designers, so consider these when building your systems:

>> Design your game around a core mechanic.

>> Set clear goals and objectives.

>> Offer feedback and rewards.

>> Make sure you can scale or add to it over time.

>> Balance your systems through testing and iteration to avoid overpowered or underpowered elements.

>> Ensure that the game is "easy to play, hard to master." The system may be complicated and deep, but it should feel simple to the casual user.

>> Link actions (hunting, foraging, flying) in the game to fulfilling a fantasy for the user.

>> Adapt to player choices, skill levels, and evolving playstyles, allowing for a dynamic experience.

Progression Systems

Progression systems are all over the place in games. A well-known progression system includes a leveling structure, but there's a place for progression in many systems if you want to encourage longer play and a sense of progress throughout time.

In our (Bodeville's) game *Garden Walk*, players plant a seed in a garden and walk to grow it. I've included a spreadsheet example in Figure 7-2. The phone tracks the steps, and each step counts toward the progress of the plant. That's a super simple example of a progression system, but they can get much more complex!

FIGURE 7-2:
A simple spreadsheet showing progression from level to level.

Id	AssetName	Species	Steps to Seedling	Steps to Teen	Steps to Mature	Steps to Breed	Steps to Wither	Drop Frequency
azalea_1	Flower1	Azalea	50	1000	8000	10000	50000	4
hydrangea_1	Flower2	Hydrangea	50	1000	8000	10000	50000	4
tulip_1	Flower3	Tulip	50	1000	8000	10000	50000	4
tulip_2	Flower3	Tulip	50	1000	8000	10000	50000	2
daisy_1	Flower4	Daisy	50	5000	12000	14000	50000	1
daffodil_1	Flower5	Daffodil	50	5000	12000	14000	50000	1
rose_1	Flower6	Rose	50	5000	12000	14000	50000	1
lily_1	Flower7	Lily	50	8000	10000	12000	50000	0.5
orchid_1	Flower8	Orchid	50	8000	10000	12000	50000	0.5

FIGURE 7-2: A simple spreadsheet showing progression from level to level.

Progression systems are useful for these reasons:

>> They give players a sense of accomplishment. Dopamine is a very effective motivator!

>> They also give players reasons to keep playing, for achievements and clear goals.

>> Narrative progression can unlock new story elements or character developments alongside their gameplay achievements.

>> It offers long-term play by offering challenges and rewards along the way, preventing the game from becoming stale or repetitive.

>> In multiplayer games, it can offer competition or progression by having players compare achievements and progress.

Even if you don't show the progression in the user interface, it can be helpful as a design tool for yourself as you design the gameplay. It helps you understand what you want players to be doing from day to day or week to week and enables you to align your feature unlocks to players' progress.

For each week or level, write out the behaviors you want the player to exhibit:

>> What are they thinking, feeling, and doing?

>> Are they mastering a skill or collecting something?

>> Are they interacting with the community to help teach them about how to solve a puzzle?

Structuring leveling systems

A *leveling system* is a game mechanic that tracks a player's progress and growth, typically through experience points (XP) or some other form of accrued points. It's intended to motivate players toward a long-term goal in a game.

Leveling must feel valuable in the gameplay, and it needs to have meaning. Rewards are helpful here, like when a player reaches a certain level, they can unlock a new area, a new feature, or get a new resource.

Here are some of the elements of leveling systems:

>> **Experience points (XP):** Players earn XP by completing tasks, defeating enemies, or achieving objectives.

>> **Levels:** Each level represents a stage of progression; players may get new items and unlock new features; or the game may take on a completely different feeling over time.

>> **Progression curves:** Leveling systems often use different mathematical models like linear or logarithmic curves to determine how much XP is needed to reach each subsequent level.

>> **Rewards:** Leveling up often comes with rewards, such as new gear, abilities, or cosmetic items.

>> **Skill trees:** Some games have branching skill trees that give players the choice to customize their characters or gameplay.

TECHNICAL STUFF

Creating a logarithmic curve like the one in Figure 7-3 in Google Sheets is simple! You set up your data like so: In column A, just enter your I values, like 1, 2, and 3. Then, in column B, you can calculate your I values using the formula =LOG(A2) to find the natural logarithm of those I values. When your data is all set, highlight both columns and go to Insert > Chart. You can choose a scatter plot or smooth line chart to see how the data looks over time.

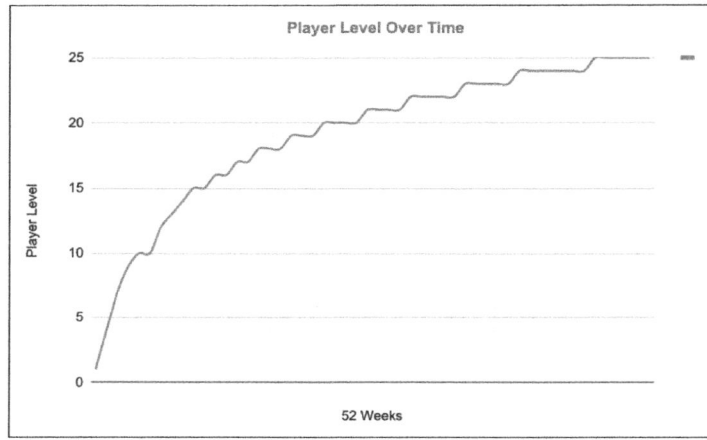

FIGURE 7-3:
A logarithmic curve for leveling made in Google Sheets.

REMEMBER

As you design a leveling system, ask yourself: Do players feel like they are working toward their long-term goals? A leveling system should challenge players and reward them throughout their progress. This helps players feel purpose while they're playing a game.

TIP

For each level in your system, write down what players think, feel, and do at each stage. This can help you prioritize features and content for each phase of the game.

Creating reward structures

Reward structures are in games to keep players motivated and moving toward their goals. When you define the actions and milestones you want players to achieve, also think about what rewards they get and when. A simple example is that when a player finishes the tutorial, they get a reward for completing it. Doing something like this early on makes people feel like they're making progress and that their choices are affecting the game.

Think about pacing when you're writing out the rewards over time. You don't want players to go through long spells of not gaining anything at all, and you want to make sure they're getting something for their efforts. It's good feedback to complete a task and get a treat for it!

TIP

In the past I've set up structures based on the gameplay patterns we intended for the game, and then observed how players engaged. The structure may dole out rewards daily or weekly, with a little randomization added into the mix to keep it interesting. It helps create expectations for players and allows you to design habits for when you want them to play your game.

Examples of progression systems

I'm playing an exercise adventure game right now that has pretty straightforward progression systems. It has an overworld that has all the places I can go on the map. It also has a leveling system that directly correlates to the challenge of the mobs in each level. I acquire new exercises as I level up, and each exercise has its own set of abilities. All of this together keeps me going and wanting to play every day. Its leaderboard helps with that, too, which I discuss in the section "Social Systems" later in this chapter.

Next time you're playing a game, think about all the rules and systems that keep you going, the next reward you're seeking, and the milestones you've achieved. Some progression systems you may have encountered include

>> **Leveling systems:** A widely used type of progression in which players gain experience points (XP) through gameplay and advance through levels, unlocking new abilities, content, or rewards at each level.

>> **Skill trees:** Players choose from various skills or abilities as they progress, allowing for customization of their characters or gameplay styles through branching paths.

>> **Prestige systems:** After reaching the maximum level, players can reset their progress to gain prestige levels, often with special rewards or benefits, encouraging re-playability.

>> **Gear or equipment progression:** Players collect or earn better gear and equipment as they progress, enhancing their abilities and effectiveness through crafting, loot drops, or purchases.

>> **Narrative progression:** Progression is tied to the unfolding of the game's story, with players advancing through chapters or missions that unlock new narrative elements and character developments.

>> **Reputation systems:** Players earn reputation points through specific actions, leading to rewards or unlocks within the game world, common in RPGs with factions or communities.

>> **Challenge systems:** Players complete specific challenges or tasks to earn rewards, XP, or achievements, encouraging varied gameplay and exploration.

>> **Collectible systems:** Players gather collectibles (for example, cards, items, or achievements) as they progress, encouraging exploration and engagement with the game world.

>> **Class or specialization progression:** Players can choose specific classes or specializations that affect their abilities and playstyle, unlocking new skills and powers within those classes.

>> **Currency systems:** Players earn in-game currency through activities, which can be spent on upgrades, items, or other progression-related rewards.

Social Systems

Social systems have become more and more prevalent in games as people have realized that gaming together is fun (obviously), and people play for longer if they play with others. A *social system* is an underlying game system that supports or encourages social connections and interactions in games. Having friends and communities in a game increases the likelihood of a player sticking around to play for awhile.

I think about social systems in games in two ways: passive social and active social. *Passive* systems allow players to engage on their time, and *active* systems give players the opportunity to engage directly in the moment.

Here are some examples of how you can design systems for passive social interactions:

>> **Observation:** Players may interact with another player's creation or achievement, like sharing photos in a game or seeing a friend's island that they spent hours decorating for Halloween.

>> **Environmental design:** Designing environments makes players feel connected by simply existing in the same space, like shared towns or hubs.

>> **Leaderboards:** Passive elements like leaderboards let players compare their progress against others without needing to interact directly.

>> **Notifications:** Informing players of friends' activities or milestones through notifications keeps them engaged without requiring immediate interaction.

Here are examples of systems for active social interaction:

>> **Direct player interaction:** Mechanics that encourage players to communicate, collaborate, or compete directly, such as chat systems, voice communication, or real-time events

>> **Cooperative gameplay:** Games that require players to work together to achieve a goal, emphasizing teamwork and strategy

>> **Player-driven content:** Features that allow players to create or modify content that others can directly engage with, such as custom maps or levels

>> **Social contracts:** How games enforce or encourage social norms through mechanics, such as reputation systems and rankings that affect player behavior

TIP

Social systems in games keep players engaged with their community and other players. If you can create a community around them, odds are they'll play exponentially more often than if it were a single-player experience.

Creating dynamics between players

Even the simplest games can encourage dynamics between players with a social feature. I mentioned I was playing an exercise game, and one of the biggest motivators is looking at my friends on the platform and their progress. I want to beat them! Chances are if you've played a game with a leaderboard, you've felt this way, too. It's not just the progression system that keeps players going; adding in social elements can encourage players to play longer and invite their friends.

As human beings, we're driven by motivators. Psychologists such as Burrhus Frederic Skinner and Edward Thorndike have defined models of external motivations since the early 20th century. A successful social system in games often balances both extrinsic and intrinsic motivations.

Extrinsic motivations come from outside the player and often involve tangible rewards like money or recognition. You can often find these in progression systems or community events. Here are some examples:

>> Achievements

>> Leaderboards and ranking

>> Reputation

Intrinsic motivations are internal and are driven by personal satisfaction and enjoyment. You do it because it's enjoyable and interesting to you, not because of any outside incentive or pressures, like rewards or deadlines. Examples include the following:

>> Friendship

>> Story and immersion

>> Agency

>> Shared experiences

TIP

In the industry, we use the term *K-factor* for measuring how many additional players each existing player brings into an app. It was adapted from medical terminology used to assess how fast a virus spreads. Although you may not need to know this term on a solo project, it can be a good measurement when thinking about getting players into your game.

Building player communities

You may just want to make a game and not worry about whether other people will play it or not. Some people simply enjoy the challenge of making a game, which is a big feat in itself. However, if you're interested in having players, building a community is a way to keep them engaged, updated, and even invested in the game's outcomes. A strong community keeps players around longer, and it gives them a voice in shaping the experience, making them feel like they're part of something unique.

Building out in the open is one of the best ways to create early interest and establish trust with players. Sharing progress, milestones, and even challenges while you're developing the game makes players feel like insiders and can attract others who want to be part of the journey from the start. Additionally, creating a space for player feedback and contribution gives your community members a chance to shape the game and gives you much needed input to react to quickly. We did this for all the games I worked on at Bodeville, and although we weren't huge by any means, I attribute our building out in the open to any success we had at reaching players.

Many game developers, such as those highlighted in the following list, actively use platforms like Reddit and Discord to build communities well before their games launch:

>> **Among Us (Innersloth):** Before *Among Us* became a massive hit, the developers were active on both Reddit and Discord. They created a space where early players could provide feedback, suggest ideas, and report bugs.

- **Valheim (Iron Gate Studio):** *Valheim* utilized both Reddit and Discord to build a pre-launch community of interested players. The developers posted early screenshots, gameplay ideas, and polls, inviting feedback from fans.

- **Hades (Supergiant Games):** The developers of *Hades* used Discord to invite fans into the game's Early Access period on Steam. They encouraged players to share feedback on Reddit, where the community became an active space for discussing new updates, sharing fan art, and reporting issues.

- **Stardew Valley (ConcernedApe):** ConcernedApe, the solo developer of *Stardew Valley,* used Reddit heavily pre-launch to share development updates and engage with players about what they'd like to see in a farming sim.

- **Ooblets (Glumberland):** *Ooblets* has an active community on both Discord and Reddit. Before launch, the developers engaged with fans by sharing funny, personal updates and screenshots, creating a warm and inviting atmosphere.

- **A Short Hike (Adam Robinson-Yu):** For *A Short Hike,* developer Adam Robinson-Yu leveraged social platforms to engage with players, especially post-launch. He shared development updates and behind-the-scenes insights on Twitter and joined indie game development communities on forums like TIGSource, where he shared early progress and gathered feedback.

If you've played any social games online, you've probably interacted with people and maybe even become friends in real life. I've met quite a few friends online on games like *World of Warcraft, Rec Room,* and *Meta Horizon Worlds.* All of these games include features in the game that facilitate relationship building and social connections, like guilds, chat, and shared events. In addition to communities on platforms like Discord or Reddit, having in-game features dedicated to creating connections can create lasting relationships within the game that often extend into the broader gaming community and even real life.

Some of the features you can build to foster a gaming community include the following:

- **Chat and friend lists:** Chat systems, friend lists, and matchmaking options allow players to communicate and build relationships directly in the game.

- **In-game interactions:** Interactions between players can encourage positive behaviors, but you have to keep positivity and safety in mind. For example, Journey had a real-time multiplayer feature that limited interactions to whistling and guiding players through levels to encourage only pro-social behavior.

- **Marketplaces:** Games like *Animal Crossing* make it possible for players to trade items, buy and sell things, or help each other out.

>> **Special events and updates:** Having regular events, new seasonal items, or big content drops (like in *Pokémon GO*) keeps things exciting and gives players something to look forward to. It also creates shared experiences that bring everyone together.

>> **Moderation:** A positive vibe makes a huge difference. Games like *Rec Room* and *Meta Horizon Worlds* have reporting systems, moderation features, and community guidelines to maintain a healthy and welcoming environment.

Social features can make a game more engaging, but they can also open the door to negative interactions between players if not handled carefully. Always think about how to keep things positive and welcoming for everyone.

Examples of social systems

As we've progressed in the game industry, including social systems in games has become expected. Many players want to play with their friends (or make new friends). So, we have a lot of good examples from games in the last ten years that allow people to connect and play together.

Here's a select few examples of how social systems are used in popular games:

>> **Guilds or clans:** Examples from games like *World of Warcraft* or *Clash of Clans* where players group together for mutual benefits.

>> **Party-based multiplayer games:** Games like *Among Us* or *League of Legends,* in which small groups of players work together (or against each other) toward a common goal.

>> **Asynchronous multiplayer:** In *Dark Souls,* players can leave messages for others to read, providing indirect interaction and shared experiences, and games like *Stardew Valley* allow players to visit each other's farms asynchronously.

>> **PvP arenas or battlegrounds:** Competitive environments like *Fortnite* or *Rocket League* that build social engagement through direct competition.

Economy Systems

Economy systems in games are designed to simulate real-world economic interactions, creating a framework in which players can earn, trade, and spend in-game resources. These systems help provide structure and value to items, currencies, and services within the game world, making gameplay more immersive. Building a virtual economy requires careful planning of in-game rewards, currency flow, and pricing to create an enjoyable, fair experience for players.

A well-balanced economy keeps players motivated to earn and manage resources without overwhelming or restricting them. You just have to ensure that items remain valuable and accessible at a fair rate. Developers often adjust how often an item can be obtained (its *drop rate*), availability, and prices of items to prevent inflation or scarcity, which can disrupt gameplay. For example, rare items may have lower drop rates to increase their value, while commonly needed resources are more abundant to support regular gameplay activities.

Building virtual economies

Virtual economies are built by designing in-game currencies, resources, and items that players can earn, trade, or purchase. Economies in games are very intriguing just like they are in real life, and they give players the ability to set goals and see progress. Everyone loves to see the numbers go up!

These economies may be tied to real money or to something you can get from completing tasks in-game. The two types of currencies we talk about when designing an economy are soft and hard. *Soft currency* is the in-game cash you rack up just by playing, like completing missions or doing daily tasks. You can typically get it often, and it doesn't require purchasing with your real-life cash. *Hard currency* is what you typically buy with real cash or earn through special events. This is how the game is monetized, and this currency is often reserved for premium items or features that can save you time or give you a significant boost in progress, like unlocking exclusive skins or speeding up something like construction times.

Some examples of types of economies in games are as follows:

>> **Player-driven:** Players control prices through trading and crafting, shaping the market. Think auctions houses!

>> **Creator:** Players can create, sell, and buy user-generated content, fueling an entire ecosystem around custom items, experiences, and games.

>> **Virtual goods:** Cosmetic items and non-essential upgrades keep things fun without affecting gameplay, like in *Rocket League* and *VRChat*.

>> **Resource-based:** Players gather resources and manage them for crafting or survival, adding a strategic layer like in *Rust* and *Minecraft*.

>> **Tokenized/blockchain:** Blockchain-based assets (like NFTs) allow for ownership and trading.

You can build an in-game economy using these steps:

1. **Choose the main currency, like coins or even something like goldfish.**

2. **Figure out your resources (like stone, wood, or seeds) and assign them value.**

   The value is not only in terms of currency, but also in terms of gameplay.

3. **Define which items are rarer than others and price them accordingly.**

   You may even create an ultra-rare item and make it a very high price to "anchor" it, making everything else look much more affordable in comparison.

4. **Create various ways for players to earn currency and resources,** such as completing quests, battling enemies, or crafting items.

5. **Create various *sinks*, where players can spend the currency.**

   These may be shops, upgrades, or customization options.

6. **Balance supply by adjusting item drop rates or prices based on how frequently players earn or use them.**

7. **Introduce new items and resources periodically to keep the economy fresh.**

8. **Prevent inflation by setting caps on currency, adjusting item values, or introducing decay.**

   Decay can also prevent players from hoarding resources or having to manage or trash them if they have too many sitting around in their inventory. This may mean an apple that you collect has a life of three days in your bag, as opposed to an old boot that sticks around forever (unfortunately).

9. **Be prepared to make a lot of adjustments and be open to feedback!**

   As I discuss in Chapter 12, you'll conduct a lot of playtesting and balancing, which means you'll be making adjustments as you go. Your game will go through many iterations, which is why I say you'll *iterate* — that is, make changes that will (hopefully) improve your game.

I mention sources and sinks in the previous steps. These are widely used terms in economy design, and balancing them well can really affect how people play the game. When revenue sources are way higher than costs, for example, the game loses its challenge and can get boring. Players won't see a reason to spend real money on currency either. On the other hand, if revenue is way lower than costs, things can be too difficult and punishing. Nobody wants to grind for hours just to make basic progress, which can lead to players dropping out of the game.

A few best practices for designing virtual economies are as follows:

>> Design as much as you can in a spreadsheet first, and maybe even simulate a few scenarios using formulas. This will help to iterate before you implement in the game. A simulation tool called Machinations (`https://machinations.io/`) can help you to simulate a process in an economy.

>> Track the numbers in your economy in an analytics tool like Firebase (`https://firebase.google.com/`).Tracking will make it infinitely easier to balance and make improvements.

>> All the items in your game should be meaningful in some way to the gameplay.

When creating your original numbers like prices for in-game resources, make sure to start on the high end. When you have players purchasing those items, making items cheaper is easier; making them more expensive is difficult without ruffling some players' feathers.

Balancing supply and demand

Just like in real life when the government makes updates to our economy, you'll have to do the same in your game. Sometimes you may find that players are frustrated when an item is too scarce or the drop rate on a basic item is way too high!

Some things you'll need to do as people play your game include

>> Adjust spawn rates, drop rates, and availability to keep players engaged

>> Keep tabs on the in-game economy to prevent inflation or deflation

>> Use price adjustments or item rarity to control supply and demand

>> Introduce events or special content to periodically influence demand

Keep an eye on player habits and how they use the economy. Use analytics to track what they buy and how often items are used. This way, you can spot trends and update things accordingly.

Examples of economy systems

Here are some examples of economies in some popular games:

» **Stardew Valley:** Resource gathering, crafting, and seasonal crop sales create a dynamic, time-based economy centered on farming and production.

» **VRChat:** In this social-driven economy, custom avatars and worlds act as valuable assets, with some creators selling these items outside the game.

» **Fortnite:** Seasonal battle passes and item shop rotations create demand for exclusive items and reward player progression.

» **Animal Crossing:** This economy is based on item trading, seasonal events, and customization options, driven by limited resources and social interaction

Balancing and Iteration of Game Systems

Game systems are full of numbers, formulas, and content. They are vehicles made to interact with each other and distribute information, creating a dynamic environment for players. These systems not only dictate the rules and mechanics of gameplay but also influence player behavior and strategy. By balancing elements like scoring, leveling, and resource management, you can create challenges and rewarding experiences.

The first numbers you plug into a system may never be the ones you ship the game with. You can make assumptions about the timing of how people will play based on research or data from other games, but they will always need some tweaking by testing them out. When I start mapping out a game system, I use my best guess for an initial number from my experience playing games and using the data I have available to me. I've been able to work on some games on a global scale and with access to extensive data, which is a nice shortcut to some reasonable starting numbers.

When I work solo or on a small team, making assumptions on the first numbers included in a system is harder. I tend to look at similar games' numbers and any feedback in forums to get a sense for where I should start. Then I take an educated guess and hope that I've allotted enough time to make those changes!

TIP

Instead of starting your numbers out small, like 1 to 10, multiply them by 100. Getting 100 apples for doing something is way more fun than getting 1 apple. Just remember to balance the system out accordingly to that multiplier.

Testing game systems

You will need to give yourself time to iterate on your original numbers in the game system. That's guaranteed. The good news is that even before your numbers hit the game, you can test them out in either a spreadsheet or a software application like Machinations, as shown in Figure 7-4.

FIGURE 7-4
An example from
Machinations, a
simulation
software for
balancing
game systems.

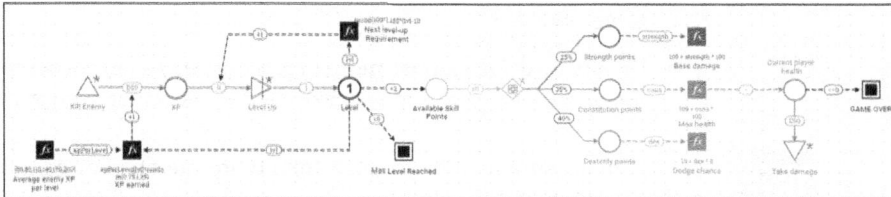

Machinations is a tool that designers can use to build a visual flow to simulate their systems. These tools are useful to

>> Test out game systems with your team

>> Simulate outcomes

>> Balance parameters on the fly

Updating game systems post-launch

Even in the games I didn't expect to make updates to (I'm looking at you Chief Emoji Officer), we ended up making some tweaks, fixing bugs, and updating some of the game systems. Not to worry though, this is a standard thing to do, and you should expect to make at least a couple of updates once it's in the store for players.

You may find issues with balancing, or you may want to add events or limited-time challenges to keep things interesting. Maybe players have way too many golden apples, and you meant for them to be extremely rare. Just make sure to communicate with your players and let them know what you're updating and maybe even why. Doing this can help fend off bad sentiment about *nerfing* (making something less effective than it was) something that was overpowered and lets players know how their gameplay will be affected in the future.

Some of the things you should expect after you've launched your game are

>> **Balancing and tweaking systems.** No matter how prepared you think you are, there will always be some player burning through your content and systems!

>> **Adding new content.** You'll want to prepare expansions or downloadable content (DLC) with new levels, characters, or missions to keep the game engaging.

>> **UX and interface adjustments:** You'll probably even encounter issues with user experience (UX) and systems' interface flow that need to be adjusted.

REMEMBER

Always make sure to allot yourself time to iterate on your game systems — *before and after* launching the game.

Chapter **8**

Incorporating Story in Games

A great story can turn a fun game into an unforgettable experience. As a gamer, I've immersed myself in numerous narrative-rich games over the years, and I reference many of these examples throughout this book. Lately, I've been focused on crafting story-based games with a social commentary angle. Building engaging stories and worlds demands dedication, iteration, and creativity, but today, it's more accessible than ever with tools like Twine for branching stories, ChatGPT for editing and ideas, and user-generated content platforms like Meta Horizon Worlds and Roblox. The popularity of the "Story Rich" tag on Steam highlights the growing demand for narrative-driven games. After all, everyone has a story to tell.

Telling a Story

You may find inspiration in different steps when coming up with a story, and you'll be able to continue building around your main concept throughout your development. We came up with a lot of the supporting characters in our game because we were inspired by people in our lives, situations that we were in, or media we were consuming at the time.

Generally, my steps for coming up with a story look like this:

1. I come up with the story's conceit. A *conceit* is the central premise of your story. Maybe it's a world where people can only communicate through emojis or a city where dreams are treated as currency.

2. Next, I think about the protagonist. Who is navigating this world? What do they want, and what stands in their way? A burnt-out office worker trying to climb the corporate ladder? A dream thief struggling to pull off one last heist?

3. Then, I build the conflict. Is the protagonist fighting against office culture, their own flaws, or an impending disaster?

4. After that, it's time to write out the beats of the story. Sometimes I write out a list of how the narrative arcs, and maybe even make a storyboard at a high level to help visualize the story, which helps me think of new characters.

5. Finally, I explore the tone and style. Is this a dark satire, a heartfelt drama, or an absurd comedy?

I explain these elements further throughout this section.

Writing story conceit

A story's *conceit* is the central premise that creates the foundation of the story. It can help create attachments to characters in the story and set expectations of the world and the interactions inside it. Think of it like the elevator pitch for your game, short enough to pitch to someone and hook them with just one sentence. It may even be your *razor statement,* a short sentence that describes your game, as I discuss in Chapter 13. Think about the following when making your story's conceit:

>> Who is the protagonist?

>> What do they want?

>> What's stopping them from getting what they want?

You've probably read or noticed the conceit in a game's marketing or storefront. The core concept of the story often appears in a game's trailer or in the store description. If it's written well, it can be a big draw for an audience and make them more likely to try the game.

The conceit dictates the emotional tone — whether it's a creepy mystery or a heartwarming, cozy experience. Think about the feeling each of these example story conceits from some popular games evoke as you're reading through them:

>> The player is a test subject trapped in a research facility, forced to solve puzzles using a portal gun while being taunted by a sarcastic AI.

>> The player awakens in a ruined world with no memory of past events. The hero must regain his lost abilities, defeat a centuries-old evil, and restore peace to the kingdom.

>> The player moves to a run-down town and starts a new life training creatures. They collect strange, adorable creatures, who help them in dance battles, farming, and improving the town.

>> The player is a fisherman in a small, eerie archipelago, where they must catch fish, upgrade their boat, and uncover dark secrets lurking beneath the surface. Strange, otherworldly phenomena occur at night, and the ocean hides ancient horrors.

Each example paints a very different picture about the ambiance of the world, from evil to adorable.

TIP

Some studios may use different names to refer to these razor statements or slogans. Even though the title may change from studio to studio, the purpose is the same: to set up the elevator pitch of the game and make it easy for people to understand the central premise. Sometimes they may even end up in the marketing, like the conceit for Dante's Inferno (Electronic Arts): Go to Hell.

REMEMBER

The conceit of a story is the core idea that drives everything from gameplay and mechanics to systems in the game. It shapes the entire player experience. If you're deliberating over whether something should go into your game or not, check back in with the conceit you defined. Referring to it can help you decide whether to include it or not.

Developing characters

Character development plays an important part of stories and games because it helps to create compelling and memorable experiences for players. Well-developed characters can drive the narrative, evoke emotional responses, and deepen player engagement. Often, games are built around characters. Just think of some of the characters from popular Nintendo games:

>> A bear and a bird in a backpack embark to defeat a witch in an adventure platformer.

>> A kid (well, depending on the game, they could be really old) in a green tunic goes on a quest to save the land from a powerful sorcerer.

>> A fox leads their team in space battles, with character-driven missions and dialogues advancing the story.

Narrative and gameplay must work hand in hand, especially through the character. A well-designed character should fit the story and align with the gameplay mechanics. When a character's goals and actions line up with the gameplay, it makes the experience feel more natural and keeps players hooked. *Ludonarrative dissonance* — coined by Clint Hocking, a game designer known for his work on titles like *Splinter Cell: Chaos Theory*, *Far Cry 2*, and *Watch Dogs: Legion* — refers to the disconnect that happens when a character's story-driven motivations contradict their gameplay actions. For example, if a protagonist is all about peace in cutscenes but then goes on a killing spree during gameplay, it feels off. That kind of inconsistency can pull players out of the experience.

TIP

Characters play a significant role by creating trust and connection with the audience. A relatable or charismatic character can make a game or story more appealing, making it easier for people to relate to the content and get invested in the experience. When characters have well-defined traits and backstories that fit the world's logic, their actions and motivations feel believable. However, characters can't be perfect — flawless characters often feel unrelatable and uninteresting. Imperfections make them feel more human, creating tension, growth, and emotional investment for the audience.

Initial creation

When developing characters, I usually kick things off with references to get some inspiration. I create a mood board and gather various assets to draw from. I may browse Pinterest, Sketchfab, or Google Images, but lately, I've been using DALL-E or Midjourney to generate a bunch of different looks, compositions, and styles.

Then, I create character guides. These guides include how the character speaks, their gender identity, social class, role in the game, and unique traits. By combining all these elements, you define what makes that character unique, including key attributes, visuals, silhouette, and voice, to ensure that they're fully fleshed out and consistent.

In *Chief Emoji Officer*, we additionally chose a theme to constrain the types of characters you encounter in the game. All the characters in the game are animals, inspired by a popular animated TV comedy in which all the characters are humanoid animals. This choice led to a ton of fun puns in dialogue and naming, and even speech patterns for the dialogue. It also helped keep the characters consistent in the world so that they all felt part of the same universe.

Names

Naming characters can be a bit of a mixed bag. Sometimes names just pop into your head; sometimes you need to see the character fully realized before the perfect name clicks. And occasionally, a road trip or a change of scenery can spark the right inspiration.

TIP

I like to flesh out the character's visuals and description first and then draw inspiration from my surroundings to find the perfect name. I've come up with great names by watching movies and pulling inspiration from the characters in that world.

Archetypes

Character archetypes are the classic roles you see in tons of stories. They're important because they provide a quick, recognizable framework for storytelling and help set audience expectations. They help players or audiences quickly understand who characters are and what role they play in the story. Here are a few:

>> **The Hero:** The brave soul who goes on a quest

>> **The Mentor:** The wise guide who helps the hero out

>> **The Villain:** The troublemaker causing all the problems

>> **The Sidekick:** The hero's loyal buddy, often there for comic relief

>> **The Everyman:** The regular person who ends up in wild situations

REMEMBER

Archetypes, like any framework, are there to give you a solid foundation, allowing you to build on them with more personal details and quirks. But don't be afraid to branch out and derive inspiration from your friends, your family, or anyone you know. Good writers use what they know and add their own twist.

Creating narrative structure

The narrative structure of your game serves as the backbone of its story. It offers a clear framework for your ideas, allowing you to figure out the big picture before writing the finer details. Although not every game includes a story, those that do rely on narrative beats and plot progression to guide the player's experience.

The fundamental narrative structure, often referred to as the *narrative arc* or *story arc*, is a framework used to create a path for a story to follow. It's not just a structure used in games, though; it's widespread in literature and film. This fundamental structure includes the following elements:

- ›› The *exposition* sets up the story, characters, and basic situation.

- ›› The *inciting incident* is a triggering event that sets the protagonist to action. For the sake of this definition, let's assume that's the player in a game world.

- ›› *Rising action* are the actions and choices the player (or protagonist) makes to move the story forward.

- ›› *Climax* is the peak of the story's tension: A critical decision or confrontation happens here.

- ›› *Falling action* is the aftermath of that climax or confrontation.

- ›› Next comes the *resolution,* in which all the loose ends are tied up and the story ends.

Here's an example of a narrative structure for one of my games, *Chief Emoji Officer:*

- ›› **Exposition:** The player is introduced into the corporate chat system, where they can speak only through emojis. They start as an entry-level employee and learn the basics of emoji-based decision-making.

- ›› **Inciting incident:** The player is taunted by Wanda, the chatbot AI, to rise through the ranks to become CEO.

- ›› **Rising action:** The player makes decisions using emojis, and the narrative develops through those choices. New characters are introduced, and new emojis are unlocked.

- ›› **Climax:** The player reaches the major decision to become CEO. This is the peak of the story, as defined by the story's conceit: "Become CEO using only emojis."

- ›› **Falling action:** The player makes their major decision and sees the outcome of it. They see how their relationships with coworkers and bosses have evolved.

- ›› **Resolution:** The player either becomes the Chief Emoji Officer or encounters a humorous alternative ending depending on their path.

TIP

As I'm writing this book, we're adding new chapters to *Chief Emoji Officer.* It's been challenging to add onto the current story structure and make it meaningful and open-ended enough to still allow for more chapters to be added. If you plan to add more or to write sequels for your game someday, keep it in the back of your mind as you're writing the structure of your narrative. You'll have to make sure not to kill off (or in my case, lay off) any characters or include other potential events that could write you into a corner.

Designing Worlds

When someone defines rules for a world, writes the lore, and establishes history and culture in a fictional environment, it's called *worldbuilding*. Worldbuilding is the process of creating the universe where your game takes place. A world has its own rules, cultures, geography, and history. It can also help give depth to the story, characters, and gameplay, making everything feel more connected and believable.

Worldbuilding techniques

When I'm thinking about building a world, I try to approach it like city planning. City planning has a significant impact on the environment and atmosphere, influencing everything from air quality and energy consumption to biodiversity and water management. While working on the demo for *Watchmakers*, I had to think about where the city's water sources came from. This influences why the city was built in that spot and what nearby cities might exist. In *Watchmakers*, Ozona's desert landscape thrived because of its magical resources, and because the inhabitants weren't human, access to water wasn't a huge priority. Still, it played a role in how I thought about shaping the relationship between Ozona and neighboring cities, the distances, and when other places were referenced in the dialogue.

TIP

As you develop your world, you may have sketched locations, created key landmarks, or defined the languages its characters speak. Make sure to start compiling all these details into a single document! I like to link it out of the main game design document (see Chapter 3). It should outline the world's rules, lore, and design elements, including its history, cultural norms, visual styles, and any governing mechanics. Keeping everything in one place helps with coherence and makes it easier to reference as your project changes and evolves.

When you're designing a world, try asking yourself these questions to really nail down the details:

>> Where are we? Are we on a planet? In a city?

>> What year is it?

>> What's the climate?

>> What does the area look like?

>> How close is it to water?

>> Is it a planned city or an unplanned city?

>> What's the biome?

>> What type of architecture is there?

>> How well kept is it?

>> What types of plants are there?

>> What colors are prominent?

>> What technology is there?

>> How does the culture innovate?

>> What research is being done?

>> What industries are there?

>> Who inhabits this world?

>> What's their purpose?

>> Where do they come from?

>> What are their beliefs?

>> What are their fears?

>> What is their language?

>> Does the physical world change or arc?

>> Does the weather change?

>> Does the culture change?

>> How does the world affect the story?

>> Does it change any physical mechanics?

>> Does it change any emotional mechanics?

REMEMBER

You don't have to answer all the questions for your world, and you don't have to show players all this information. Even on much larger projects, like the global, map-based pet simulator I worked on, we wrote backstories and information to help us make sense of the world we were designing. Doing this influenced how we designed points of interest in the world, the characters, and the resources in the game. For instance, it helped us answer why the creatures were returning to specific locations and what resources they could obtain from those places. All this information sits in design documents for the team to reference. It wasn't ever intended to be player-facing but can be helpful in answering design questions for the world.

Creating immersive worlds

Crafting your entire world will take time. You can see just how many different parts of worlds people make and their great examples in r/worldbuilding on Reddit. You may be answering questions all throughout your story development, and as you build situations and events, you may need to revisit questions about characters' motivations or questions about how the world behaves or why it exists. Gathering the visual bits (my favorite part), including sketching and building the world, is a great step toward building out your world. Most games will need a visual world, unless you're into text adventures like me.

For me, I like to spend quite a bit of time curating references on Pinterest, and sometimes I find inspiration that takes me in a whole different direction. This process helps to understand the mood, colors, layout, composition, perspective, and style of the world. You can even buy reference packs from places like Gumroad, the Unity Asset store, or Unreal Engine Marketplace if you want to get a head start with pre-made assets. When you have a general sense of how you want your world to look, it will start to take shape.

The next steps of world creation, which I explore throughout this section, involve the following:

>> Sketching a top-down view of your world

>> Creating a golden path

>> Blocking out the layout of the world's map

A top-down view of your world

Start by sketching a *top-down view of your world.* This is like drawing a map from above, showing the overall layout and key locations. This view helps you visualize the geography and major landmarks, and how different areas connect.

Figure 8-1 shows a rough layout and user flow of a map and includes all the places where I wanted to provide puzzles for a virtual reality (VR) experience I made while working on *Meta Horizon Worlds.* I started with the focal point of the level, a caged alien that the player must save, and worked backward from that main goal by listing steps the player needs to take to get there.

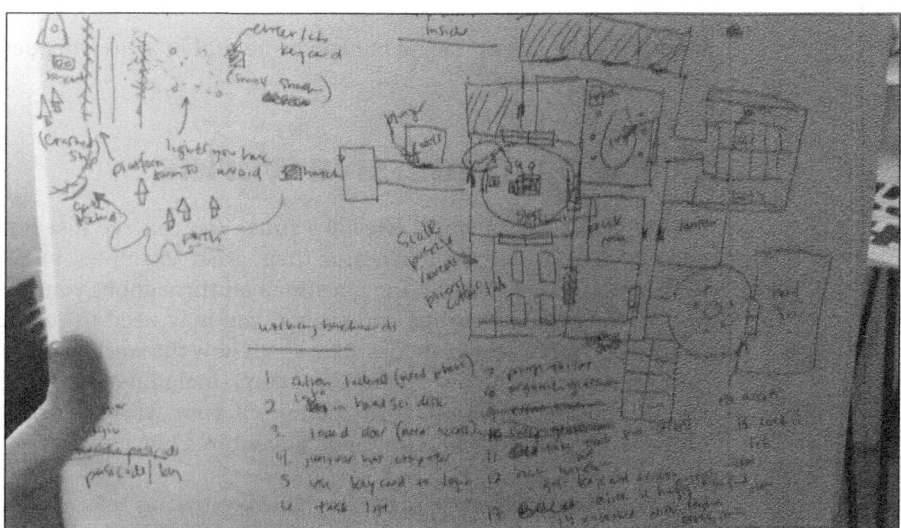

FIGURE 8-1:
You can use
simple tools to
create user flows
for your games.

A golden path

Next, outline a *golden path* that represents the ideal journey you want your player to take. This path highlights the main route through your world, focusing on the core actions the player must take to reach their end goal.

For everyone who can't read the chicken scratch in Figure 8-1, here's a condensed version of the player flow:

1. Player notices hungry alien locked in a cage.

2. Explore and find janitor closet.

3. Find locked head scientist office.

4. Use keycard to log in to janitor's computer to show the task list.

5. Show task list.

6. Plunge toilet.

7. Take out trash.

8. Get access to program to hack access to keycard.

9. Get access to head scientist office.

10. Alien is hungry, so find it food.

11. Cook food in lab.

12. Solve a weighted scale puzzle to get pliers.

13. Use pliers to release alien from its cage.

14. Feed alien.

15. Grab alien and take it back to the rocket and finish the game.

The layout of the world's map

When you have a rough layout of your world and the points of interest, *block out the layout of your world* in 3-D or 2-D space, as I've done in Figure 8-2. Blocking out maps in worlds is commonplace in the industry to get a feel for the space, identify points of interest in the world, and to guide the player toward interesting places or goals. It's best to use simple shapes or modular pieces to create a rough version of your environment. This stage is about getting a tangible sense of space and how different areas will interact, and less about the details, if it all. It allows you to experiment with the placement of objects, structures, and pathways before you spend time on assets.

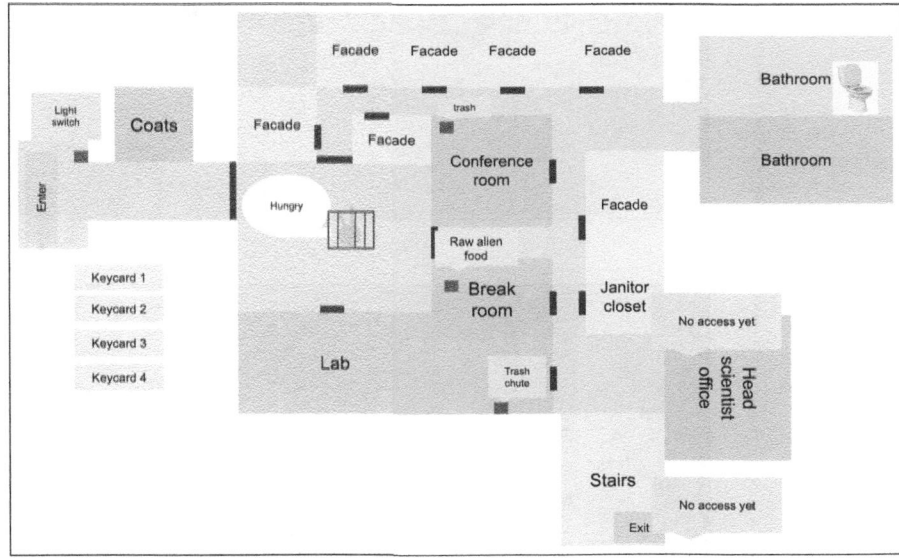

FIGURE 8-2:
A top-down level layout, made with simple shapes in Google Slides.

REMEMBER

Don't feel as though your first iteration is final or needs to be perfect! Your map and its contents will shift as you iterate on the mechanics and content explorers interact with. Often, my first pass is vastly different than my final piece. I tend to make spaces too large, making them feel empty. A smaller space with denser interactions will make the world feel more alive and interesting.

Eventually you'll be able to add art assets, iterate on the environment, and add all sorts of props and interactions depending on your game's mechanics. Figures 8-3 and 8-4 show a couple of screenshots of how our VR experience turned out from the layouts shown in Figure 8-2 — after defining the layouts in 2-D, we built out these environments in 3-D.

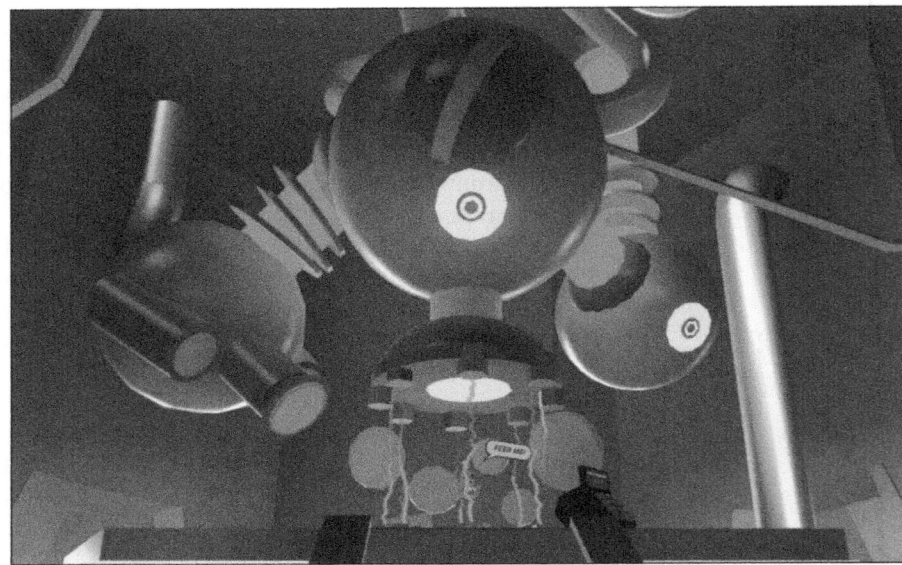

FIGURE 8-3:
The player notices a hungry alien locked in a cage.

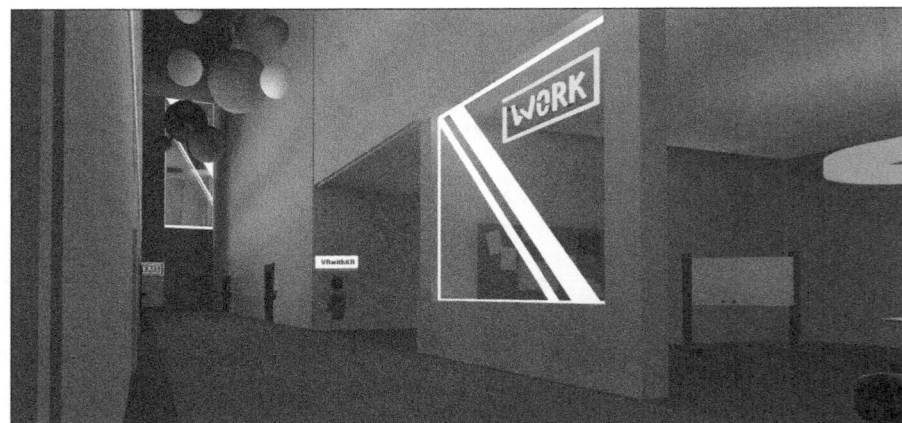

FIGURE 8-4:
The player grabs the alien and takes it back to the rocket to finish the game.

Being consistent in world design

Consistency helps create a sense of reality in your game world, making it easier for players to become immersed. Humans are always seeking out patterns, so just like in the real world, when things follow predictable patterns, the experience feels more believable and engaging. A world consists of

>> Aesthetics, architecture, and art

>> Lore, history, and culture

>> Characters and communities

>> Man-made and natural rules of the world, such as economy and physics

>> Sounds

Sounds are consistently an afterthought in game development, but they can do a really great job of establishing location and time. An excellent example is bugs. Bugs make a lot of noise, and as someone who grew up in Florida and lived in Texas, cicadas (the constantly buzzing bugs) really establish a location, a temperature, and a nostalgic feeling. If you watch a lot of Japanese media or anime, you may notice that cicadas are often used to establish the sound of summer.

Beyond the basics, think about additional patterns and elements that can enhance consistency in your game world:

>> Color schemes

>> Architectural styles

>> Symbolism and motifs

>> Dialogue patterns and the way characters speak

In *Chief Emoji Officer,* we crafted distinctive speech patterns and assigned emojis for each character to enhance their unique identities and bring the satire of corporate life to life. Because this game is primarily text-based, this is one of the patterns we could use to enhance the world. By incorporating corporate lingo and office jargon, we not only differentiate the characters but also amplify the game's satirical tone. Here's an example:

Thom Pence (Finance)

Thom has a noticeable lisp that adds a hissing quality to his speech. He frequently elongates "s" sounds with multiple "s" to enhance his menacing and overly greedy demeanor. His dialogue is laced with greed and financial manipulation of users. Example dialogue:

Let's discusss the budget, shall we? We need to maximize profitsss and minimize expensesss, no matter the cossst. Remember, every dollar saved is a victory in the world of finance, and I plan to squeeze every lassst cent out of thisss operation!

REMEMBER

Create a world document that outlines the rules, lore, and design elements of your game world. Include details in this document like the world's history, cultural norms, visual styles, and any specific rules that govern how things work. Keep it handy when you add new characters, dialogue, systems, environments, or really anything else so you can keep the world consistent.

IN THIS CHAPTER

» Learning what art style is

» Digging into why art style is important

» Creating your art and audio styles

» Finding tools for defining art and audio style

» Remembering ethical and cultural consideration when designing games

» Learning from real-world examples

Chapter 9

Developing an Art Style in Games

A game's art style is the first thing you notice when you look at a game! It sells the game to players, and it sets the mood and tone. *Art style* is the visual identity of a game, and often people won't even make it to the gameplay if they don't like the art style. In a nutshell, art style is important because it

» **Helps with marketing.** A recognizable art style will set your work apart from others.

» **Helps form communities.** Players are drawn to games with art that they enjoy, so your game will draw like-minded players. Think of how fans of one stylish indie game often flock to others with a similar vibe.

» **Clarifies scope for development.** Curating the options for your artwork can help the art team focus, create better art, and create more of it.

In this chapter, I provide an explanation of why art style matters and how to develop your own — while keeping in mind issues like scope, ethics, and cultural considerations.

Defining Art Style

Defining art style for your game is important because creating systems for what your art should look and feel like can help keep the art cohesive when it comes to developing it. If your art is cohesive, it can help make your game recognizable on the store and create a visual brand for your work. What makes the games that you've played instantly stand out to you? It could be one of many things:

>> The colors used

>> The theme or setting

>> How characters look and act

>> How all the elements in the game come together

>> Stylish and easy-to-use interfaces

Identifying the elements of art style

Art style is the overall look and feel of a game's visuals, created by a curation of artistic choices. Art style isn't about how good the graphics are but how the game conveys the mood and atmosphere to the player. Art style can vary widely, ranging from realistic to abstract, to cartoonish or pixelated.

Each art style is made up of different attributes:

>> **Color palette:** The combinations of colors you use that sets the mood and vibe.

>> **Line work:** How lines are drawn. They may be thick, thin, smooth, or rough.

>> **Texture:** How the surfaces are rendered. They can be smooth, bumpy, hairy, or patterned.

>> **Shape language:** What shapes are the assets composed of? Are they blocky, round, or organic?

>> **Perspective and composition:** How everything is arranged in the frame and how players see it.

- » **Character design:** The look of your characters, including their proportions and features.

- » **Animation style:** How movement is shown. It can be choppy or smooth.

- » **Lighting and shadows:** How light and shadows are used to create moods.

- » **Artistic techniques:** The methods you use to create the art, like drawing by hand or using 3-D software.

- » **Cultural influences:** Inspirations from different cultures that give your art style its unique flavor.

- » **Iconography and symbols:** Specific symbols or images that add meaning and help tell your story.

WARNING

Drawing inspiration from different cultures can add depth and richness to your art, but please be mindful about the context, history, and significance of the elements of the culture you're using. Consulting with cultural experts of the community can help you understand and be thoughtful regarding what you're including in your work.

REMEMBER

Art history can be a huge inspiration for your art style. If you're trying to achieve a dark, intense mood, you may pull inspiration from the heavy contrasts in Baroque paintings. Or if you want something playful and bright, you may draw inspiration from Pop Art. Learning more about Impressionism, Cubism, or Surrealism can help you find more inspiration for unique colors, whimsy, and visual effects.

TIP

There's a whole art world out there beyond games. I recommend checking out *Art History For Dummies* (Wiley) if you want to learn more!

Understanding how art style evokes a game's mood

Game studios often start a game by prototyping mechanics and then develop an art style on top of it. But games can come from anywhere, and mechanics aren't the only way to start making games. Art style can actually inspire a game's direction, like if you were to make a Salvador–Dalí inspired game. Either way you go about it, art style is an important part of games as a visual media. Think about the moods these two games evoke:

- » **Brotato:** A game in which you play a potato warrior who battles hordes of enemies while collecting resources and upgrades. It has a colorful, cartoonish pixel look with goofy character designs.

>> **Vampire Survivors:** A game in which you play a vampire slayer, battling monsters while collecting resources and upgrades. It has a retro pixel art style with darker, moodier color palettes and gothic themes.

These games have similar gameplay and both are considered to be *roguelites*, replayable games that have skill-based gameplay in which every run is different; you lose progress when you die; and you unlock permanent abilities, characters, or resources over time. Some of the differences include the setting, theme, art, and player fantasy. The differences in the art style set apart the atmosphere and mood; they may attract different players and demographics; and their aesthetic sets expectations for the gameplay and narrative.

The different art styles really set the mood for each game. *Brotato's* goofy visuals bring a sense of fun and humor, and *Vampire Survivors'* darker tones amp up the tension and excitement. The art style plays a big role in player fantasy and narrative. It makes the story and world feel more immersive, especially when you throw in some epic metal music to match the intensity!

REMEMBER

Art style is important in games! Even a game seemingly lacking an art style like *Dwarf Fortress*, a text-based simulation game, has a cohesive art style that sets expectations for the players' experience.

Figuring out your art style

Figuring out what makes up your artwork is going to take practice. The best way to do this is to continuously make work, analyze what makes it "you," and iterate from there. No one is born a talented artist (even though society sometimes tells us this), and everyone can be a talented artist with practice. The best artists I know practice often, every week, and sometimes even daily. Picasso made around 13,500 paintings, and he didn't just make a few excellent works of art in the first three tries. He experimented and tried new things to get to a result he was proud of.

I am no expert artist! I have a lot of work to do on that front, but I've learned from some great artists in the industry on what their process is, which involves these steps:

1. **Define the feeling you want to evoke from a viewer or player.**

   This can be nostalgia or sadness.

2. **Research existing works of art to figure out what you do and don't like based on the atmosphere or theme you're trying to achieve.**

   Collecting references can be useful for figuring out where you want your art to go. I create *mood boards* by using Pinterest or Figma to collect a bunch of different references. I then use the mood boards to analyze the commonalities and the things I want to inspire my work.

3. **Create concept art.**

   Concept art is the visual exploration of how a game looks and feels. It can help define the environment, characters, props, or overall visual style before you start making all the assets.

   There may be an iteration phase during which you try different shapes and rendering techniques.

4. **Make a few mock-ups of scenes or items in the game, like key locations, characters, items, or user interfaces.**

5. **Start putting together an art style guide (ASG).**

   An *art style guide* is a document meant to help you define how the game looks. It can help align everyone on the team and help the artists create cohesive art assets. See more about the ASG in the later section, "Exploring Elements of Art Style."

6. **Collect feedback.**

   You can share your artwork with your friends, your peers, potential players, or online to get feedback and make improvements on your work.

7. **Iterate on all the above.**

8. **Produce or find the final assets that work within the established ASG guidelines.**

Creating consistency in your artwork

Many games strive for consistency in their artwork because it enhances *immersion*, meaning the player feels fully absorbed in the game's world.

Back in the early days of puzzle games, sometimes you could tell what items were interactable because they were rendered brighter than the rest of the environment. For example, imagine a book on a shelf that you needed to check out, and sometimes it'd be obvious which one because it was a different shade than all the other books on the shelf.

This can be a good and a bad thing! I can't tell you if it was intentional on the developer's part or just a product of the technology at the time, but this color differentiation made it easier for the player to find items in a large world (good thing) or ruined the surprise of exploration because having one book brighter in the room kept you from being able to explore on your own (bad thing).

A great example of a game that maintains strong immersion through consistent artwork is *Limbo* by Playdead. The game's black-and-white silhouette style creates a haunting atmosphere, and instead of using bright colors to highlight interactable objects, it relies on contrast and environmental cues. This allows players to stay engaged in the world without feeling like the game is hand-holding them and telling them exactly what to explore.

Creating consistency in your artwork not only will enhance immersion but will also help you create assets quicker after you figure out your artistic guidelines. For one of my games that had more than ten characters in it, the first character took the longest for me to make. I had to figure out the shape of the character, what the face would look like, what colors to use, and what clothing it would wear, and then I had to model and animate it all. I made the first character at least five times, which took quite a bit of work and time. But once I figured out all those details, I had a base for all the other characters, and I could even adapt that asset for the other characters.

TIP

Shapes, colors, and motifs don't just affect your in-world assets, but they can also influence your user interface's design. You may include the theme or cultural influence of the game into any motifs in your UI, or you may choose to use complementary colors to make the UI pop off the background.

Creating consistent artwork takes time and many iterations. Here are some ways to get there:

>> Create an art style guide (ASG) to define rules and guidelines for uniformity.

>> Use consistent color palettes, character designs, and environmental aesthetics. I always say if you're going to make it ugly, at least make it consistently ugly!

>> Regularly review and refine assets to maintain a cohesive look.

REMEMBER

I talk about iteration a lot in this book because nothing starts out perfect! Designing a game takes *iteration* — redoing what you've done or refining it as you go — and making improvements over time to achieve something. The same goes for art. Remember to continuously analyze and improve your work, and you'll get to that image you have in your mind.

Adapting art style to gameplay and narrative

Making sure that the art style supports the gameplay leads to a more immersive environment. Take for instance a game about war. War is a heavy topic, so bright colors and a highly stylized environment may not suit the theme.

Here are some things to consider when deciding on an art style that matches your gameplay:

>> **The emotions you want to evoke, like drama or light-heartedness, and what artistic elements you need to achieve this.** A dramatic game about war may have muted colors and serious dialogue. A light-hearted game about war, on the other hand, may have brighter colors and comical or satirical dialogue.

>> **The speed of the gameplay and how you can increase legibility.** Think of something like Superhot, a fast-paced virtual reality game, that uses red for mobs to make them stand out on a white background.

>> **What players expect from the genre.** For some genres like RPGs, players may expect detail-rich worlds. On the other hand, a casual puzzle game can have less detail.

Telling a story through visuals

You can use visuals to illustrate a story throughout your game, lead players toward something, and foreshadow upcoming events.

Lighting and color play a large part in setting the scene. A dark, dreary place or moody lighting can seem tense or gloomy, or warm colors and a bright space can create a sense of calm or happiness. Think about the scene of a boss battle: A red-lit arena with shadows and sharp contrasts instantly signals intensity, but soft lighting with even tones may tell a totally different story.

If you've played *Journey*, one of the first things you see is a distant mountain. It's always in view, reminding you of your goals and the adventure you'll have on the way up there. Environments can also allude to the story's arc — abandoned towns and buildings overrun by nature can visually hint at a past tragedy, or an oasis and lush setting can portray a time of peace.

Choosing Tools and Software for Art Style Development

When working on your art, you'll create sketches, graphics, textures, and possibly even models and animations. You'll likely utilize various tools in this process, but the tools themselves aren't the main focus. You can even achieve your desired results with just a pencil! It's easy to get caught up in learning a new tool or to feel like your workflow would improve with the latest software you just discovered. It's great to learn new tools, but you should prioritize working in what you're most comfortable with.

Here's a collection of tools and programs commonly used in the industry for creating game art:

>> **Procreate:** A free digital painting app for the iPad. It's great for sketching, illustration, and concept art, and I even make some user interfaces with it.

>> **Adobe Photoshop:** This is the go-to option for 2-D art, textures, and digital painting.

>> **Adobe Illustrator:** Perfect for making logos, UI elements, and illustrations with vector graphics.

>> **CorelDRAW:** Another solid choice for vector graphic design, great for illustrations and layouts.

>> **Blender:** A free and open-source tool that's awesome for 3-D modeling, sculpting, and animation.

>> **Autodesk Maya:** A professional-grade software for 3-D modeling and animation, widely used for characters and environments.

>> **3ds Max:** A tool from Autodesk, often used for modeling, animation, and rendering.

>> **ZBrush:** Specializes in digital sculpting and painting, making it perfect for super detailed characters and assets.

>> **Spine:** A handy tool for 2-D skeletal animation, great for making animations for games.

>> **Toon Boom Harmony:** Great for 2-D animation, commonly used in animated series and games.

>> **Adobe After Effects:** Great for motion graphics and visual effects, helping you create dynamic animations and transitions.

>> **Substance Painter:** A cool tool for painting textures right onto 3-D models, giving you detailed and realistic materials.

>> **Quixel Suite:** A set of tools for creating and applying textures, seamlessly integrated with Unreal Engine.

>> **Aseprite:** A popular pixel art tool for whipping up and animating 2-D sprites and pixel graphics in your games.

Exploring Elements of Art Style

Throughout this chapter, I mention an art style guide (ASG) a few times. I repeat myself because documenting all the elements and rules of your art style will help you keep things like characters, user interfaces, and environments consistent during your development. With the teams I've worked on, an ASG was started and revised throughout the game's development. So, it's okay if you don't have all the information filled out in the beginning, and if you're adding and changing while you're making your art. You'll find better ways to achieve what you want along the way, and you may even find that you want to take a bit of a different path.

Here's some of the info you may want to get started with early in your ASG documents:

>> **Introduction:** Summarizes the document and provides a brief overview of the visual intent for the game.

>> **Characters:** This includes concept art for the characters, bios and descriptions of the characters, and a lineup that shows the scale of the characters compared to each other.

>> **Storyboards:** This is like a comic strip, or a 2-D representation of what some of the key action shots look like, as well as how they flow.

>> **User interface:** Description of UI intent, breakdown of the UI elements, and mock-ups of the UI elements.

>> **Environments:** Description of the environmental intent and environment concepts.

>> **Camera:** Demonstrates intended camera angles using environment and character mock-ups.

>> **References:** Various inspirational works from other games, shows, media, or anything else you get inspiration from.

As you progress in your artwork, you'll be able to add more detail and guidelines to your art style guide. Some of the detail may include

>> **Lighting:** What color the lighting is and how it affects the dynamic and static objects in the game.

>> **Specific rules for environments, characters, or props:** If you're making a procedural character with long ears, what's the minimum ear length and what's the maximum ear length (see Figure 9-1)?

>> **Color palettes:** What colors are used and where? Are environments a different color palette than characters and props?

FIGURE 9-1:
Use rules for visuals to define attributes of characters in your game's world.

TIP

When you start analyzing your work, it can be helpful to put all your assets in a scene next to each other and compare them like in Figure 9-2. Are some characters too tall or too short? Do all the colors work together? Are all the eyes the same across the faces?

FIGURE 9-2:
Putting all your assets side by side can help you understand what does and doesn't work together.

Here are some examples of art style guides you can use to get started with your own:

>> **Adventure Time: The Art of Ooo:** This is an art book for a cartoon, but it has a lot of details on how the characters should be drawn, down to how and where the elbows should bend on the arm for the main characters.

>> **The Art of Cuphead:** This book shows personalities of the characters, how their animations work, and how the environments were developed.

>> **Liberated Pixel Cup:** This style guide is a set of artistic guidelines designed to help creators make consistent, open-source pixel art that fits together in a cohesive way. It was originally created for the Liberated Pixel Cup, a game development and art competition that encouraged open-source contributions to freely available game assets.

https://lpc.opengameart.org/static/LPC-Style-Guide/build/styleguide.html

>> **Team Fortress:** This style guide is a presentation by Valve from GameFest 2008, detailing the art pipeline and rendering techniques used in the Source Engine. It covers shade implementation, lighting, materials, and asset creation, with insights into how Valve optimized visuals while maintaining performance.

https://cdn.cloudflare.steamstatic.com/apps/valve/2008/GameFest08_ArtInSource.pdf

>> **Capcom:** This style guide outlines how Capcom artists used anatomy to refine game character proportions, animations, and effects to enhance readability.

https://game.capcom.com/cfn/sfv/column/131606

REMEMBER

Every team's needs will be different, and a 100-page style guide will surely take a lot of time away from working on the game and the art assets if it's just you working on the game. Only use as much documentation as you need to remember what your intentions are. Maybe you only need one page! Larger teams, with more artists to keep consistent, may need longer documents to communicate with external stakeholders, like publishers or partners.

Visual elements

Some visual fundamentals to know about when making the art for games include

>> Color theory

>> Shape language

>> Texture and material

Color theory

Having a basic understanding of color theory enables you to effectively communicate a variety of things in game making, like function, how the world works, or setting the tone of the game.

Colors have been a topic of fascination for ages, leading to various color theories. One of the most iconic inventions in this area is the color wheel, first introduced by Sir Isaac Newton in the mid-1600s during his studies on the visible spectrum of light. He organized all the visible colors into a circle, creating a handy way to see how colors relate to each other. Later, American painter Albert Henry Munsell expanded this idea by adding three dimensions to color: hue, value (lightness), and chroma (saturation).

The elements of color are

>> **Hue:** This is the base color, which can be one of the standard colors like yellow, blue, or green, without getting into its different shades or tints. Avoid mixing too many colors in one piece of art, as it can create a cluttered look that confuses players.

>> **Chroma (saturation):** This is the intensity of a color. *Saturation* describes the intensity of a chosen hue. Bright, prominent colors have high saturation, and dull colors have low saturation.

>> **Value (lightness):** This property refers to how much light a hue reflects. Lower values mean darker colors; higher values lead to brighter ones. Lightness indicates how much "black," "white," and "gray" mix with a hue.

>> **Temperature:** This is the perceived warmth or coolness of a color. In principle, all colors from strong red through yellow hues are considered to have "warm" temperature. Contrary to that, all prominent blue through green hues are perceived as "cold" ones.

TIP

The elements of color can be used to create patterns to teach players about how to interact with your game. For example, maybe all the cool-colored objects in the space are static objects, and the warm-colored objects are dynamic and able to be interacted with.

Creating color palettes can be a bit daunting, but this has become a lot easier with presets in programs, palettes on Pinterest, plug-ins in Figma like Color Wheel (`https://www.figma.com/color-wheel/`), and tools like Adobe Color (`https://color.adobe.com/create/color-wheel/` —and it's free!).

Fortunately, you have a few ways to generate a decent color palette using some color combination schemes, as shown in Figure 9-3. They include but aren't limited to

>> **Complementary:** Pairing two colors from opposite sides of the color wheel creates strong contrast. It's perfect for making assets pop, like when you need to clearly separate background elements from the foreground.

>> **Monochromatic:** Using different shades and tints of a single color. This style works best when you want a more toned-down look.

>> **Analogous:** This combination is based on the idea of picking one main hue and selecting the adjacent colors on the color wheel. Opposite to complementary scheme, the aim here is to produce a low-contrast calm art.

Complementary   Monochromatic   Analogous

FIGURE 9-3:
Color combination schemes can help you find a harmonious color palette.

Keep in mind who you're creating your game for when it comes to choosing colors. Different cultures can have differing meanings and perceptions for colors. An example is the color red. In Western countries, red evokes excitement, danger, urgency, and love. It evokes danger and caution in the Middle East, and in China, red symbolizes luck and happiness.

TIP

Shape language

Another visual element you can use to convey ideas in your game is *shape language*. The shape of something can convey a character's role, emotions, or the vibe of a place without having to explain it in words. It gives objects some "personality."

Here's how you can use different shapes to give objects some personality of their own:

>> Circles and roundness convey friendliness, whimsy, and safety. They feel approachable and soft!

>> Square and rectangle shapes are solid, grounded, and dependable. A character or building designed with a blocky shape can feel strong.

>> Sharp edges are edgy or dangerous. Sharp shapes are often used to make things more intimidating, like villains or weapons.

Texture and material

Texture and material can provide weight, realism, or history and culture. Think of the difference between a metal box and a wooden crate. They have the same silhouette and maybe even the same *mesh* (the 3-D geometry that gives the box its shape); you'd think one is heavier than the other, right? A metal box probably doesn't belong in the 1800s in a jungle, but maybe a wooden crate does. Use these elements to style your game and add immersion based on the story you're trying to tell.

Animation style

Animation is important because it provides feedback for player input. If something doesn't move when you interact with it, it can really take you out of the experience. But in the worst case, you may not even be able to play the game. Take for example, a fighting game. Fighting gamers rely on immediate feedback when they've successfully kicked someone in the face. A confirmation like that can mean another combo they can complete. If they were missing that feedback, it would be pretty difficult to know whether the move was registered by the game. On the flip side, if you're plucking plants out of the ground to tend to a farming simulation, it may just be a more boring experience. The feedback can feel and look really nice, but you can still play the game.

Ask yourself these questions as you're integrating and prioritizing animations in your game:

>> Does the animation communicate core gameplay?

>> Does it express character personality?

>> Does it enhance the game's tone?

>> Does it make interactions more believable?

There's a wide variety of animation styles and tools out there these days. I've seen people make stop motion games, sprite-based frame-by-frame animation, and animations in Maya with 3-D models. Here's some things to consider when choosing your animation style:

>> **Realistic versus exaggerated animations:** Realistic animations feel grounded and lifelike, and exaggerated ones often make characters feel more expressive and playful.

>> **Fluidity:** Smooth, flowing animations can make movements feel elegant and polished. Snappier animations add quirkiness.

>> **Frame rates and timing:** Higher frame rates add realism; lower rates can feel stylized. Timing can also help actions feel punchy and quick or more intense.

Audio style

There's a joke about how audio always comes last when developing games. Somehow it often gets overlooked until the end, but think about how much audio impacts our everyday life. We use our ears to figure out what time of day it is, where we are, and what's around us. You can do the same in a game, and if you add audio, it'll make the game that much more immersive.

Audio style includes the music, ambient sounds, sound effects, and any voice acting in the game. It's a creative and technical process that involves planning, recording, editing, mixing, and implementing audio assets. Just like in a movie, audio in a game sets the tone, builds atmosphere, and provides important cues to the audience. But unlike in a film, game audio is interactive and it responds to the player's actions in real time. Each of these elements can set the tone of the game, give hints about gameplay or events in the game, or give feedback on player input. Some ways you may signal a change in gameplay include

>> An enemy is nearby.

>> An item has been collected.

>> The environment is changing.

>> A character's health is damaged.

A consistent audio style ties the game together and help players know what to expect in an environment. If your game allows different planting or has events during a specific season like *Stardew Valley*, maybe you'll change the music for each season to signal to the player there's been a change in the environment.

Here are some considerations when designing audio for your game:

>> **Consistency:** Make sure that audio is consistent with the game's tone and world. If your game is spooky, the sound effects, music, and voice can all add to that atmosphere.

>> **Player feedback:** Well-placed sound cues make actions like getting a power-up, hitting a target, or discovering something secret feel rewarding.

>> **Layering:** Layering sound effects, background ambiance, and music creates depth and richness.

>> **Emotional connection:** Use audio to reinforce emotions. If your game has intense moments, amp up the music and sounds to match the stakes, like in a boss battle.

>> **Spatial awareness:** 3-D audio and spatial cues can help players locate something, giving a sense of direction in the game world.

>> **Silence:** Silence can be just as powerful as sound. Strategic use of quiet moments or pauses can create tension or let players focus on a specific element.

You can use a variety of tools to produce and edit music and audio. I currently use GarageBand for editing audio files (it's free), but other widely used audio production tools are available, like FL Studio, Albeton Live, and the open-source tool Audacity. These tools are great for

>> Recording and editing voiceovers or sound effects

>> Cutting, trimming, and looping audio clips

>> Basic noise reduction and audio cleanup

>> Applying simple effects like reverb or equalization

TIP

I once was tasked to create dedicated voiceovers for all dialogue in a game. Every time we changed the dialogue, we had to rerecord the voiceovers. It was a mix of bad planning and lack of experience on my part, but I learned from my mistake. After that, any game I made with voiced characters leaned heavily into stylized voiceovers — think Animal Crossing *murmurs* or Star Fox–style one-shot voice clips — instead of full sentences. Doing so saved time, added charm, and kept things flexible. I recommend considering the scope when you do full voiceovers for any dialogue in your games.

ANALYZING EXAMPLES OF ART STYLES

Fortunately, today's games have such a wide variety of art that it's easy to find something you like — from hyper-realistic games like *Red Dead Redemption* to overly stylized games like the *Untitled Goose Game*.

Some big-name games are known for their iconic visuals. *Breath of the Wild* has a dreamy, painterly look that makes exploring feel magical. The world feels full of life because everything has movement and color. Another example, Hades opts for slick comic-style characters and vibrant colors. The underworld brings drama and the character's designs feel epic.

Both games took years to make. The art and gameplay took Hades three years to craft, and *Breath of the Wild* took seven years on top of the backlog of work from Zelda games throughout history. Making one of these games takes dedication in the form of a large part of your life. Practice is what will get you there!

In *Untitled Goose Game,* the simple, cartoon-like visuals focus on the humor of causing chaos as a goose. These unique styles make even smaller games feel like one of a kind and help them stand out. Implementing a look like this can simplify a lot of the finer details in the game. This one took about three years to make.

I may get reamed for this, but *Vampire Survivors* has an extremely interesting art style, and the audio makes the entire game feel metal and epic. At first and on first glance, the style can feel chunky and not cohesive, but the sheer amount of detail put into each character and description of levels makes up for some of the lack of cohesion. This game took a year to make.

Considering Scope When Choosing an Art Style

Some art styles take less time to implement and can be more forgiving when it comes to cohesion than others. After you define a look and start working in-engine, you'll need to make some (or all) of the following assets:

- >> **Shaders:** These are scripts that dictate how the surfaces of your models interact with light. They can create effects like glossiness, transparency, or even special effects like outlines.
- >> **Materials:** Materials hold the properties that define how objects look in your game. This includes color, texture, and shininess.
- >> **Models:** These are the 3-D representations of your characters, environments, and objects in the game.
- >> **Sprites:** In 2-D games, sprites are the images used for characters and objects.
- >> **Animations:** These bring your models and sprites to life, adding movement and personality.

>> **Textures:** Textures are images applied to 3-D models or sprites to give them detail and depth.

Before choosing an art style, make sure to consider how each one has a different time investment. Some art styles, like minimalist or flat-shaded designs, can save time. I opted for a flat-shaded look for Watchmakers because my skills and practice in 3-D modeling are still developing. I used this approach because I could achieve a stylized look without the need to spend time on details.

Here are some things to think about when deciding on an art style:

>> **2-D versus 3-D:** 2-D games generally require less time to develop and can be more forgiving when it comes to consistency. Because creating 2-D assets can often be less complex than their 3-D counterparts, it allows for faster iterations and adjustments.

>> **Consistency:** Choosing something requiring less detail, like low poly or pixel art, can save time on efforts. The faster you can get to a final piece of art, the faster you can make guidelines for consistency.

>> **Technical constraints:** Consider the limitations of your chosen engine and the capabilities of your team. Some art styles may need more advanced technical skills or larger file sizes, but some can be implemented with less work.

>> **Player expectations:** If you're going for a more cartoonish or whimsical aesthetic, players may expect a more casual gameplay experience. A darker or more realistic art style can create a more serious tone.

REMEMBER

The biggest consideration for me when figuring out how to scope my art is 2-D versus 3-D. 2-D just takes less time because it has fewer moving parts for the asset and any animations associated with it. 3-D is very fun to make, but just keep the required extra effort in mind when choosing to make a 3-D game.

Budgeting for art style

The best way to go about budgeting for art is to figure out how much you can afford to spend. Remember that if you choose to make it yourself, it may take you more time depending on your skillset, which is time that can be used to build other parts of the game. Then when you have the budget, start looking for artists within your price range. A highly qualified artist with lots of experience will have much higher rates than an amateur looking to build their portfolio. Or maybe you have a friend or someone you've worked with before that can make a deal with you.

Depending on the type of game, art can take much more effort than the engineering. For instance, an open world game may have two artists for every engineer. Which game you're making can completely change how much money or time you'll have to budget.

Here's a step-by-step process to figuring out your art budget:

1. **Roughly figure out what assets you need (the more detail the better).**

   For one of my games for which I hired an artist, I listed narrative panels and every accessory I needed for the game, plus the variations for them in a spreadsheet. I then shared that spreadsheet with potential artists and created a statement of work based on that list.

2. **Look for asset packs on game engine asset stores that you can use straight from the package or that you can adapt for your game.**

   This can save you a lot of money!

3. **Contact an artist and ask about their rates.**

   You may want to find a couple of different ones on websites like Pinterest or ArtStation or Reddit subs like r/INAT.

TIP

You may also need to consider fees for tools; in Chapter 5, I list various art tools, including some free ones. I switched to completely free toolsets when I went indie to save some money! (Also check out Chapter 19 for free tools and assets, as well as other free resources.)

Collaborating with artists and designers

Collaboration is tough and takes work. This is true for any partnership or team! For designers and artists, the work is so close together that it can take a lot of communication about expectations and progress.

Proactive communication has always been the best bet for me, and some of the ways to do that include documenting, showing your work, frequently communicating, and testing together.

When you document, try to write together and get feedback on your ideas, systems, and assets. Most studios use tools like Google Docs or Notion to write collaboratively.

Showing your work means sharing your ugliest stuff. It took me a while to be okay sharing the ugly stuff, but as a designer — and depending on the team — it's not my job to do the artistry, and I need to rely on an artist to do it better. You'll want to share prototypes, block outs, rough passes, pencil sketches, and all other forms of "ugly work." Doing this boosts productivity, as there's less room for big misalignments or surprises.

Proactive communication involves sharing early, widely, and often on all project progress and updates. If your team uses Slack or Discord, send updates on your work to make sure everyone is on the same page and that there's visibility and alignment of the current status of the project and next steps. This helps keep the team from regressing or revisiting decisions.

Testing together is a huge part of communication. Sure, something may not be ready to test. But even if it isn't, it's still useful to let other people see it early so that they know what to expect. Testing at this stage shouldn't be treated like a normal playtest; you're actively collaborating with someone else to develop the game, and it's okay if they see it in the raw or if you don't have defined testing goals for it. This helps raise awareness of the current state of the project and leads to more productive and more specific conversations.

Managing art production timelines

Creating artwork generally requires multiple rounds of revisions and adjustments. Having concept art in the beginning helps the team align on goals for the assets, but technical issues always pop up along the way. For example, lighting setups may look great in concept but don't translate well in-engine due to limitations of the *renderer* (the part of the game engine responsible for processing how light interacts with surfaces of assets). You may have to prepare for trade-offs for what you wanted initially. Unless you're a team who's worked together for a while and already has a distinct art style, you need to allot more time for art production and experimentation.

Deadlines and milestones are helpful in figuring out when assets can be created and reviewed. Prioritize tasks based on what the gameplay demands most urgently and consider the release schedule.

Some ways to think about how to prioritize art are as follows:

>> Is it part of the core game loop?

>> Is it a character that defines the intellectual property or story?

» Does it impact the success of any game mechanics?

» Am I okay with external playtesters seeing the art in an unrefined state at this stage in the game?

TIP

Consider the level of detail when creating timelines for your artwork. For example, if you're making an open world, you may have multiple assets for one tree, because players will see that tree at different distances. If you're developing artwork for a mobile phone, the assets may be very simple and require less detail because of the size of the asset.

Addressing technical constraints and optimization

Meeting the quality of an art concept can be difficult due to technical limitations for the platform. On every game I've worked on, we've always done an *optimization pass.* This means refining game assets to improve performance, ensuring that they run smoothly on the target device without straying too far from the intended visuals.

A few of the games I've worked on had a dedicated technical artist to build tools and pipelines to assist with optimization. It's a pretty big deal in the industry, and even more so on platforms like mobile or on virtual reality headsets. One of the basic needs is that the game must run properly for someone to play it.

Some technical issues to consider as you develop the art are as follows:

» **File size:** Huge file sizes for high-res assets threaten to increase the file size of the mobile game, often past Apple's file size limits.

» **Screen size:** It's harder for players to appreciate realism and detail on a smaller screen. 3-D models often sacrifice detail for legibility.

» **Resources required:** Realistic games require artists who specialize in things like lighting and animation. Employing these specialists can increase the cost of production to the point where it's out of reach for most indie developers.

TECHNICAL STUFF

To make file sizes smaller, consider reducing textures, reducing poly count, creating *addressables* (assets loaded at runtime), changing lighting, and limiting animation to make files sizes smaller.

Ethical and Cultural Considerations

Thinking about ethical and cultural considerations in games and media makes the world a better place for all of us, and it also helps the reputation of gaming as a medium. The best way to be considerate about ethics and culture is by learning and analyzing as much as you can and working with a variety of different people.

I was once designing a feature in a game in which a player chooses one item out of three and gets a curated object from that item. At the time, I didn't realize this was coming close to a loot box, and our company's policy was against designing loot boxes and gacha (a feature of a computer game in which players can pay to get a new character, ability, object, at random). A team member called out the issue, and I worked with our lawyers on the design to make it more transparent and fairer for players, so that no one item was more valuable than another.

When you're designing a game or a feature, take these things into consideration:

>> **Games are meant to be engaging.** But some people have trouble with addictive tendencies; excessive screen time and addictive behaviors are problems that have become increasingly prevalent as gaming has progressed. You can implement time-tracking systems, daily play-time limits, or reminders to take breaks to promote healthy gaming habits.

>> **Data collection for anyone, but specifically vulnerable populations like children, shouldn't contain any personally identifiable information.** Federal laws regulate the collection of personal information from children under the age of 13. If you're looking to learn more about this, consider taking CITI training:

   `https://about.citiprogram.org/series/responsible-conduct-of-research-rcr/`

>> **Age-rating and age-appropriate content ratings can help parents and kids understand what types of content to expect.** Content ratings groups, such as the following, break down what type of violence, language, and mature themes may be in a game so that parents (and players) know what to expect:

   • For North America: Entertainment Software Rating Board (ESRB), `https://www.esrb.org`

   • For Europe: Pan-European Game Information (PEGI), `https://pegi.info`

   • For Japan: Computer Entertainment Rating Organization (CERO), `https://www.cero.gr.jp/en/publics/index/3/`

For mobile games, the Apple App Store and Google Play Store use the International Age Rating Coalition (IARC; https://www.globalratings.com), which automatically assigns ratings based on different regions.

>> **Monetization should be carefully designed.** You need to be aware of predatory tactics, pay-to-win mechanics, loot boxes, gambling, and child-targeted monetization tactics — and generally avoid them. Transparency, clear pricing, and spending limits are great considerations when designing anything for purchases in games.

>> **Art and aesthetics are perceived differently across the globe (and probably also across the universe).** Different cultures have unique interpretations and values that influence how members of that culture view visuals, themes, and narratives. For instance, I once was developing a prototype for a game in VR where you pointed at people to accuse them of something. In many cultures, pointing is quite rude, and some folks may not appreciate being pointed at. Being aware of these differences fosters inclusivity and helps you be intentional about how your work is perceived by people different from you.

Addressing issues such as addiction, representation, violence, mental health, and ethical monetization during development will lead to healthier gaming habits, a healthier industry, and healthier people.

Representation in art style

As with any media or creation by people, showing diversity and practicing cultural sensitivity in your game design is important. The world is diverse, and people like to play games that relate to them — and that don't insult or appropriate their culture (whether that's done intentionally or not).

Here are a few ideas to help you along this path:

>> **Create a diverse team.** Remember that anyone can make games; it just takes practice and dedication.

>> **Research cultures and collect references.** Conduct basic cultural research for your game. If you intend to localize it for a specific market, you'll need to do a lot more research to make sure it aligns with the culture or adapt it for that area.

>> **Create characters, not caricatures.** You want your characters to be like real people — not stereotypes — and to represent a wide range of ethnicities, body types, genders, and abilities.

>> **Consult with experts.** Partner with cultural consultants or artists from specific backgrounds to help you and your team learn different perspectives. This will help you create respectful and accurate portrayals of people and cultures in your games.

>> **Focus on storytelling that celebrates diversity and representation.** Instead of just checking boxes, think about how diversity naturally fits into your world and characters.

>> **Provide training on cultural sensitivity and the importance of representation.** A little education goes a long way! Running workshops or sharing resources with your team can help avoid harmful tropes and encourage thoughtful, inclusive design. Even a simple discussion about unconscious bias can make a difference.

TIP

The better you understand the audience for your game, the better you can provide the kind of gaming experience they enjoy. I recommend getting feedback as you develop characters.

As you collect that feedback, strive to understand how various elements of your game may impact the audience. Visual choices can read differently with various audiences. Consider how elements like colors, shapes, and character designs may be interpreted in different cultural contexts to create a more thoughtful and engaging experience for all players.

When developing a virtual reality game, for example, we initially implemented a mechanic that required players to point at characters. However, we soon learned that pointing with one finger can be considered rude or even offensive in many cultures. As we progressed, we began collaborating with a content team that highlighted important cultural elements we needed to be mindful of. This experience underscored the importance of researching cultural nuances to avoid misrepresentation in our games.

Ethical challenges

When you make art, you may have intentions to mimic the real world or comment on society in some way. The act of making art carries the potential to offend, and moral dilemmas are present — not more than in any other employment, but they may be a little less obvious.

I cannot even begin to have all the answers here, and I think this topic comes down to: "How much are you willing to risk for the impact?" Many folks use pen names in writing because they don't want to risk their reputation for the content they want to write. But the world is greyscale, not true or false, right or wrong. I think it's important to contribute how you can, no matter who you are, and you are entitled to do so.

Regardless of how much risk you're willing to take, these questions are worth pondering as you create art in your games:

>> What is offensive?

>> How can you be authentic?

>> What is breach of copyright?

>> What is talent worth?

>> What should be censored?

REMEMBER

When you make something, you're contributing to history. Consider this point when you choose your topic or content. There's a chance you'll become known for it (for better or for worse), and it could have an impact (positive or negative) on others.

IN THIS CHAPTER

» Learning what user experience (UX) is

» Understanding why UX is important

» Making a game your players will love

» Designing interfaces and tutorials

» Considering design choices for different platforms

» Making games accessible

Chapter **10**

Creating an Engaging User Experience

U ser experience is the complete picture of what a player experiences when they play the game. It includes the tutorial and intro to the very end of the game, and all the steps in between. Designing this means understanding what you want the player to experience and feel at each step at a high level, and designing the details (like music and interactions) to make an experience that's easy for the player to understand and progress through.

Defining User Experience in Games

User experience (UX) is about how players feel when they're playing your game and how easy (or frustrating) it is to navigate through everything. A great UX can keep players coming back for more and make them want to stick around longer when they do.

In the context of games, UX design looks at factors like the following:

>> **Interface design:** How buttons, menus, and other elements are laid out so players can easily find what they need

>> **Gameplay mechanics:** Making sure that the rules and systems feel fair and fun

>> **Feedback:** Giving players clear responses to their choices, like sound effects or visual cues when they accomplish something

>> **Accessibility:** Making sure the game can be enjoyed by players with different abilities, like those who may need text-to-speech options, larger buttons, or enhanced readability

Importance of UX in game design

When we talk about user experience (UX) in game design, we're talking about how players interact with a game and what their experience feels like. UX design is the practice of putting intention into how the player engages with your project, how they feel, and what happens during their gameplay.

Putting work into the UX of a game can improve:

>> How much fun players are having

>> How many people play your game

>> How quickly a player learns how to play

>> How long people play your game

REMEMBER

A great user experience keeps players coming back for more, making your game not just enjoyable, but also very memorable!

Impact on players and retention

A good way to be intentional about the user's experience is to map out the intended path for your players. My process for this is to create a flow chart of the experience and then a more visual storyboard that follows that chart. These allow me to think through each step of the game, and I can then create data along with it to improve the experience when I start playtesting.

A *golden path* in game design is the ideal route you want players to take to enjoy your game the way you intended. It should show off all the cool mechanics, story moments, and features without players getting lost or frustrated. Games are often nonlinear, which makes it difficult to make a game fit into a perfect sequence of events. Think of the golden path as more of a guide of the intention and a way to see where players like to go off the rails.

Questions to ask yourself when creating your golden path are as follows:

>> How much do I want to guide players versus letting them explore?

>> Where would I include analytics to track a choice a player makes?

>> What should players be feeling at certain milestones?

>> What signals can I give players to show that they are making progress?

>> Are there any potential points of friction where players may get stuck?

>> How will the game escalate in difficulty or complexity as players advance?

>> Will the game accommodate for different playstyles?

>> What mechanics should players have mastered by the end of the game?

Here's an example of a golden path for a game about taking care of a pet:

1. Player gets a notification on their device about the game.

2. Player opens the game, which opens to the pet's interests/quests.

3. Player taps on a quest.

4. Player walks the pet.

5. Player gets XP.

After you have that golden path, you're able to create a user flow like the one shown in Figure 10-1. Based off that, you can create a *funnel chart,* a simple way to track how players move through different parts of your game. Funnel charts visually represent player behavior at each stage of their journey, from when they first learn about your game to when they decide to continue playing or leave. By analyzing a funnel, you'll be able to identify where players are dropping off and improve the experience to keep people interested.

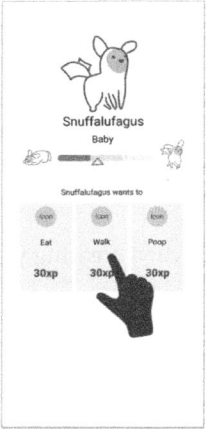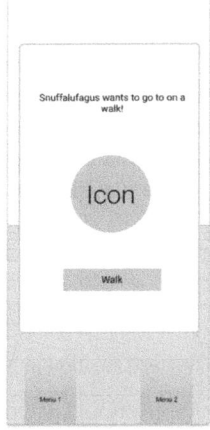

FIGURE 10-1:
A user journey for a golden path, which is the intended path for a player to take.

Let's say you have 300 players in your game and four steps. The following table shows an example of a funnel chart for that game:

Step Name	Player Count	Completed %
Step 1	300	100%
Step 2	70	23%
Step 3	30	10%
Step 4	29	9.6%

Take note of any steps that have large drop-offs and figure out why it's happening. Having some players drop off over time is expected, but a big chunk of players leaving on one particular step can signal a game-breaking bug or issue in the flow that you need to figure out!

Being intentional about designing for user experience helps retain players because you'll be able to understand where players quit your game and what tasks they are (and aren't) completing throughout.

REMEMBER

Finding Out Who Will Play Your Game

Figuring out your audience is helpful for user experience, specifically because it helps you curate the look, feel, and pacing for the audience's needs. In Chapter 13, I go into how you can find your audience for your project at a more practical level, but here I cover tools and best practices for finding your audience. There are a couple of ways to get information about the players who will want to play your game, and then you can create more detailed profiles describing your target audience.

Gathering information through surveys

When I'm kicking off a new game project, I like to make a survey about the concept (see Chapter 13 for more about creating your game concept) to get some initial feedback on it. This includes any mock-ups, prototypes, or concept art. This is a chance for me to share my concept so that it helps me understand how players may describe my game and spot any similar experiences that may inspire me. I find my initial testers through friends, family, relevant sub-Reddits, and my peers who may be interested in my game.

Here are some of the questions I usually include in my survey:

1. What types of game do you usually play?

2. How would you explain this game to a friend?

3. What other games does this game remind you of?

4. Why are you interested or not interested in this type of game?

5. What types of things would you want to see in this game?

6. What genre do you think this game fits into?

TIP

Google Forms (https://www.google.com/forms/about/) is free and easy to use for sending surveys to players. I pretty much always use Google Forms to ask players about my games.

TIP

You can learn a lot about potential players from places like Reddit, Steam reviews, articles, blogs, and social media. You may find out what other games they like to play, what they liked about a specific feature in a game, or how they strategize gameplay in games with similar systems.

Researching the market

Researching the market can be very important when you end up working on a game that's not necessarily made with you as a player in mind. Once, I was working on a game aimed at helping elderly people with dementia complete routine chores around the house. I was a 20-something undergrad student when I worked on this, and the rest of the development team was about the same age. We were a little off the mark when it came to the demographic, as you can probably tell. We needed to do research because we were making something for people who used technology quite differently than we did.

After we figured out the goals of the project and the mechanics we were hoping to use to achieve them, we made mock-ups of the screens. We organized a focus group to learn how they interact with tablets and apps. The researchers at the company helped organize this and recruit players for the focus group by posting flyers at the locations where they may be visiting. They were able to recruit a handful of people to talk to about the project. We found out a lot about how to design our game's interface to be more accessible, especially for those with vision issues.

When you're doing market research, you want to get information about your potential players or users by asking questions like these:

>> Are these people the right target audience? Why or why not?

>> What are their motivations for playing?

>> What genres, mechanics, or themes are popular with them?

>> What other games are they interested in that you can learn from?

>> Which business models work best for their lifestyle?

>> Do they have any accessibility considerations?

>> How much are they willing to pay for a game?

>> How much time can they dedicate to playing a game?

Typically, when you work on a larger team, you have someone — usually a researcher, cognitive scientist, user experience (UX) researcher, or maybe your producer — dedicated to finding and recruiting people who would be a good fit for your research. If it's just you as a developer, you may need to start searching locally and across the web for people who fit your audience.

Creating personas

A *persona* is a fictitious character profile that helps you picture who your players are. It keeps everyone on your team aligned with your audience, making sure your game meets their needs. If you're working solo, it can be a way to set aside some time to dig into who will play your game so that you can think through where you can find them, what they like in terms of art style, what other games they like, and what features they enjoy that may fit into your game.

Personas don't take too long to make, and they can be helpful in the long term when you go to promote your game because you'll already have some assumptions and research about what your players like and where they hang out.

Make sure not to make too many assumptions about who would play your game and use your market research from the previous section to inform your personas to truly understand your target market. A good persona is informed by data from potential players.

Items to include in a persona are

>> **A picture of the fictious person:** Sometimes I use a stock photo on larger teams so that the person isn't associated with any specific team member. When I'm working solo, sometimes I use a friend's photo if I know they play the type of game I'm making.

>> **Their demographics, like age, location, and occupation:** This can help give you a general sense of their obligations, how much disposable income they have, and how much extra time they have to play games.

>> **Their motivations:** Why do they play games? Is it to exercise or socialize or compete?

>> **Some of their favorite games:** Doing this can get you thinking about why they like those games. Is it for specific features or aesthetic or themes?

I like to make a template for personas. I have my students make them often, and if I'm working on a team, I'll make them so we're all aligned. I just use a simple Google Slide like the one shown in Figure 10-2. You'll want to use this format once you get started building your own concept in Chapter 13.

PERSONA PROFILE

ALEXIA MANDEVILLE
THE CASUAL SOCIALIZER

AGE: 325
LOCATION: The World
OCCUPATION: Magical Wizard

MOTIVATIONS
- Alexia enjoys socializing with friends over a casual puzzle game or exploring a farming sim
- If she's not using a game to hang out with friends, Alexia likes games to be easily finished in a few sittings

BIO
Alexia is a professional game designer that works from home. She mainly plays games on her Nintendo Switch. She likes games that have a story and social aspect to them. She also enjoys yoga, camping, biking around town, and and drawing.

GOALS
- Get outside more often
- Do more artwork
- Engage in more online communities

FAVORITE GAMES
 Katamari 塊魂 Damacy

FIGURE 10-2:
A persona can help you align with your team on who will play your game.

Designing for Your Players

As I sit here writing this, I'm deep in the *Stardew Valley* grind (once again). This game is an excellent example of designing for a specific audience of players. Its developer felt that improvements could be made to a previous role-playing series, but the foundation of that series had already attracted a large, dedicated fanbase. By tapping into what made that series great and adding a personal touch, the developer created something familiar with a twist.

The conventional advice in the gaming industry right now is to "never design a game for yourself." Although there's some truth to this, it's not a hard-and-fast rule. In the case of *Stardew Valley*, the developer began by designing something they themselves wanted to play, drawing inspiration from an existing property. It turns out that a large group of gamers wanted the same thing. When you build on what already interests players, you don't need to reinvent the wheel; you just need to find a new way to make it spin.

REMEMBER

Although it's important to design with your players in mind and not exclusively for yourself, the more important sentiment here is to get information and feedback from somewhere other than your own mind, as I discuss in the preceding sections. After all, you probably hope your game reaches an audience beyond just yourself!

Tailoring gameplay mechanics to your players

When you play a role playing game (RPG), what features do you expect? You're probably thinking of things like character customization, quests, narrative, or skill progression. These features are part of what makes RPGs enjoyable and relatable. You could very well prioritize some unexpected feature, like fast-paced combat or rhythm-based gameplay; you just may need to allocate more time to testing or communicating the expected gameplay accordingly in the marketing materials.

For our game *Grift: Scam Tycoon*, we decided to do a bit of that. We made an idle dollmaker with incremental qualities. Or at least that was the original goal. The incremental gamers told us it was flat out not an incremental game. It wasn't "idle" enough for the idle gamers. And I don't think we leaned into the dollmaker aspects enough to make it attractive for the dress-up gamers. You can learn from my mistakes!

Some pros to tailoring gameplay mechanics to players are as follows:

>> Players are more likely to connect with and stay immersed in a game when its mechanics align with their preferences.

>> Adjusting your game mechanics to fit what your audience likes can build a solid community around your game and make them feel included.

>> Every game genre comes with a set of expectations. If your mechanics stray too far from these expectations, players may get confused about what the game is.

Choosing features of the genre

Get to know your audience and check out similar games to see what players love. Think about the feeling you want your game to have and focus on features that boost that experience. From there, you can analyze existing games to see what they've included and what you can improve or where you can add a twist.

For example, in a platformer (a genre of game where you jump from platform to platform), you may prioritize some of these features from the beginning:

>> Tight, responsive controls that allow players to make precise movements like jumping, running, and interacting with the environment

>> Interesting, thematic levels that complement the main gameplay mechanics and include obstacles, enemies, puzzles, and goals

>> Progressively difficult levels throughout the game

>> Great audio and visual feedback to help the player learn from their actions

>> Power-ups that can be found in the environment that allow the player to have new abilities or tools

Here's a process I use when deciding which features to incorporate in the games I've worked on:

1. Decide on a core game loop and the main features the game will include.

2. Define the game's goals and my own personal goals.

   - Do I want players to have a lot of agency?

   - Do I want to challenge myself to make a game in a genre I've never made?

   - Do I want to make money?

Setting goals helps you prioritize your work. You'll encounter lots of feedback, ideas, and even distractions while you're making a game. You may come up with a better or different idea while hashing out the details of one feature set. Goals can help you decide whether the new idea is more important than the one you were working on.

3. Choose a handful of genres or tags (tags used to categorize games on distribution platforms) to bucket the game into.

    It's even better if you can order the list by priority, with the most important genre at the top of the list. This helps you prioritize features in your game to align with the expectations of that genre.

4. Research features of the genres within that list.

5. Prioritize features based on what fits into the core gameplay, aligns with my goals, and what players will expect.

Designing effective tutorials

A *tutorial* is where you're able to teach players what you want them to learn and engage them in the game from the start. Across game studios I've heard it called other terms: onboarding, the new user experience (NUX), and the first-time user experience (FTUE). Whatever it's called, a good tutorial can make players feel engaged and motivated to continue playing; a poor tutorial can lead to frustration and churn.

When designing a game's tutorial, I keep these things in mind:

» 5 seconds to fun

» Scaffold or layer information

» Introduce long-term and short-term goals

» Improve through testing and iteration

» Embed tutorials into the gameplay (rather than having a separate tutorial)

» Include a way for players to get back to the tutorial (if you allow them to skip it)

It's important to get the player to fun as soon as possible! This doesn't necessarily mean it has to be five seconds, but it's a way to remember to get the player invested as soon as possible to keep them motivated. This can be in the form of agency of choice, a fun mechanic to play with, or allowing them to make progress and offering a quick reward. In *Chief Emoji Officer*, we added an Easter egg right in the start. After the player chooses their avatar, they can make an immediate choice using their emojis. If they pick the wrong one . . . well, I'll let you find out.

A good way to get early feedback is to create a storyboard or visual user flow of the steps of the tutorial, as shown in Figure 10-3. You can then show new players the steps and understand what you need to add or make more concise. Don't be afraid to experiment with different onboarding approaches and gather feedback from players to see what works best.

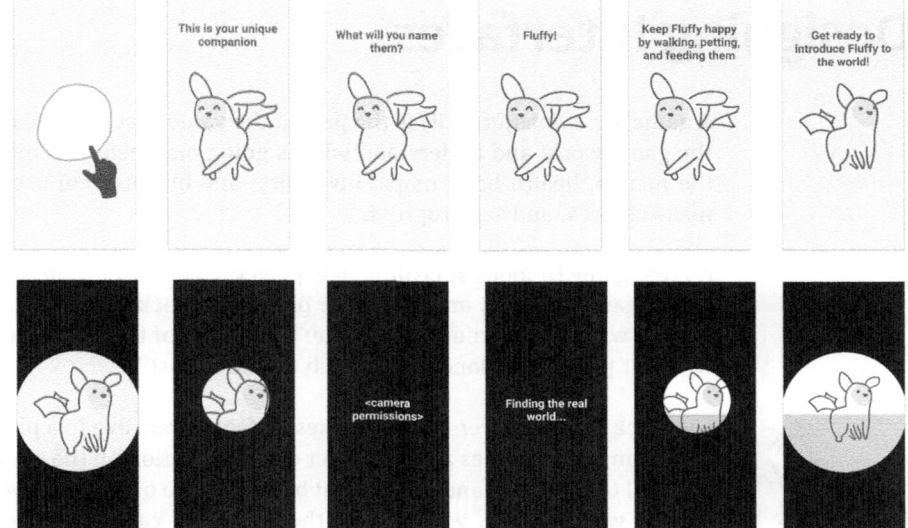

FIGURE 10-3: Use a storyboard to iterate on a visual user flow without having to implement it in the game.

Appealing to your players

In the preceding few sections, I show how players expect your game to work, the features that are included, and how players are ramped into the game. Another big part of players' expectations is how the game looks and the storefront.

If you've looked at mobile gaming stores any time recently, you've probably seen the candy-colored screens that saturate the market. Mobile games are filled with saturated color palettes and cute characters right now. Maybe that fits your game, or maybe it doesn't.

If it does, it's important to make sure that your game still stands out. What makes your cute, colorful characters different from the thousands of others available to players? Maybe it's their personality — do they sing death metal at karaoke after work? Or maybe it's the story — does the game have a story that provides commentary on society or pop culture? This goes for all types of games, not just ones on mobile. The important thing is knowing what's out there and making sure your game brings something unique to the table.

Grift: Scam Tycoon definitely didn't fit a cute scheme. We wanted an edge, and we wanted the artwork to stand out among what was already out and bring something a little different. Our scam theme allowed for this grittiness, so we chose a dark comic style, using a dark academia color palette that was very different than what's on the market for mobile games.

Designing Interfaces

A game's *user interface* (UI) is the part of the game that helps players interact with the game world and understand what's going on when they make decisions. It's the menus, health bars, maps, inventory, and buttons you use to move around, make choices, and see progress.

A great game UI looks appealing, lets players know important information related to the game's world, and gives the player feedback for their actions in a game. Players will want to know things like: How much of that resource do I have? When will that process be done? How much does this cost?

TIP

Feedback for the player is what makes UI feel responsive to a player's input. Even something as simple as a hover effect or an animation on the press of a button can make UI feel reactive and usable. Just be sure not to overdo it, especially for actions players will do a lot. What's cute the first time can get old quickly if it slows things down.

The most important questions to ask yourself when designing an interface are

>> Does the player have all the information they need to make a decision?

>> Is there any unnecessary information on this interface?

>> Is the UI consistent with itself?

>> What information is most important to the player in this moment?

REMEMBER

If you're asking a player to buy something for 100 coins in a shop, for example, they need to know if they have enough coins. When you're making a screen or a menu, think about the important data for the player. Is it how much time they have left in the day? Or is it how many more slimes they need to kill before they can score that new sword? Players need to be confident in their decisions and see what happens when they make them.

When you think of a UI, the first thing that comes to mind is probably the 2-D UI on the screen. But there is a lot more to game UI, and quite a few ways to relay information to players than just the screen-based information. UI can also be 3-D and in the game world.

UI can take various forms in games, as shown in Figure 10-4 and described in this list:

>> **Diegetic:** This type of interface is part of the game world and can be seen by both the player and the character. For example, when your character reads the in-game bulletin board or checks the mail, both actions are shown as part of the game world. Your character physically walks up to the board or mailbox, interacting with it the same way they would in real life. This makes it feel like a natural part of the environment.

>> **Non-diegetic:** These are the screen-based game elements that only the player can see, like health bars or score counters. Think of the life hearts you see when you're battling a boss. When you experience damage, you can see them change, but the player character doesn't. I also call this *screen-space UI.*

>> **Meta:** Meta UI shows how the game world affects the character without being something they directly interact with. For example, when the screen gets darker or starts shaking when your character is low on energy or health.

>> **Spatial:** This UI is in the game world but doesn't always fit the narrative. For example, when you see a marker over a character to show that it's interactive. These can be speech bubbles or tooltips that pop up when you're near something interesting.

FIGURE 10-4:
Examples of
interface types.

| Diegetic | Non-diegetic | Meta | Spatial |

How do you figure out what's the best approach for designing your UI? In our game *Watchmakers,* we decided to include any puzzle interactions in diegetic UI, meaning it exists within the game world and is part of the narrative, as shown in Figure 10-5.

For example, there's a puzzle in which you have to press some buttons in a specific order. We had tried a version in which you interact with a rock and a screen pops up to show you the puzzle in screen space, so that you can use your cursor to select the buttons in order. Ultimately, we ended up putting the buttons on rocks in the world.

FIGURE 10-5:
We included our
puzzle in diegetic
UI so that the
main character
was aware of
interactions in
the world.

This process involved trial and error, but a guiding principle was to ensure that the UI felt intuitive and cohesive with the game world and story. When designing UI, consider whether players should engage with elements in-world (diegetic UI), in a 3-D overlay (spatial UI), or in a separate 2-D interface, or maybe the player character should engage with the interface.

Here's why our first approach didn't work out:

>> The screen-based puzzle UI covered up the playable character, which felt wrong and like you were being taken out of body.

>> It felt very weird to go from interacting in the world to interacting on a screen, from a narrative perspective and the "how do the mouse and cursor work now?" perspective. We'd have to turn off player interactions on the main character. It opened another box of problems to solve.

Here are some things to think about to help figure out where to start incorporating UI:

1. Is the UI something my playable character (or however the player is represented) would know about? If so, then keep it in the world.

2. Is the UI something only I need to know about as a player to help progress in the game? If so, then maybe the UI can be spatial, meta, or non-diegetic.

3. Does the UI relate to a specific object in the game's world? If so, then maybe spatial UI is the way to go.

4. Does the UI reflect something that happens (or feedback) from an event in time? If so, maybe meta UI is the way to go.

Diegetic and spatial interfaces are popular in virtual reality (VR) and augmented reality (AR) because they blend the game world with the real world. The goal of immersive experiences is to make the players feel as though they're in that world. Using screen space UI can risk taking them out of it, reminding players that they're in a game instead of a fully immersive environment.

REMEMBER

A good UI should be responsive and predictable. Players shouldn't have to relearn how it works every time they interact with something. Patterns should be consistent so that things behave the same way throughout the game. Part of design is teaching the player what to expect!

Learning interface design principles

User interface design is about using typography, images, and other visual design elements to turn a basic interface into something easy to understand, usable, and maybe even delightful. A successful UI is one that people want to interact with. For games, there's another added element of delight and sometimes even whimsy, depending on your game's mood and aesthetic.

Here are some principles to keep in your pocket when designing interfaces for games:

>> **Clarity:** Is the purpose of each element in your game easy to understand?

>> **Consistency:** Stick to patterns and layouts that feel familiar. If players learn how one button works, they should be able to expect the same behavior across the game.

>> **Feedback:** Actions should have clear responses. It can be a sound. visual effect, or animation. Players should know when their input was received.

>> **Accessibility:** Consider all types of players, including those with different abilities. Make sure text is readable, controls are easy to use, and important elements are always visible.

>> **Hierarchy:** Information and visual elements are ordered and sized by importance so that the player can direct their attention in that order.

>> **Aesthetic harmony:** Match the UI design with the game's theme and mood. A sci-fi game will look strange with medieval-looking buttons, and vice versa.

TIP

To keep your UI consistent, consider making a quick style guide you can reference while you develop your game. Try to think about which colors, shapes, and terminology will signal across the game. Style guides include text, color, elements, and icons styling.

For example, in *Grift's* style guide, shown in Figure 10-6, I use greens for interactive items, yellow to highlight, and black for the menu. Another example is to make all the interactable objects in a VR game warm colors like reds and oranges, and all the non-interactable objects cool colors, like blues and greens.

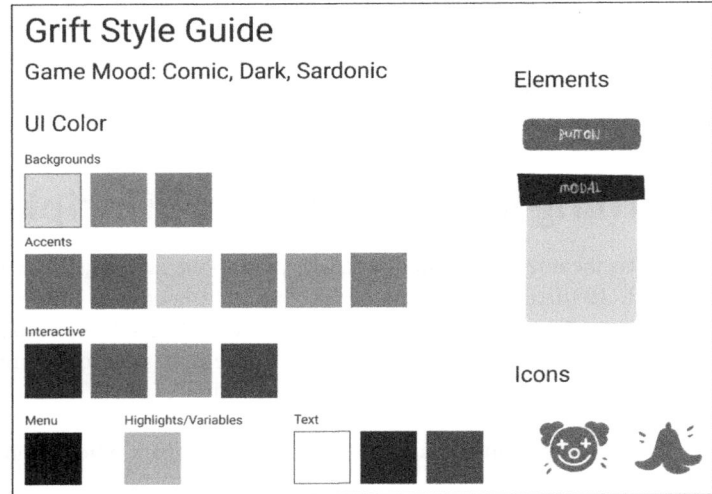

FIGURE 10-6:
Use a simple style guide to keep colors, elements, and icons consistent in your game.

Tending to accessibility considerations

As we all know, people have different needs from each other; we all have our own strengths, weaknesses, abilities, and sensitivities. When you think about *accessibility,* consider how someone may not be able to see like you do, may not be able to hear like you do, may have only one arm, and so on. Making an *accessible interface* means making it user-friendly to a wide variety of people. When you consider accessibility when designing your games, you simply open your game to many more people to enjoy. It's a way to ensure that as many people as possible can jump in and have fun.

Some considerations for accessible game design are

>> Controller remapping: Let players customize controls so they can play in a way that feels comfortable for them.

>> Font size: Make sure text is large enough to be easily read, especially in menus or dialogue.

» **Color-blind support:** Use color-blind modes or ensure that critical information isn't communicated through color alone.

» **Subtitles for dialogue:** Include subtitles so players can follow the story even if they can't hear the dialogue.

» **Contrast checking:** Ensure that there's enough contrast between text and background, so it's easy to read.

Choosing tools and techniques for accessibility

Quite a few tools are out there for checking accessibility. Many of the best practices for accessibility are derived from established guidelines like the Web Content Accessibility Guidelines (WCAG) but adapted for games. These tools help you check things like color contrast, font size, and alternative control options, so you can spot and fix issues early in development.

Here are some tools to help make interfaces more accessible for games:

» **Use accessible design frameworks:** Many game engines, like Unity and Unreal, have plug-ins or built-in tools to help with accessibility, such as contrast checking, text-to-speech, or audio cues.

» **Controller customization tools:** Allow players to remap controls or use alternative input methods. Tools like Rewired (Unity) or custom remapping frameworks enable players to modify keybindings or control schemes for various input devices.

» **Font and UI scaling tools:** Include options to scale up fonts and user interfaces. Built-in accessibility features in Unity's UI system, for example, allow dynamic resizing based on player preferences.

» **Color accessibility tools:** Use tools to simulate how your game will look to color-blind players, such as Color Oracle or Unity's Color-Blind Shader. These can help you tweak colors and improve contrast to ensure that all players can distinguish important elements.

» **Subtitles and captioning tools:** Make sure you have robust options for subtitles or closed captioning. Tools like Unity's TextMesh Pro allow for easy subtitle implementation, while also offering styling options to improve readability.

If you're interested in learning more about accessibility guidelines, a good place to start is the web accessibility guidelines from Web Content Accessibility Guidelines (WCAG) from the World Wide Web Consortium (W3C). They develop standards and guidelines to help everyone build a web based on the principles of accessibility, and websites are a bit more established than games in this regard.

Designing responsive interfaces

A *responsive interface* is one that adapts to multiple devices and screen sizes. Designing responsive interfaces means designing UI for those multiple devices and screen sizes, while also considering where controls are located on devices. A responsive interface can be the difference between someone being able to play your game and not.

I primarily use Mac to develop games, so when we decided to launch *Watchmakers* on Windows as well, I had to start testing on an old Windows machine I had laying around. Most of the time, the game worked great on Mac. The buttons were all in the right places, text was where it should be, and that's because my teammate and I were always testing on Mac. It wasn't until I booted it up on the Windows machine that I saw all the problems with the UI. Buttons would be off the screen, and you wouldn't be able to progress through menus.

Safe areas are the parts of the screen where you want to make sure important UI elements are placed, so they don't get cut off or hidden behind notches or overlays. I dive deeper into safe areas because forgetting about them while making a game can keep lots of people from being able to play your game.

In mobile games, your most important information, like health bars or buttons, can get cut off and be unusable if you don't account for these areas. When you're designing a UI, consider safe area standards that are designated by device manufacturers and think through where information should go so that it doesn't conflict with areas like notches or the dynamic island on some phones.

Here's a high level look into how I design for mobile devices:

1. **Understand what set of devices I'm designing for.**

When I start designing an interface, I think about the set of devices I want to ship on. For example, if I'm making a mobile game, maybe I want to only distribute my game on iOS for iPhone 8 and above. This will help me determine how to create responsive interfaces.

2. **Find a safe area template for Figma or my design tool of choice.**

These are available in the Figma design community for free, like this one:

`https://www.figma.com/community/file/988392183086784844`

3. **Consider whether the devices I'm shipping on have interesting device requirements like the notch, dynamic island, or foldable devices.**

4. **Lay out all my design elements and information within the safe area and accounting for anything from Step 3.**

5. **Bring the elements into my engine of choice. (I use Unity for this example.)**

6. **Use the Device Simulator in Unity (shown in Figure 10-7) to test my UI across devices.**

That way I don't have to make builds to test, and I can even show the safe area/zone.

FIGURE 10-7: The device simulator is a useful tool for testing across mobile devices.

Safe area scripts are available for Unity on the Unity Asset Store for free. The purpose of them is to resize canvases according to the safe area for iOS, if you want a catch all that fits your UI within the limits. For Android, Unity has settings to keep all the UI within the safe areas.

Designing for platforms and devices

Consider all the different controllers, devices, peripherals, and screens devices have. It's simple to design for one; there's only one way to view and interact with the game. After you add multiple platforms or devices, you'll need to start thinking about how each device behaves differently. You need to consider how the experience will feel across various screen sizes, input methods, and hardware capabilities. I once worked on a VR platform that was also available on PC. We had to design multiple ways to sit in a chair. One player could literally just sit down, but the other one had to click the chair and we'd play a "sitting" animation.

Some things to keep in mind when designing across devices are as follows:

>> What's the input? Will players touch the screen or use a mouse and keyboard to play? A mobile device is touch-based, so controls need to be intuitive with large, easy-to-press buttons. But for a Steam Deck, you'd optimize it for the onboard controls.

>> What's the device capable of? An older Android device won't perform the same as the latest gaming PC or console.

>> How big is the screen? A mobile device doesn't have as much screen real estate as a desktop PC. For consoles or TVs, you need to make your text readable from a distance.

>> Are there any platform conventions? For example, console players may expect shoulder button shortcuts for menus, and mobile players may prefer swipe gestures.

Other considerations should be made for platforms, including fees, requirements, and design standards. For example, Android and iOS have different UI guidelines that developers need to follow, which you can find in their developer documentation. These standards cover things like safe areas (to avoid notches and edges), navigation patterns, and even how gestures should work.

Some of the best games started out on one platform. This is my preferred way to distribute games. Make a great game on one platform and expand it to multiple platforms and devices over time.

Looking at Examples of User Experience in Games

User experience can make or break a game and greatly affect the perception of your game. Games like *The Legend of Zelda: Breath of the Wild* and *Celeste* are often highlighted for their intuitive controls and responsive mechanics. These games have fine-tuned their controls and interfaces, spent time and intention adding feedback to every player input, and made sure players know how to play.

Analyzing successful UX design

Games that have good UX typically have intuitive menus, responsive controls, or user-friendly tutorials that enhance the player experience. Not all of this was perfect from the first implementation, though. The practice of UX design incorporates lots of testing with players and understanding what they expect and where there are issues.

Some games that have good UX are

>> **Celeste:** This platformer has fine-tuned controls to make every jump feel great. You can also change the difficulty to fit how you want to play. The standard version can be quite punishing.

>> **Stardew Valley:** This game is welcoming for new players because it introduces new mechanics over time and has simple menus for each associated system that are clearly labeled.

>> **Breath of the Wild:** Instead of lengthy tutorials, this game teaches you through exploration.

>> **Overwatch:** Each character is visually distinct, making it easy to understand their abilities.

REMEMBER

It's possible that some games launched with some issues or knowing they needed to improve UX. Many of these games have been around for quite some time and even years. It can take time to test and make improvements, so it's okay to still make updates after launch. Doing this will result in better reviews and players who keep coming back.

How UX design impacts players and reviews

A well-crafted UX can lead to positive reviews, and poor design can lead to frustration and even negative reviews. Reviews impact who will play your game, the exposure it gets, and whether players keep coming back.

At the very bare minimum, prioritizing UX helps us make sure that things are functional. *Maslow's Hierarchy of Needs*, a psychological theory that explains human motivation in five tiers from basic survival to personal fulfillment, is a good way to think of designing your products. When you're designing something, basic requirements must be satisfied before players can engage with deeper aspects of the game. At the most basic level, players need things to work and function. It's only then can they enjoy the depth and complexity of a game. In Figure 10-8, I show an adaptation of Maslow's Hierarchy, tailored toward UX in games, with these tiers:

>> **Meaningful:** Adds value or purpose; something that resonates or has significance.

>> **Convenient:** Easy to use or access, saving time and effort.

>> **Usable:** Simple, intuitive, and effective in getting the job done without confusion.

>> **Reliable:** Dependable and consistent; works the way you expect it to every time.

>> **Functional:** It does what it's supposed to do — nothing fancy, but it works.

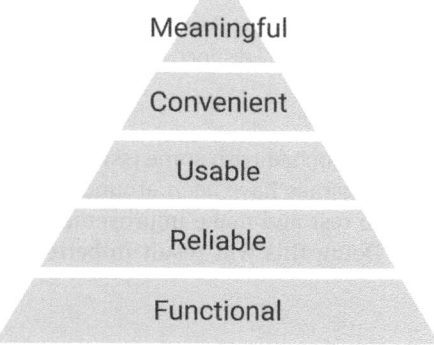

FIGURE 10-8:
A hierarchy of needs to help prioritize features and issues in your game.

3

Balancing Your Game

Learn what game balance is, find out how to create challenge, and dig into the data that goes into games.

Discover the practice of playtesting and why it's so important to test early and often. Find out how to recruit testers and sort through feedback to iterate on and improve your game.

Chapter **11**

What Game Balance Is

G ame balance is the art of making sure your game feels just right. You'll want to balance your game so it's not too easy, not too hard, and definitely not unfair. A lot of changes happen when games publish an update. They may *nerf* — lessen the power — of a weapon or character ability or go the other way and make it way too powerful. I'm sure you've heard of the term *overpowered* or "OP."

In this chapter, you learn what game balance is, explore principles for helping you maintain a mix of difficulty and fairness in your games, and look at the data behind it all.

Defining Game Balance

Although balance often relies on data, it's also about intuition. Sometimes, knowing when a game *feels* right is just as important as what the numbers show. If something seems off, playtesting can help, even if you don't have access to a massive pool of players. Early on, you'll rely on your own instincts, as well as feedback from a handful of testers to find what works. Intuition develops over time and takes practice; trust your gut and know that you'll be able to make changes after some more testing.

Also know that not everything will end up perfectly balanced. There will always be something that ends up overpowered or a bit off, but players tend to develop the best strategies for the ways they want to play with the systems and data you've given them.

Balancing a game means that you, as the game designer, spend time making sure players can be engaged with all the characters, items, or resources in your game without frustrating them or making things feel like a cakewalk. Some of the tasks you'll be doing for this include

>> Setting expectations for pacing, difficulty, and player progression

>> Testing the game and gathering feedback from a variety of players with different skill levels

>> Fine-tuning levels, enemies, or obstacles to match player abilities

>> Balancing strengths and weaknesses to avoid overpowered elements

>> Adjusting costs, rewards, or resource generation to maintain flow

REMEMBER

Balance isn't a one-and-done deal; it's something you tweak as players engage with your game. Once players get their hands on your game, observing how they interact with it will provide invaluable information for balancing stats.

Balancing game economy and systems

Balance goes into many games. A huge amount of data goes into games, so any games with resources, rewards, or progression will need some time and effort put into tweaking it.

Some considerations when you're balancing your game are

>> Determining how long you want a play session to be

>> Making sure players aren't drowning in resources or starving for them

>> Giving rewards that feel meaningful and keep players motivated

>> Watching out for loopholes that let players break your systems in unintended ways

>> Finding that sweet spot where players feel challenged — but not like the game is out to get them

>> Making sure that your systems don't favor one player, character, or strategy so much that it ruins the fun

For example, if you want a fight to last a minute, and a character has 100 HP while each attack takes three seconds, the math would look like this:

100 HP ÷ (60 seconds ÷ 3 seconds/attack) = 5 HP/attack

This means each attack should deal 5 HP of damage on average to achieve your desired fight length. That's your starting point. From there, you can adjust for other factors like attack range, area effects, buffs, debuffs, or knockback. Some moves may take more or less than three seconds, so you'll need to adjust for those. How do these values scale as players progress? Every variable starts as an educated guess and is refined through playtesting. The goal is consistency, like ensuring that each character outputs roughly the same 10 HP per three seconds under normal circumstances.

REMEMBER

Generally, these variables are best guesses at first and then honed through a lot of playtesting!

TIP

When you're making changes to your game's data, cut it in half or double it. Doing this will let you see big changes and understand where you need to make small tweaks versus large changes.

Looking at examples of good and bad game balance

Game balance can make or break the player experience. Here are examples of how balance works in games available now:

>> **Chess:** Despite having asymmetrical starting conditions (white moves first), chess is considered one of the best-balanced games. Each piece has clear strengths and weaknesses, and strategy can often overcome these differences.

>> **Overwatch:** Blizzard's hero shooter uses team roles (damage, tank, and support) to balance gameplay. Each character has unique abilities, but no single hero dominates when played against others of equal skill.

>> **The Legend of Zelda: Breath of the Wild:** The game allows players to approach challenges in multiple ways. Resources like weapons and stamina are balanced so that players feel rewarded for exploring.

The following are examples of opportunities to implement better balance:

- ➤➤ Some games may favor players who spend money to progress. This can create situations that feel unfair to players who may not be investing money into the game. A good way to balance this out is to offer items that aren't paid that help progress in the game. Make sure players that don't spend also have access to ways to advance.

- ➤➤ In games with class or role systems, certain classes may emerge as disproportionately strong in specific contexts. This can make other choices feel less viable until those overpowered classes are balanced against the rest of them.

- ➤➤ Some games may have systems in which one resource becomes overly abundant while others feel scarce, or where sudden difficulty spikes disrupt the intended pacing of the experience. When in doubt, double it or half it. Making big adjustments like this can reveal balance issues faster than small tweaks.

Learning Design Guidelines for Game Balance

Game balance is based on the choices and resources available to the player. Just like in an economy with supply and demand: There's a resource, which a group of people are producing and selling, and which another group is buying and using. The balance of these things is relative to one another, so you have to balance them against each other.

In games, this idea helps you balance resource availability. Too much supply and it feels like the resource doesn't matter. Too little, and players may get frustrated. Finding that balance keeps things fun and meaningful.

If you think about other factors that go into our real-life economy, it can help you define how you design the game.

Reviewing guidelines of fairness and equity

Fairness in games means giving every player a fair shot from the start, no matter which options they choose. This is super important in PvP games where players are directly competing. But even in PvE games, players should never feel like the game is rigged or the enemies are unbeatable. When a game is unbeatable, it kills the fun.

REMEMBER

Fairness doesn't mean that the game has to be easy. A good game can be challenging, unpredictable, or even feel a little unfair at times, as long as it's possible to reach the goal and win.

One key concept is the illusion of winnability. A great game keeps players hooked by making them feel like victory is always just within reach. The game has to stay challenging enough to keep players motivated but not so hard that it feels impossible. For beginners and pros alike, the goal is to create a sense that the game is winnable, even if it's not something they can totally master. That's what keeps them coming back for more.

Balancing skill and luck

You want players to feel like their skills and decisions matter but also leave room for those unexpected moments that keep things exciting. Too much reliance on skill can make a game feel intimidating, and too much luck may make it feel meaningless. The sweet spot lies in giving players enough control to feel rewarded for their efforts while adding just the right touch of randomness to keep things fresh and unpredictable.

TIP

Allow the players' skills to influence outcomes more consistently than luck, which can provide surprises (without determining success entirely).

Considering ethical matters

Certain mechanics, like microtransactions or sudden spikes in difficulty, can impact the gameplay in ways worth thinking about.

Take microtransactions, for example. If your game's core loop involves doing X, Y, and Z, but players can only complete Z by paying, it feels less like a game and more like a cash grab. Pay to win isn't fun. A fairer approach is ensuring that players can progress without hitting a paywall.

Players trust you to create a fun experience, so it's important to think about the ethics of your design. Are your mechanics encouraging genuine engagement, or are they exploiting frustration? Being thoughtful builds a stronger connection with your audience that will pay off in the long run for the success of your game.

Digging into the Data in Games

Data is your best friend when it comes to game balance. It's how you know what's working, what's not, and where to make adjustments. Think of resources and their values in a game, as shown in Table 11-1.

TABLE 11-1   **Weighing Resources and Their Values**

Resource	Rarity (1–10, int)	Harvest Time (in seconds, int)	Primary Use (Notes)
Wood	10	3	Crafting, building, fuel
Stone	9	5	Tools, building, furnaces
Coal	7	2	Fuel, crafting torches
Iron Ore	6	4	Tools, armor, crafting components
Diamond	3	7	High-tier tools, armor, enchantment table

In Table 11-1, these variables reflect the following:

» **Rarity:** How easy or hard it is to find the resource in the game. A 1 means it's super rare (like diamonds), and a 10 means it's everywhere (like wood).

» **Harvest time:** How long it takes to gather the resource when you have the right tools.

» **Primary use:** What the resource is mainly used for in the game, like crafting, building, or trading.

Table 11-1 is just a starting point. Your spreadsheets will have hundreds of rows and columns of data. Defining these values is just the first step; you'll need to integrate them into your game engine.

For every variable, you need to understand what type of data it represents in code. A game variable can store different types of values, and knowing these distinctions will help when implementing balance adjustments in your game. A game variable can store the following types of values:

» **String (Text):** Strings are just text. They can store all kinds of info, like a scene name or a character's name. Handy for keeping track of stuff in quests or checking and showing it later.

>> **Bool (Trigger):** Think of bools as on/off switches. They're great for tracking whether something has happened, like completing an event or flipping a trigger.

>> **Integer (Number):** Integers (ints) are whole numbers without decimals. Use them for things like amounts of resources or items.

>> **Float (Number):** Floats are numbers that can handle decimals. Use them for things like calculations, formulas, or tweaking numbers in a system. These can be used to represent things like position, velocity, acceleration, texture coordinates, and colors.

>> **Vector3 (Position):** These store 3-D positions *(x, y, z)*. Perfect for events or targeting spots in a scene, like spawning or moving objects around.

TIP

When I'm defining data in a game, even if it's just in a document or spreadsheet, I find it helpful to define the type of value of the data. It helps create expectations for what kinds of data will fill in that value, and it helps whoever is implementing the data understand how to implement it in-engine when that time comes so that the format shows up correctly. A float and an int will display differently on your user interface.

If you can, avoid embedding your values directly into the code. Having all your data in a spreadsheet keeps it more organized and in a central location, rather than dispersing it throughout all of your scripts.

One way to manage your game's data is to keep it in a spreadsheet and build a way to import it into the engine. Figure 11-1 shows a tool that we built for Bodeville so that we could import and export the data for our game, *Grift.* Being able to keep data in spreadsheets (see Figure 11-2) allowed us to edit the data in Google Sheets, which also let us run formulas on the data to help us balance it out between playtesting.

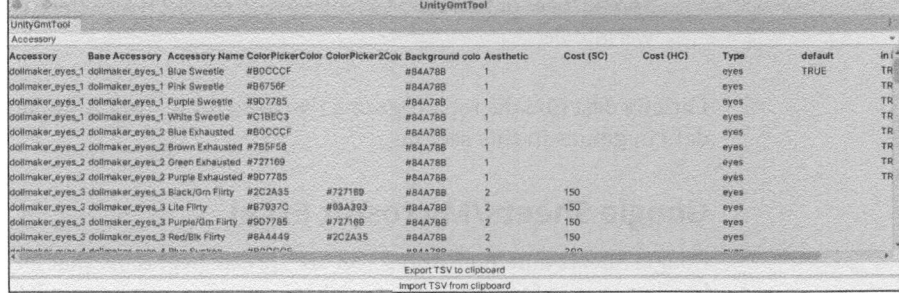

FIGURE 11-1:
The data storage we used in Unity for *Grift.*

Accessory	Base Accessory	Accessory Name	ColorPickerColo	ColorPicker2Color	Background color	Aesthetic	Cost (SC)	Cost (HC)	Type
dollmaker_eyes_1_blue	dollmaker_eyes_1	Blue Sweetie	#B0CCCF		#84A78B	1			eyes
dollmaker_eyes_1_pink	dollmaker_eyes_1	Pink Sweetie	#B6756F		#84A78B	1			eyes
dollmaker_eyes_1_purple	dollmaker_eyes_1	Purple Sweetie	#9D7785		#84A78B	1			eyes
dollmaker_eyes_1_white	dollmaker_eyes_1	White Sweetie	#C1BEC3		#84A78B	1			eyes
dollmaker_eyes_2_blue	dollmaker_eyes_2	Blue Exhausted	#B0CCCF		#84A78B	1			eyes
dollmaker_eyes_2_brown	dollmaker_eyes_2	Brown Exhausted	#7B5F58		#84A78B	1			eyes
dollmaker_eyes_2_green	dollmaker_eyes_2	Green Exhausted	#727169		#84A78B	1			eyes
dollmaker_eyes_2_purple	dollmaker_eyes_2	Purple Exhausted	#9D7785		#84A78B	1			eyes
dollmaker_eyes_3_blackgreen	dollmaker_eyes_3	Black/Grn Flirty	#2C2A35	#727169	#84A78B	2	150		eyes
dollmaker_eyes_3_lite	dollmaker_eyes_3	Lite Flirty	#B7937C	#93A393	#84A78B	2	150		eyes
dollmaker_eyes_3_purplegreen	dollmaker_eyes_3	Purple/Grn Flirty	#9D7785	#727169	#84A78B	2	150		eyes
dollmaker_eyes_3_redblack	dollmaker_eyes_3	Red/Blk Flirty	#8A4449	#2C2A35	#84A78B	2	150		eyes
dollmaker_eyes_4_blue	dollmaker_eyes_4	Blue Sunken	#B0CCCF		#84A78B	3	300		eyes
dollmaker_eyes_4_purple	dollmaker_eyes_4	Purple Sunken	#D451B8		#84A78B	5		150	eyes
dollmaker_eyes_4_white	dollmaker_eyes_4	White Sunken	#C1BEC3		#84A78B	3	300		eyes

FIGURE 11-2: The associated spreadsheet we used to import values into the data storage in-engine for *Grift.*

Ideally you want data storage that allows you to change a variable and have that change ripple out to all scripts in your game. This keeps iteration time short and enables you to make and see changes in your game super quick! You don't want to invest more time making it than would be spent changing the values by hand, but making a data storage like this helps reduce unintended changes by giving you one file to rule them all.

Using simulation and modeling tools

Every game designer should learn Excel, Google Sheets, Machinations, or some other tool at some point. These can be very useful to iterate on your data even before getting it into the engine. Testing, simulating, and modeling data in games can help game designers identify potential balance issues, test different variables, and refine mechanics before writing a single line of code. Here's a quick look at what these concepts mean:

- **Testing:** Checking how a system or mechanic behaves under different conditions. For example, adjusting item prices in a spreadsheet to see if players can still afford upgrades at different points in the game.
- **Simulating:** Testing a scenario to see possible outcomes. For example, simulating a combat system may involve plugging in different attack values to see how long a typical battle lasts.
- **Modeling:** Creating a structured representation of a system, often in a spreadsheet or tool like Machinations, to predict how different variables will interact.

I briefly describe the top programs I've used for testing, simulating, and modeling data in games in this section.

Google Sheets/Microsoft Excel

Google Sheets and Microsoft Excel are spreadsheet tools that let you organize data in a list or grid format. At its most basic, you can use a spreadsheet to keep things like a list of art or sound assets in a video game and a list of their current status. The data lives in rows (numbered) and columns (lettered), and where they meet is called a cell. Each cell is like a tiny box for one piece of info, and you refer to it by its row and column — like "A1" or "B19."

Here are some ways to use spreadsheets in your game design:

>> Randomizing mechanics or testing data, like simulating loot drops

>> Working with numbers requiring precision, like currencies or scores

>> Managing checklists or progress trackers

>> Calculating totals without manual addition

>> Providing values for variables, which you can use in formulas across multiple sheets to adjust balance dynamically

>> Creating graphs for analyzing trends in data, like how often players earn a specific item

TECHNICAL STUFF

Create multiple worksheets in your spreadsheets for better organization, or to archive older values that you can refer to later. You can reference a cell or range of cells in another worksheet in the same workbook. Just put the worksheet name followed by an exclamation mark (!) before the cell address. For example, to refer to cell A1 in Sheet2, you type **Sheet2! A1.**

REMEMBER

A spreadsheet is truly an indispensable tool here. Information and data can get complicated quickly, so a good spreadsheet helps you visualize everything and learn more efficiently.

Machinations.io

Machinations.io is a platform designed for game designers to model, prototype, and balance game systems visually. Instead of a bunch of data, it lets you use a flowchart to see how the data flows in the system. This can be helpful to plan and test game mechanics like resource systems, economy loops, and progression paths without the need to write code.

A lot of templates and examples are available on their website, but here are some common use cases:

>> Balancing in-game economies like currency systems or crafting mechanics

>> Designing progression systems like experience points or skill trees

>> Modeling player interactions like multiplayer systems

>> Testing risk/reward scenarios like loot drops

Home-grown tools

Home-grown tools, which are customized tools, will be different for every project. In the past I've worked with engineers to develop simulation tools in-engine. For example, we built a way to test breeding creatures for one of the games I made. It allowed artists and designers to see how procedural creatures looked after adjustments and allowed us to see what the spawn of two creatures looked like if we mixed them together.

For solo developers or people just getting started, I recommend investigating ScriptableObjects (`https://docs.unity3d.com/Manual/class-Scriptable Object.html`). These are data containers that you can use to save large amounts of data. A benefit of using them is that they're already integrated into Unity with documentation to help you get started.

Collecting data

The two types of data that can be collected in games are *user feedback*, such as opinions and descriptions of experiences, and *user behavior*, which is how the player behaves and involves the data around how they behaved in the experience. User feedback is often a retelling of how the player remembers what they experienced, but the behavior tells you what actually happened.

With user feedback, the more feedback you're able to get, the less weight each individual opinion carries. Some players may give feedback in direct opposition to another player's feedback, so it's helpful when you can get a variety of feedback and analyze overall trends. When you have fewer players, it's easier to chat with each one and process an individual's feedback. But if millions of people are playing, keeping track of every single opinion is impossible.

When you have a bigger player base, sending out surveys and polls will be necessary to collect and sort through all this feedback. This way, players have a way to share their thoughts while still letting you see the big picture. After a test, you can ask players about specific parts of the game and give them options to choose from, like difficulty ratings or sentiments about agency.

Some best practices for writing surveys to collect data at scale are

>> **Have a goal in mind for your survey.** You may be focusing on the first time user experience, or how players engage in quests. It's best to keep focused so that your survey doesn't get too long and confusing.

>> **Keep it shorter.** I like to keep my surveys to fewer than 15 questions. The longer you make your survey, the higher the risk of survey fatigue and players not submitting the survey.

- >> **In early testing, free-form responses are your friend.** You'll get a lot of good information if you let people answer freely, especially before you have your analytics set up.

- >> **In early testing, ask whether players had any technical issues in the beginning.** If they did, this will skew their responses to the next questions and may even keep them from being able to answer them.

- >> **Don't make questions mandatory.** Players often won't be able to answer a question you've made mandatory, and this skyrockets the risk that they don't submit the survey at all, leaving you with no information.

- >> **Don't ask leading questions so that players are biased toward a specific answer.** Ask "How was the difficulty of the boss?" rather than saying "Did you feel the boss was difficult?"

- >> **In later testing, do start making multiple-choice questions based on what you've been observing.** This makes the surveys easier for you to parse and easier for players to answer.

- >> **Use neutral language.** Instead of asking "What sucked?" ask "What were your first impressions?"

- >> **Include a catch-all at the end of your survey.** The question "Is there anything else you'd like the developers to know?" allows the players to add anything you may not have thought to ask in the survey.

When it comes to user behavior, you want to track stats by collecting analytics data through tools like Firebase, Unity Analytics, PlayFab, or Google Analytics. This data will help you figure out where things need to be adjusted. For example, suppose you have a bunch of quests that can be completed. Tracking this data, you'll be able to see what percentage of players chose specific quest lines and adjust from there.

Analyzing data

Data analysis is the process of looking at data to find patterns, trends, or useful insights. You can start by gathering the data and then cleaning it up (like fixing errors or formatting it). For example, if you're analyzing level difficulty in a game, you may track how many times players fail each level, how long they take to complete it, and where they tend to quit.

After that, you explore the data, often using charts or graphs to see trends. If you plot level completion rates and notice a sharp drop-off at Level 7, that could indicate a difficulty spike. Once you have some ways to view the data at a higher level, you can then interpret the results to make smarter decisions or solve problems you've previously defined or have found through your scouring of the data. If players are quitting at Level 7, for example, is it because enemies are too strong, the controls are unclear, or the difficulty curve is too steep?

Data analysis helps make games better. It shows you

>> Where players are having fun and where they're stuck

>> How to fix or improve things to keep people playing

>> How to balance making money with keeping players happy

There are quite a few ways to analyze data. Some tools you may run into are

>> Analytics platforms like Firebase, Unity Analytics, PlayFab, or Google Analytics, or custom telemetry systems

>> Tools like Google Analytics/Firebase, Tableau, Power BI, Periscope, or Google Sheets/Excel to create dashboards for visualizing the data

>> Software like Python, R, or SQL for deep dives into player data and statistics

TIP

Knowing SQL, a programming language used to store, organize, and pull data from databases, has been extremely helpful for me as a game designer. I'm able to write queries on the fly to find out information on the fly. I learned SQL on the job as a data analyst working in information technology, but you can practice online: https://www.sql-practice.com/.

Even when you have all the data collected, it's best to get information both from dashboards and from players' input. Often, the data can show a problem, but it doesn't tell you why it's a problem. You'll have to dig deeper to understand why the issue is happening. For instance

>> **Player retention:** If you notice players are dropping off after a certain point in your game, data analysis can help you figure out why. Are they frustrated with the difficulty? Is the level too long? Are there bugs causing issues?

>> **In-game economy:** If players aren't spending as much money on in-game purchases, data analysis can reveal trends. Are certain items priced too high or too low? Are players getting stuck at certain points and abandoning purchases? Or maybe the value of in-game items isn't clear enough.

>> **Level design:** If you notice players are failing certain levels more often than others, data analysis can help you find patterns. Are the levels too hard? Are they getting frustrated with a specific mechanic or obstacle? Gathering data on player performance can provide insight into how to adjust difficulty or improve the level design.

>> **Feature engagement:** If a new feature isn't being used as much as expected, you can dive into the data to see how players are interacting with it. Are players unaware of it? Is it too complicated to use?

TIP

I recommend starting with Firebase (`https://firebase.google.com/`) when collecting data on a small team. It's easy enough to learn how to use, has a lot of documentation, and is free for all the major features. It's integrated with Google Analytics as well. You can connect Bigquery to write ad-hoc SQL queries on the data.

TECHNICAL
STUFF

You can find information about using Firebase events at `https://firebase.google.com/docs/analytics/events`. Firebase is good for logging an event and sending parameters with it. My process involves implementing this in Unity and then using BigQuery, Google's cloud-based data warehouse that lets you quickly analyze massive datasets using SQL queries, to unnest the information so that I can write queries on it. Here's a good reference for that:

`https://lace-chantelle-rogers.medium.com/bigquery-the-art-of-unnesting-google-analytics-4-event-parameters-8597e5a0ac2f`

Chapter **12**

Analyzing Feedback and Making Adjustments

P*laytesting* is the process of evaluating a game by having players play it during development. An imperative part of creating interactive experiences and games, playtesting requires that you observe how players interact with the game, gather feedback on their experience, and identify any issues with gameplay mechanics, balance, difficulty, or user interface. I touch on all of these topics in this chapter.

This process helps you refine and improve the game based on real-world feedback, helping you make sure it's fun, functional, and engaging before its final release. You need to learn how to do it effectively to make a great game. Playtesting offers you and your game the benefit of uncovering issues you may have missed as the developer, including

» Bugs or glitches

» Gameplay issues and friction

» Unbalanced difficulty

» New ideas or creative directions you hadn't thought of

REMEMBER

Creating a game you love is important, but feedback plays a big role in shaping the final product. It helps teams iterate quickly and improve processes. If you're a solo designer, the feedback process can help you transform an okay experience into an excellent and fun experience for your intended audience. However, feedback isn't everything. Ultimately, you should make the game you want to play if you're not making games as your career. It's your life and your art — have fun with it!

Knowing When to Start Playtesting

You don't need to wait for a perfect build or even a polished demo to playtest or get feedback on your game. Playtesting can begin as soon as you have something tangible to show. Personally, I upload mock-ups as soon as they're drafted to see how people respond. You could create a mock website, post mock-up images to Reddit or social media, or create a storyboard of the game's flow to get a sense for what players may expect.

If you're working on your game regularly or already have a release flow, a manageable cadence that won't burn out your players is one month. Monthly playtests help maintain momentum, allow you to track progress, and gather valuable input without burning out your audience. For this, I typically send a short survey asking general questions to capture broad feedback. Then, for bigger milestones or major features, I schedule short, targeted playtest sessions to focus on specific areas that need improvement.

The following are few questions to ask yourself to see if you're ready to get external feedback:

>> What specific feedback am I looking for?

>> Have I made significant progress on a feature or concept?

>> Are there any glaring problems to solve?

>> Am I ready for honest, potentially critical feedback?

>> Do I have a reliable way to document the feedback?

For internal testing, on both large and small teams I've been part of, we playtested at least once a week. This not only gets you quick feedback on the game, but also helps people understand what's made it into the build.

REMEMBER

The earlier you start collecting feedback, the more data you'll have to iterate and refine your game. Playtesting isn't just about identifying bugs; it's also about seeing how players interact with your world, characters, and mechanics and finding opportunities to make your game even better.

Exploring Types of Playtesting

Playtesting can take many forms. Different methods offer unique insights into various aspects of your game, and each format serves a specific purpose. Here are some of the various formats you'll want to use in your development:

» **Focus groups:** Focus groups are typically used to get qualitative feedback on major milestones in your game or during pre-production, when you want to get general feedback on the concept of your game. They are a small group of participants who discuss their experiences and thoughts.

» **Interviews:** Interviews offer a more personal, in-depth look at how individual players experience the game. By talking one-on-one with players, you can ask follow-up questions and get more details on their experience with specific parts of the game and acquire deeper knowledge into how your players are using your game.

» **Blind playtesting:** This is a method that allows the developers to see how players interact with the game without any guidance. Playtesters are not given any instructions or guidance from the developers. It's a great way to observe and see any challenges players may encounter.

» **A/B testing:** A/B testing involves testing two different versions of a game feature with two groups of players. It's commonly used to decide between design options or gameplay features by comparing how players respond to each version. App stores typically have a way to do A/B testing for the storefronts in your game, but for in-game content, you have to develop multiple builds or use a tool to distribute to different groups of players.

» **Surveys:** A more structured way to collect feedback, surveys are often used after playtesting sessions. They're a great tool for quantitative and qualitative research. They're easy to create and allow you to collect data from a very large sample size using something like Google Forms.

Make sure you go into every session with a goal. For instance, if you're testing a tutorial where you teach players how to interact with your game, you may set your goals as follows:

» The player can finish the tutorial, which helps them learn the game.

» The player had *x* delightful moments.

» The player understood the short- and long-term goals of the game.

You can use any or all of the playtesting methods. If you're using surveys, don't let your survey length get out of hand! Make sure you consistently tailor and trim it, or players will get bored or burnt out of completing surveys. Here are some of my top tips for writing surveys:

>> **Make questions optional.** This way if a player doesn't want to answer a question or doesn't know how to, they can skip it, and there's less risk that they'll ditch the entire survey.

>> **Put "Did you have any technical issues?" at the beginning of your survey.** If they had issues, players may not be able to answer subsequent questions because they weren't able to experience the game.

>> **Don't make surveys too long.** This is important, so I'm repeating it. I stick to 10 to 15 questions so that players don't have to spend too much time on them, and there's a greater chance they'll complete the survey.

The method of playtesting also depends on the length and type of game you're making. It's difficult to assess three hours of narrative gameplay with a short demo. Instead, pick focused mechanics or short narrative sections to test with players.

TIP

As someone who was working on a game during the pandemic, I can confidently say you can accomplish all these methods remotely! Depending on the platform, you can distribute builds to your players, ask them to record their gameplay videos, and fill in surveys asynchronously.

REMEMBER

A good way to learn about your game is to simply watch people play. You don't even need to ask questions; just observe and see what happens!

Finding People to Playtest

Finding people to playtest on a small team can be very challenging. You don't always need to compensate people to find playtesters, but one way to get feedback is to provide an incentive for playing. At the larger studios I've worked at, we've provided compensation for shorter, more focused playtesting sessions or focus groups and had a closed beta for insight into longer play sessions so we could look at longer-term retention.

I've found the most success as a solo developer by posting screenshots or questions about gameplay on Reddit. Depending on your connections or followers, you may have more success on other social media. Another place to find testers is on Alpha Beta Gamer (https://www.alphabetagamer.com/), a website that helps developers find playtesters by showcasing upcoming games and providing links to demos or sign-ups for closed tests.

Yet another way to find playtesters is to attend local community events for game developers. When I lived in Orlando, Florida, we had Indienomicon and various local community game jams or events where you could demo your game. There are also events like Protospiel, which is for board and tabletop games. Much larger events like Penny Arcade Exchange (PAX) in Boston and Seattle have tables available for game makers to demo their games. If your city doesn't have something like this, you can always consider creating one yourself!

Depending on your distribution platform, you can use a few testing tools such as the following:

>> TestFlight is for iOS games.

>> Google Play Console has open, closed, and internal testing releases.

>> Oculus for virtual reality games has Alpha, Beta, and Release Candidate channels.

>> Steam provides the Steam Playtest feature, which allows developers to give access to players via access keys.

The closer your players are to your target audience, the more valuable their feedback will be. It's important to pre-screen playtesters for focus groups (especially if you're paying for it), or if it's ad-hoc feedback you're getting, understand what type of player the person is. Although feedback from all types of players can be insightful, prioritize input from those who match your target audience.

For example, I once playtested a virtual reality game with a medieval-inspired art style. As both a playtester and a game developer, I acknowledged that I wasn't the target audience, so I advised taking my feedback with a grain of salt. I preferred different types of games, and although that game eventually became a hit, my feedback felt less impactful compared to those who aligned more closely with its intended players.

While leading design for a virtual reality party game, we conducted several playtesting sessions with diverse groups. Early on, we encountered players who weren't engaged with our game and preferred more action-packed games with fast gameplay. Their user experience feedback was valuable, but it signaled the need to focus on players who enjoyed casual or party games. We then sought out feedback from a more representative group, which provided insights more relevant to our game's systems and content.

Keep a list of games that serve as good comparisons or references in your back pocket and ask your players if they've played them. This can help you gauge their preferences and refine your game accordingly.

Get as many people as you can to playtest your game but categorize them into people who fit in your target audience and those who don't. Then, when it comes to using the feedback, you know which to focus on.

Questioning Playtesters

Watching someone play your game without any guidance can be incredibly valuable, particularly when you have few remaining questions about your core game loop and want to assess whether the game is engaging, understandable, and user-friendly.

However, in the early stages of development or when certain systems are still being refined, it's more effective to design your testing sessions and surveys around specific questions you need answered. This way, you get exactly what you need answered at the stage of development, it fits in with your priorities at that time, and minimizes some of the off-topic suggestions players will have. You need to know the answers to the following questions:

>> Do players understand the value of x resource?

>> Can players describe what the long-term goals are in the game?

>> What are players' thoughts on x feature or system?

>> How does the timing of the progression feel?

>> Can players describe a reason to return to the game?

>> Do players knows how to use x feature or flow?

The following are some good practices for asking survey questions:

>> Be clear and specific.

>> Ask open-ended questions.

>> Avoid leading questions.

>> Focus on specific areas of the game.

>> Encourage honesty.

You may be tempted to ask players to rate the "fun" level of your game, but I recommend avoiding this approach or knowing a few caveats when you do use it. A "fun" score often leads to overly positive responses as players may hesitate to provide honest feedback to avoid hurting your feelings. They may also feel like they're being led to rate the game as a fun game, depending on the way you phrase the question. Instead, try some of these questions when writing your surveys:

>> "What did you enjoy most about the gameplay?"

>> "Were there any parts of the game that felt confusing or frustrating?"

>> "What did you think about the new combat system?"

>> "Did you experience any issues with the game's interface?"

>> "What did you think of the game's graphics?"

>> "What was your overall impression of the game?"

>> "Would you recommend this game to a friend? Why or why not?"

>> "Do you have any other feedback for our game?"

TIP

I like to include that last question as a catch at the end of a survey, just in case players had feedback they felt didn't fit any earlier question.

Make sure to ask non-leading questions that target specific aspects of your core game loop and features you're developing. Leading questions are designed in a way that subtly influence the respondent toward a particular answer. If you ask, "How much did you enjoy the game's awesome graphics?" you're suggesting that the graphics are indeed awesome and are steering the respondent to agree. Non-leading questions help you gather unbiased feedback and identify areas for improvement. Some examples are

>> Do: "What did you think about the controls?"

>> Don't: "Don't you think the controls are too complicated?"

>> Do: "How difficult was the level?"

>> Don't: "You found the difficulty level challenging, right?"

A few best practices for asking effective questions are

>> Explain acronyms and industry jargon.

>> Start with general questions and ask specific follow ups to get more detail on their answers.

>> Ask specific questions about how players may use certain features instead of asking about the game's fun or engagement.

>> Ask how people may accomplish tasks to understand where players encounter challenges moving forward in the game.

Observing Playtesters

Surveys and written feedback are helpful, but they don't always reveal the full story of why a player has a certain opinion or why they feel a certain way. Sometimes they may even forget steps they took or struggle to articulate the experience. By directly observing playtesters, you can see their genuine reactions, note where they get frustrated, understand their decision-making, and identify issues they may not even realize exist. Here are some things you'll want to watch out for:

>> Where players hesitate, get confused, or become frustrated.

>> Emergent behaviors, like when they start jumping up a wall instead of using the platforms you laid out for them.

>> Moments where players lean in, smile, or react emotionally, because it shows that the game is working!

TIP

Try not to help players through a problem they're having when you're observing how they play the game. I typically wait until they're at their wit's end if they're encountering a problem. If they've been struggling for a bit and not making progress or don't have any ideas to move forward, then you can make a note of that and then help them through it. It's always good to see how they approach solving a difficult issue.

Sorting through the Feedback

One of the most difficult things to do as a designer of the game's vision is sorting and prioritizing feedback. The designer must decide when to disregard feedback, keep it for later, or dig into the underlying problem the feedback is revealing to create solutions for the team.

If you're making a game, you're going to be inundated with feedback. If you work at larger companies making games (as I have done), the feedback comes from all angles. You'll probably get feedback from playtesters, stakeholders like managers or executives, cross-functional teammates, the developers on your team, and maybe people on external platform teams working on any games' tools.

At one company, I organized the weekly org playtest of about 150 people and two dev team playtests of about 10 people, on top of doing game reviews with execs and receiving feedback from external playtesters. That's a lot of incoming information to sift through and make actionable. Figuring out which feedback to prioritize can be overwhelming, especially as you receive feedback from people who hold more power than you at your company. Here are the best ways I've learned to prioritize playtesting feedback or table it when necessary to help the team move forward:

>> Playtest with the target audience.

>> Structure playtesting sessions and surveys to answer questions about specific mechanics or systems.

>> Define the underlying problems.

>> Identify how the feedback fits into your current priorities.

TIP

When players propose solutions to issues in your game, try to focus on the underlying problems they're addressing rather than the solutions themselves. Often people jump to their own solutions, but as a designer, you have all the context for the game systems and priorities. Understanding the root problem behind their suggestions helps you grasp what they're trying to solve, rather than just implementing their proposed solutions.

Additionally, people sometimes get caught up in hypothetical problems, particularly if they haven't played the game extensively or if they lack tangible issues to address. It's important to guide feedback toward tangible problems related to specific unanswered questions within your game build. Get them playtesting!

After you've gathered feedback from playtesting, the next step is to evaluate how this input aligns with your current development priorities. Feedback can be diverse and abundant, and without a clear framework for integrating it, you risk overwhelming your team or losing focus. I typically map out the next x months' game systems and questions to be answered, and when we get any other feedback, I do one of the following:

>> Enter the idea into an "ideas backlog" if it's an entirely new game system or mechanic.

>> Iterate on a game system, mechanic, or user experience if it's a current system that just needs some tweaking.

>> Identify if it's a missing ingredient by looking at all the game systems and figuring out the gaps and problems. If any of the feedback solves those problems, it's something to consider and brainstorm with the team.

As you can imagine, working as a solo developer or even on a team of two, the feedback may be much more manageable depending on how big your player base is. We did playtesting for *Chief Emoji Officer* in Google Forms very early on, as soon as we had written a story and had some art to show for our characters and user interfaces. The following table shows real feedback we received from playtesting.

Who were your favorite characters or least favorite characters? Why?	Were there any parts in the narrative that stuck out to you as funny or interesting? Why or why not?
I did not get many opportunities to explore the characters and ultimately hated any high-level worker, such as the managers and HR, who could easily get me fired for disagreeing with them.	No, the story felt very forced and was not engaging because of it.
Alex and Karen were my favorites because you could kinda develop romantic relationships with them.	Making close relationships with Karen and Alex was interesting to me because I did not expect the game to take a romantic turn.
Alex Fox, I really enjoyed his misspellings and then correcting afterwards, I felt like it added a layer of personality above that of the rest of the cast.	I thought it was interesting how (in the narratives that are not soft-locked right now) you had to skirt the line between going with the flow and being a voice for reason in the company. It certainly was making a statement and was an interesting argument to be told subtly in the story branches.
I think my favorite was Joey; they just seemed like a fun person.	It was funny for Joey to be so attracted to the avatars; it was also funny he managed to leave it at the bar.
Harry Bear, he was an elusive icon I wanted to know more about. I thought the icon was very cute. Joey was also quite funny.	I found it interesting the risky choices you had to make to continue forward. Having to side with Karen was interesting and made me feel like I was turning to the dark side.

The actual spreadsheet of information has hundreds of records, which enabled us to see that players either hated specific characters or loved them and liked risky decisions and that we had some stability issues (among many other observations). Players also gave us great references to other games and media we used to inspire new situations and themes.

REMEMBER

The feedback you get from playtesting shouldn't derail you from your vision. Instead, use it strategically to find the correct audience and analyze the trends you see within the feedback to adjust gameplay mechanics, user interface, and content. I've seen teams completely pivot based on feedback, sometimes leading to an existential crisis. This creates unnecessary anxiety and should be avoided. Instead, focus on iterating and refining systems before making drastic changes. Nothing is perfect or fun right from the start, and improvement comes with time and improvements.

Iterating on Your Game

Iteration is the process of repeatedly refining and improving something over time. In game development, it involves testing different versions of a game, identifying areas for improvement, making changes, and then testing again. This cycle continues until the game reaches the desired level of quality. To iterate, you'll need to get as much feedback as you can from people and analyze the trends of that feedback as a whole to make decisions. The best time to get feedback is as soon as you have a concept or first draft, even if in its ugliest state. Then by getting lots of feedback from tens to hundreds of people, use that body of information to analyze trends to make decisions that fit your vision.

Analyzing trends in feedback

Instead of zeroing in on every individual comment, try to spot patterns that show up across multiple players. This will help you figure out if there are bigger issues or areas that need improvement. By spotting these trends, you can focus on the changes that will make the biggest difference. It's a great way to make sure that your game is getting the tweaks it really needs based on what players are consistently saying.

TIP

Although I really like open-ended questions in surveys because you can learn unexpected things from them, the easiest way to analyze data is to make sure it's formatted consistently across answers. This means that using multiple choice questions or rating-scale questions can be useful to help organize and filter lots of data.

There's always room to improve

No matter how polished a game feels, there's always room to improve it. This can range from optimizing performance to fine-tuning gameplay balance or adding small details that enhance immersion. Many games have day 1 patches, or provide updates for bug fixes and improvements post-launch. Every game I've worked on had updates to improve upon the initial launch.

Perfection is the enemy of progress, so I highly encourage you to share your work as much as you can at multiple levels of fidelity and launch when you feel like you've achieved what you set out to do. A game you make or art you create is never truly "finished"; — you just bring it to a point where you're ready to share it with the world.

Being flexible and open to changes is a very important skill to learn when making games.

Deciding when your game is complete

One of the toughest challenges for game developers is determining when the game is truly finished. It's a complex decision that often involves balancing various constraints and priorities with delivering a high-quality game (that people want to play) on your timeline. Here are some considerations:

>> **Find the sweet spot between finishing on time and over-polishing everything.** Deadlines can push you to wrap up the game even if you think it needs more work.

>> **Set clear goals and stick to them.** If you don't, you may find yourself continuing to add new features or making changes, which can lead to endless development.

>> **Focus on useful suggestions that align with your overall goals.** Incorporating feedback is important, but too many changes — especially unnecessary ones — can delay the release.

>> **Consider what you can achieve within your budget.** Financial limits can affect your timeline. Everyone knows time is money!

Sometimes I get worn out working on the same project and feel ready to jump to the next one. I usually check if I've met the quality standards for the current project and put in extra time if needed to reach that bar. Each developer or team needs to assess their own situation and decide what factors to prioritize. However, more often than not, constraints like finances or time are the bigger factors at play.

4

Designing Your Own Game

Find out what it takes to bring your concept to life! You'll learn how to set goals and how to determine if you may be biting off more than you can chew for one (maybe your first) project.

Explore the steps from concept to launch of a game and what happens during each phase.

Learn practical tips for creating routines and keeping your motivation high to finish your game and make it to launch.

IN THIS CHAPTER

» **Getting your idea on paper**

» **Identifying a reasonable scope for your project**

» **Defining goals for your game**

» **Documenting your designs**

» **Finding your players**

Chapter **13**

Building Your Game Concept

I f you're reading this book, you've probably had an idea for a game. Being inspired and coming up with new ideas can be one of the most exciting parts of making games! The previous chapters describe the process of designing the details of a game. But now, you can get started on your own idea! So, get out that old notebook in which you wrote your ideas down or whip out those notes you may have taken from Chapter 4, because it's time to start creating!

In this chapter, I guide you through how to get your idea into a solidified concept you can use to start designing your own video game. You discover some of the first steps designers take to bring their ideas to life. Experienced game designers know that ideas are just the first in a series of steps to creating an interactive game. Some of these concepts may sound basic, but research, goal setting, and writing out the details can help keep you on track throughout your project so that you can take it over the finish line.

I cover how to set clear goals for your project and establish metrics to measure your progress. Seeing progress can motivate you to continue your game development journey! I also cover creating a plan and identifying who will play your game.

By the end of this chapter, you'll have a clear roadmap to guide you through the development process, ensuring that your game comes to life and ends up in the player's hands.

Refining the Concept

Sometimes even getting a concept on paper can be hard! The game design process, a series of creative and analytical steps, helps you craft a vague idea into a well-defined concept.

Getting inspiration

Ideas are plentiful when you're in a place where you're already solving lots of creative problems or have time to think and digest the world. When you're designing a game, you're constantly solving problems. That means you're coming up with many solutions, some that may be a good fit for your problem at hand and some that you may table for later. The ones that you decide to save for later may very well be your next project!

Solving creative problems doesn't just happen when you're working on a creative project like a game. It comes from intentional thinking and giving your mind time to think. I mention this because the best places that I've found inspiration are on road trips, in the desert, while camping, and on the beach. Basically, anywhere I'm away from the day-to-day grind and I'm able to take in the world! These settings allow me to observe, reflect, and draw connections between seemingly unrelated ideas, leading to unique solutions.

TIP

If you're searching for inspiration, go out into the world and explore with an open mind. Embrace new experiences, observe the world around you, and allow your creativity to flourish.

Researching techniques

Research is a large part of development for designers. Some fun things I've spent time researching to develop a game or feature of a game include the following:

>> **Conversations that scammers typically have online:** This research helped me flesh out text-based conversations in a game about online scams.

>> **What time people are typically using the bathroom in the morning:** This research helped me figure out the best time to schedule events and notifications in a mobile game because we all know we're playing games during that special quiet time in the morning.

>> **Southern Texas flora and fauna:** Researching environments and biomes helps you design virtual environments, drawing inspiration from a certain locale.

Research can look different at each stage of development. Expect to spend maybe a day conducting research in the beginning, and throughout development you may spend a few hours of research for each feature you design. Your studies may entail reading and studying players' feedback, exploring web forums, or even collecting information from friends. During development, there will be even more of that, but development also includes testing and iteration or data analysis. In these beginning stages, though, researching online via forums like Reddit or checking out other games in the space is a good starting point to develop your concept.

When I begin research for my concept, I start by looking at other games, pop culture, and media. What has other media done and not done? What trends are happening, and what are people currently interested in? What's missing? This market research and competitive analysis can help you understand what makes other games successful, how they position themselves to their audience, and what types of players are playing those games. But don't limit yourself to just other games! Inspiration can come from fashion, cartoons, movies, even a landscape.

TIP

You don't have to hyper-organize this process, and you can often couple it with brainstorming techniques. I typically drop a bunch of screenshots and notes into a slide deck for reference, or create a Pinterest board of images, noting what I do and don't want to be inspired by for each game or media.

Brainstorming techniques

Brainstorming doesn't have to involve people in a room chatting through ideas. In fact, that's one of the least effective ways to brainstorm and can exclude the quieter folks in the room. Traditional brainstorming sessions often favor more extroverted individuals who are comfortable speaking up, leading to a dominance of certain voices and ideas, unless someone is being intentional about calling on quieter attendees.

Consider incorporating a variety of techniques into your workflow that cater to different thinking and working styles you'll encounter in your journey. One of these structured techniques will get you started poking holes in and iterating on your concept:

>> **Mind mapping:** A *mind map* is a chart that visualizes the connections of ideas. Start with a core idea and map out connections for sub-features and tangential concepts. Mind mapping can help to uncover relations between different game elements.

>> **Wireframing:** Wireframing is a technique that involves creating rough sketches of the screens or layout of an interface. Visualizing your idea on paper allows you to quickly iterate on your idea, focusing on layout and navigation.

>> **Design analysis:** Analyzing the design of games on the market can spur inspiration and create an understanding of what you like and don't like and why. Look at similar games on the market and break down their most fun bits, focusing on how you think the designers may have created them.

>> **Storyboarding:** Storyboarding is a technique that involves creating a step-by-step visual narrative of the player's journey, as shown in Figure 13-1. By illustrating each step of the gameplay, you can better understand the flow of interactions or user interface and identify areas that need more work.

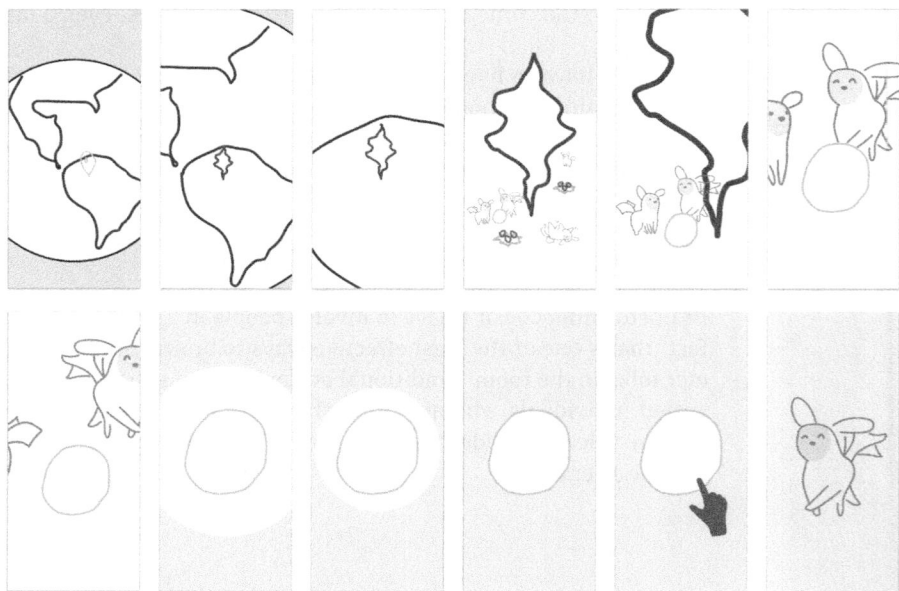

FIGURE 13-1:
Use a storyboard to help you visualize a player's journey.

Crafting the perfect idea

The perfect idea doesn't exist! If you've checked out the previous chapters, you may know by now that an idea is just the tip of the iceberg when it comes to game design and development. You and I could take the same idea and execute on it, but our projects would turn out completely different, because we have different experiences and skills. This is why it's important to do the work on your idea to get it into an executable state.

REMEMBER

Your execution will impact how the project turns out and will always be unique because it comes from your own life experience and perspective. That's why it's important to go through these early steps to get your idea on paper. It's the first step toward execution.

Validating your concept

After you've brainstormed and refined your concept, the next step you should take is *validating* it. Validation ensures that your concept resonates with your target audience and has the potential for success in that market. This involves gathering feedback, conducting tests, and analyzing the data you've gathered to make informed decisions about your game's viability.

Here's what to expect when you start gathering feedback on your concept:

>> People will get really excited about certain parts of your idea!

>> They will also point out parts of the idea that don't make immediate sense to them.

>> People will suggest things that may be unrelated to the direction you're taking in your project.

TIP

Receiving feedback can be one of the most challenging parts of game development. Over the years, I've learned not to take feedback as a personal attack on my artwork. Now, I thank the player for the feedback, incorporate it how I can, and analyze it with the larger body of feedback to address any trends I find. Stay open and receptive to feedback; it's a valuable tool for improving your game that can highlight areas you may not have considered.

A quick way to get feedback on a concept is by developing a short pitch, including the core gameplay mechanics, unique selling points, who would play it, and an overview of the storyline or setting. Sharing a slide deck with reference images helps my testers get a sense of the atmosphere and theme of the game. You can start by asking family and friends for input, or even asking people in online forums like Reddit to tap into a more specific audience. Some elements you may want to include in a pitch are

>> Reference images that convey the game's atmosphere and theme

>> Objectives in goals that the players will achieve in the game

>> Competitive analysis of similar games and how yours is different

>> Target audience including who will enjoy or benefit from the game

>> Core gameplay mechanics including the main actions and interactions in the game

>> What makes your game unique

>> What stage of development the game is in; whether it is in the concept stage or more developed

>> An overview of the game's plot or environment

Setting the Scope

Scope is the size of the game you're intending to make. It involves outlining the boundaries and limits of your project to ensure it's manageable, feasible, and aligned with your goals. All the parts of a game, like the artwork, the sounds, the engineering, and the design, contribute to the scope of the work. Scope directly translates to the time it takes to implement a feature of a game. When you develop a feature, you first have to think about what that feature is, what it looks like, and how it interacts with other features in the game. Then you have to implement it and make sure it's usable and free of glitches. Chances are that your first imple-mentation of the feature won't be the final iteration — you'll still need to take time to playtest it to make sure players understand how it works.

A well-defined scope keeps you focused, ensures that you can finish your game, and helps prevent *scope creep*. Scope creep occurs when you add more features throughout development. A bigger game means more development time and more complexity, which contributes to the stability of the features and the players' experience and understanding. Every single feature you implement will take you more time and thought than you expect.

One of my recent games, *Chief Emoji Officer,* was meant to be a game of small scope. The core of it was a simple chat interface, in which players can react with emojis in a Slack-like interface to become the Chief Emoji Officer. Although the game ended up being quite technically simple, we took months to prototype and find the core of the gameplay. A bulk of the work was in writing the content and finding meaning in the choices throughout the story. The implementation of each feature wasn't what took the most time. Instead, we spent many hours testing with players, rewriting chapters and characters, and making sure the pacing and the tone of the story felt right. In the end, we successfully kept the scope of the work on the smaller side, but the game still took about five months to distribute onto the mobile app stores.

TIP

For your first game, start small. By starting small, you can go deep on your gameplay rather than going wide. For instance, think of the game *Pong*. *Pong* is a game where you move a block from right to left, bouncing a ball between yourself and an opponent that has the same controls. If you choose to make something as simple as this, you can go deeper and add all sorts of mechanics or content on top of it, like adding in various types of balls with different qualities and speeds or battling with multiple balls. If you choose to make something more complicated with many more features, you end up going wider and having to split your time developing all the features at once.

You'll learn so much developing your first game and start to understand what you want to change next time. It can also feel very empowering to finish your first game, so I highly recommend getting there as soon as you can! When you finish, you'll be energized to start your next idea and have a better idea of how you'll approach creating your next game.

Scope will always be bigger than you initially imagine. It's just human nature to underestimate time and effort; many of us in the industry have learned to overestimate. And, fortunately, you can better understand the scope of your idea if you list any features, tasks, or ideas you have for your game. It can be anything from core gameplay mechanics to icons to sharing features for social media. Don't worry about organization just yet; focus on getting a list on paper. Next, prioritize the list. Categorize your items into three buckets: Need, Want, and Backlog. In the next sections, think about how you may re-prioritize the list according to your strengths, the core experience you want the player to have, and your timeline. The top items will help guide you to create the core of your game in the next chapters.

REMEMBER

If a new feature or idea doesn't align with the core experience, don't be afraid to say no or push it to a later phase. I was once the lead designer on a team of sixty; people would come to me with new feature ideas. We would chat about the feature and understand whether it was a good fit for improving a problem we were currently facing. If not, we put it into the backlog document for future use. That way, we still had the idea recorded for later, and we could consider it when and if it solved a problem in the future.

Defining your strengths

Scope may look different for each person or team. Maybe you're very good at character art, or you really enjoy programming. Use these strengths to your advantage when developing your idea and lean into the parts you think are fun to do or are skilled at.

Make a list of what you excel at. For me, I enjoy designing user interfaces, game systems, 2-D art, and character art. I am not as well practiced in 3-D modeling, 3-D game mechanics, or environment design. With the goal of completing a project, I lean toward making a 2-D game with characters in it. Choosing a 3-D experience would mean that it will take longer for me to complete the project as I haven't yet built up the muscles of 3-D creation.

REMEMBER

If you want to create a game to stretch your skills and practice new techniques, go for it! I'm not saying you shouldn't choose to do something you aren't practiced in. Learning is all a part of the process. But when you're defining the scope of your project, you need to acknowledge what you can do quickly and what would take you longer.

Keeping it simple

In game design, simplicity is often key to making an enjoyable game that players understand. Throughout development you'll have a ton of ideas, but focusing on the core of the game enables you to make a cohesive, manageable, and polished experience for players. A simple design means fewer elements competing for attention, which can make a game feel cleaner, more accessible, and more enjoyable. For example, if you're designing a platformer game, the core experience may be running and jumping across various platforms. For this game, you want to focus on developing responsive controls and interesting levels for the platformer. After you've created the main experience, you can add depth through content and lean into the main parts of the experience that you want to stand out.

Here's a concept you may be familiar with. Imagine you're a plumber who can jump, and your goal is to get to the end of a level filled with enemies. You can run, jump, and collect items. By concentrating on these core elements, as a designer you can focus on developing the architecture of the level and the types of enemies that you encounter there. Games don't need to be overly complicated to be enjoyable. The plumber game for example is a fun experience. When you've nailed the core experience, you can then add more abilities to add challenge and story. By embracing this philosophy, you'll develop a game with a scope you can manage, and you'll ensure that your game is more accessible to a wider audience.

TIP

Keep it simple by nailing down the core mechanics first. Focus on what makes your game fun, like running and jumping in a platformer, before adding extra stuff. This helps keep the game clear and enjoyable, making it easier for players to get into it.

Planning your project

I love a good plan. Putting a plan on paper not only helps calm the mind, it also keeps you honest and accountable for your work—and that, of course, helps you to stay in scope. You should spend some time thinking about your plan, but it doesn't need to be meticulous. Just enough to have a guiding light toward a goal. This exercise can help:

1. **Set a date for when you want to have your project done.**

This can be an event either online or in-person at a conference. Platforms like Steam or Nintendo hold sales or events like Steam NextFest to help upcoming developers get eyes on their upcoming games that could be a good fit for your game. If you're more interested in doing something in-person, events like Penny Arcade Exchange (PAX) or Game Developers Conference (GDC) are great ways to have your game tested by other developers and players.

2. **Set milestones for your project.**

I cover typical milestones in more detail in the later section "Creating milestones and deadlines," but you should at least set a few milestones involving scaling up the playtesting for your game. Set a milestone for having your friends playtest it, and then strangers, and then lots of strangers! Having eyes on your game is helpful to iterate and get fresh input on your work.

3. **Work back from the final launch date you've set and assign dates for each milestone.**

The dates are guidelines for your project. It's okay to slip up, because estimating time months or maybe even years in advance is almost impossible to do. Life happens; other things become priorities, and that's okay.

TIP

I force myself to double an estimate for things I think will take x amount of time. Underestimating is human nature; the industry standard is to overestimate time to account for outside factors.

4. **Write down the features you want to have in your game for each milestone and what you want to test.**

Look at the list of the features you wrote down that you intend to have in your game. You should already be able to organize these items into each milestone. The items under "Need" will go into the first milestone; the items under "Want" will go into the next milestone; and then items in the "Backlog" can fit into another milestone or be saved for a later date.

After you get all your important dates and milestones on paper, you can revisit your timeline while you're creating your game to help provide a path forward when you inevitably get stuck. Game making gets tedious, and sometimes just knowing that you have a plan can keep you motivated.

REMEMBER

As with anything, it's important to set realistic goals so that you're able to complete them. A lot of difficult tasks may pop up in game development because it includes many different technologies and skills. If you don't know how long something will take, add more time into that milestone. Remember to overestimate how long something will take when setting dates.

Determining the Goals

When I start a project, I typically set some goals even if I'm working solo. Establishing clear goals helps me stay on track and see the project through to completion. It provides a roadmap that guides my progress and ensures that I remain focused on the essential aspects of the project. Or it can help me understand the gaps I need to fill to reach the goal, or it can help provide clarity around when I need to pivot if I am not able to reach my goal. For a larger development team, setting goals is even more critical as it helps keep everyone aligned toward a common objective. This alignment ensures that all the team members are working toward the same vision, which is essential for maintaining coherence and efficiency throughout the development process.

For the purposes of this book, I go over how to set goals for your own games that will be helpful as a solo designer or as a designer on a small team. In major game development studios, goal setting often involves a more structured and rigorous approach in which long-term objectives are broken down into milestones that are signed off on by stakeholders and producers. Milestones offer a more manageable approach that keeps the project on track and allows for regular assessments of progress. It also feels great to hit a milestone, and it'll give you that extra motivation to keep going! Next, I share what's worked for me on a smaller and more flexible team, incorporating the learning I've taken away from larger studios.

Defining metrics

A "metric" is just a fancy word for a measurement of something. A metric is a quantifiable measurement used to evaluate, compare, and track performance. For games, we use metrics to understand player behavior, what the players think is fun, financial performance, and how to balance the data in the game. You want to use metrics because they are a great way to help you understand how to iterate and improve your game.

Here's a list of the most common metrics for games with some examples of how you may use them:

>> **In-game behavior data:** This data ranges from capturing the levels players completed, timing around how players progressed, achievements earned, or a funnel analysis of how players move through your game. This data is the most important to track in the beginning of your development journey because it's useful to understand how systems need to be tweaked or user flows should be adjusted.

>> **Daily active users (DAU):** This is the number of unique users who use the game every day. This can be helpful in the beginning when you're researching your genre or games that are comparable to your own. You can get a clear sense of how many people are playing those games and what's hot on the market now. This information on its own isn't too important, but it's the basis of many of the other calculations you may want to eventually figure out.

>> **Monthly active users (MAU):** The number of unique players who engage with the game over a month. This can be used with DAU (DAU/MAU) to understand engagement and stickiness. A higher ratio means better engagement.

>> **Retention rate:** This is the percentage of players who continue to play the game after a certain period, like one day, seven days, or thirty days after they install it. This is more widely used in live games like *Peridot* or *Pokemon Go*, or even on platforms like Roblox.

>> **Churn rate:** This is the percentage of players who stopped playing the game over a specific period. It can be useful not only to understand churn rate, but also to talk with players who churned to figure out why they stopped playing so that you can potentially fix those problems.

Games have many more metrics, especially for monetization and marketing, but I leave those to their own sections of the book. The metrics I list previously may not come into your plans as you get started, but thinking about them earlier rather than later is a good idea.

TIP

Formulate your initial metrics around the core loop of your game. For example, in *Grift*, our core loop was to create characters and use those characters to chat with (or scam) non-playable characters. We had a large set of items to use to dress the characters, so we wanted to get a sense of which items players were using and when. A lot of artwork went into those items, so it was in our plan to optimize for the favorites of the bunch. We also didn't want players to progress too quickly through the experience and burn through all the items. So, we tracked that and made sure to create enough dialogue in the story to mitigate players churning after using all the most coveted items up too quickly.

REMEMBER

It could be overkill for your project to create goals based around these metrics. But at least setting goals around active users will help you get more feedback, push you to recruit players, or even market your game. Feedback from these players is essential to improving your project!

Creating milestones and deadlines

It can be difficult to find motivation and urgency in a project without a deadline and milestones. Personally, if I don't set these up in the beginning or at least loosely define a deadline, I often drag my feet to finish the work. "There is always tomorrow," I tell myself.

I highly suggest setting deadlines for yourself, and it's even better if you can tie the deadline to an external obligation. Here are some ways that I've used scheduled deadlines to keep motivations high during development and make sure the project gets shipped:

>> **Schedule an event:** Conferences and online events are great ways to keep you accountable during your development. For one of my last game demos, *Watchmakers,* we set a deadline around Steam's NextFest to generate some buzz around the game and keep us working toward a deadline. We were held accountable because the demo was due on a specific date prior to the event, and our incentive to complete it by that deadline was high as NextFest only happens once per year.

>> **Schedule a meeting:** Having an external obligation to someone can help get you to the finish line. This person can be a friend, a family member, or maybe even an investor!

>> **Schedule playtesters:** Knowing that you have a cohort of players waiting to try your game and provide feedback can be a great motivator! Not only will you have something to show, but you'll be able to get feedback that will help improve your game. It can be scary to show it off, but getting positive and critical feedback is a huge step toward the finish line.

Here's an ultra-condensed and summarized example of some steps in my plan for a new game for which development was only a couple of months long (it was a game of small scope):

>> Month 1: First prototype

>> Month 1: Playtesters round 1

>> Month 1: Post video on Reddit for feedback

- » Month 2: Alpha: Major screens need to be in the game

- » Month 2: Art needs to be complete

- » Month 2: Playtesters round 2

- » Month 2: Beta: no game-breaking bugs

- » Month 2: Draft trailer and get feedback

- » Month 3: Contact streamers/press with trailer

- » Month 3: Launch

- » Month 3: Run ads

Most companies define milestones to align on the development stage of a game and its timeline. These definitions can be very useful to help align teams on what should be within each milestone, which will be specific to the game and the team's skillset. Typical milestones for game development include

- » **Concept:** You'll be figuring out your game's core idea and mechanics. Put together some initial concept art and a design doc to lay out your vision and goals.

- » **Prototype:** Create a basic version of the game to test out the main gameplay ideas.

- » **Pre-production:** Plan out the details, including features, art style, and technical needs. Set up a production schedule and budget to keep things on track.

- » **Alpha:** Get a working version of the game with the main features. Focus on internal testing to catch major bugs and gameplay issues.

- » **Beta:** Share a nearly complete version with a select group for feedback. Use this time to fix remaining bugs, balance the game, and polish it based on what players say.

- » **Soft launch:** Release the game in a smaller, controlled market to test the waters.

- » **Final build:** Wrap up the game with all features and polish. Test thoroughly to make sure it's stable and performs well before launching.

- » **Release:** Launch the game to the public. Plan your marketing, distribution, and launch events.

- » **Post-production:** Keep an eye on player feedback and address any issues that come up. Release patches or updates as needed and think about adding new content or expansions based on player feedback.

Documenting Your Game

Documenting your game is a good habit when making games. It not only helps you keep track of your ideas and design choices, but it also forces you to think through your concepts more thoroughly before jumping into implementation. Documentation serves as a reference point, allowing you to revisit and refine your ideas as your project develops. Read more about design documentation — like a game design document (GDD) — in Chapter 3.

Unless you're working on a large team over an extended period, documentation isn't going to make or break your project, but it still plays a valuable role in solo projects. The major reasons I encourage maintaining documentation in solo projects are to

1. **Prevent losing track of ideas that evolve over time.**

   Life comes at you quickly; writing things down will help you keep track of your thoughts or pick up where you last finished. Often, I'll include links to inspiration or references, tutorials I used, or assets to be able to reference them later. This also keeps a clear record of your creative and technical decisions. Creating habits like this can also be helpful if you ever need to refer to the license for an asset you included in your project, in case you need to give credit if you're including it in the final project.

2. **Help identify design challenges before they become issues during implementation.**

   Jumping straight into implementing a feature or system can cause you to focus on how you're creating it instead of understanding the entire flow or why you're including it. Writing down the purpose and how you want the player to interact with the feature or system can be your first step in iterating on the design. You may quickly realize that an extra step of clicking a button or jumping through a hoop doesn't make sense in the entire flow.

3. **Enable you to communicate your ideas to others.**

   At this stage in your game development path, you may not be sharing your work with others or working on a team. But you may want to show your friends or family to get some quick feedback on your idea or get suggestions about what they would like to see more of. Documenting your work can serve as a valuable tool if you decide to bring others into the project later or when you're ready to share your game with a broader audience.

Documenting your designs

I start by documenting my games in a basic document. I don't fret over software, templates, or formatting, I just allow my creative energy to transfer onto the document in the early stages, however it flows!

An example of how this may surface in my creative process is a paragraph summary of what the game is and how it should feel and play. Sometimes I collect picture references, create sketches, or write a bunch of random keywords down. Your creative process could look different! After you understand your concept, you'll be able to organize it into key information. Let's work through a simple exercise to get your documentation started:

1. Create a razor statement.

A razor statement is a short sentence about what the game is. My last game's razor statement was "Become CEO using only emojis." This statement doesn't need to be player facing, but in my case, players found it straightforward enough that I used it for marketing materials. The next section covers how to best craft razor statements.

2. Create three to five design pillars.

Choose the values of your game. Your game may focus on story, or action, intrigue, or jump scares. It's good to keep this at a maximum of five pillars, otherwise it can be difficult to keep your game focused and can lead to scope creep. See the later section "Defining design pillars" for more.

3. Define the genre.

I start by defining a genre because it can really help shape how your game evolves and what it's inspired by. Genre acts as a framework that informs your design choices, narrative direction, and gameplay mechanics. It also serves as a reference point for players, helping them quickly understand what kind of experience to expect from your game. Players may expect lots of storytelling in a role playing game (RPG) but none in a fast-paced shooter.

4. Define the gameplay time.

Determine how long players will be playing your game. Is it a big time commitment of 60 hours, or is it playable in one sitting? The two have very different scopes and considerations for content, and each attracts different types of players.

5. Define the core game loop.

The core game loop is the heart of your game. It's the main set of actions that players repeat over and over. The best game loops consider how each action or "verb" leads to the next one and loops back to the start. For example, a game loop can be as simple as the one shown in Figure 13-2, or have more steps, like this:

Explore ⇨ Gather resources ⇨ Fight enemies ⇨ Gain ground ⇨ Explore ⇨ Back to the beginning

To define a good core game loop, start by figuring out what you want the player to do most of the time. Are they fighting enemies, collecting resources, solving puzzles, or building things? Whatever it is, this will be the central activity that keeps the player engaged and that you'll build all other systems upon.

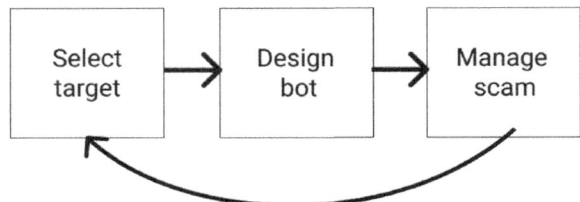

FIGURE 13-2:
A simple core game loop.

When you have these items written down, you probably have a clearer picture of what you want your game to be. These things can and will change as your game develops. You may find that you want to change the pillars or even the core game loop because you find something that's more fun.

TIP

You can find many templates for a game design document (GDD) online, and not each one will be the same. Find one you like and adjust it to your preference. In the industry, each one will be tailored to a studio's needs and preferences.

Creating razor statements

A *razor statement* is a single, concise sentence of what your game is. It serves as a quick, memorable pitch that distills what makes your game unique and engaging. Razor statements typically highlight key elements such as gameplay mechanics, design choices, or the player fantasy that drives the experience.

An effective razor statement should communicate the primary appeal of your game in just a few words, making it easy for others to immediately understand what your game's all about. It's a sharp, focused summary that cuts to the core of your game's identity and purpose.

226   PART 4 **Designing Your Own Game**

Examples of effective razor statements include the following:

> "A relaxing cat-collecting game in which players attract and discover adorable feline visitors in a charming backyard setting."

> "A quirky game in which you roll up everything in sight to create massive, colorful balls and restore the cosmos."

> "A moody fishing game in which you explore mysterious waters and uncover an eerie narrative that's been kept secret from the town."

Each of these examples demonstrates the main idea about what makes the game special, making it simple for anyone to grasp what the game's about and why it's worth playing. This makes it equally as simple for you to remember the essence of the game you're trying to create!

Defining design pillars

Design pillars, which I introduce in Chapter 3, are the key ideas that guide your game's development, keeping everything on track with your goals. By writing down clear and simple design pillars, you create a helpful framework that keeps gameplay, story, visuals, and overall player experience consistent.

For example, if one of your design pillars is "corporate satire," every element of your game should reflect and critique corporate culture in a humorous or ironic way. For example, let's say your game is *"Chief Emoji Officer,"* a satirical mobile game in which players navigate the world of corporate communication using only emojis.

The gameplay could involve navigating over-the-top office scenarios using humorous emoji-based communication, and the narrative may feature exaggerated characters and absurd corporate challenges that satirize typical office life. Cool game idea, right?

Another pillar you could choose is "meaningful choices." This could mean that players face decisions that shape their experience and the game's story. By making choices meaningful, each choice could lead to different outcomes, affecting the player's reputation, career progression, or even the overall storyline.

Here's example design pillars for *Chief Emoji Officer:*

>> Corporate satire: emphasize humor and irony of corporate culture.

>> Emoji communication: Communicate with emojis, and emojis only, to challenge players to interpret scenarios.

>> Meaningful choices: Players' decisions impact the game's narrative and progression.

TIP

After you choose your pillars, keep them in sight! You can create a poster for your wall or a desktop background. The essence of the game you originally wanted to make can be surprisingly easy to forget. Keeping your pillars around is a good reminder to stay focused on the values of the game.

Finding the Audience

Understanding who would play your game can significantly shape its development and marketing strategy. Of course, if you're creating a game purely for your own enjoyment, that's perfectly valid, and you may want to skip this step. However, if your goal is to share your game with others, the first step is knowing who your potential players are and where you can find them. By pinpointing your audience early on, you increase the chances of getting your game into the hands of those who will appreciate it!

The work you do to find your audience will help you create communication tools like a *persona,* a fictitious player used to help define and communicate who will play your game. I go over how to create personas and put the research from this section into practice in Chapter 10.

Doing your market research

Using the information you define in documenting your game (see the previous section) — like genre, gameplay time, and game loop — you can start your research by examining similar games. Include titles within the same genre and those that share similar gameplay mechanics or themes. Pay attention to how these games structure their game loops, pacing, and overall player experience. Take note of things they do well and what can be improved. Read through the reviews to see what players liked about them and what they critiqued. All these things can offer valuable insights into who will play your game and what they liked about the games they've played in the past.

TIP

Consider the art style, narrative approach, and difficulty levels in these similar games. How do these elements align with or differ from what you're planning for your own game? This comparative analysis can help you refine your ideas, pinpoint unique selling points, and anticipate potential challenges you may face during development and release.

Identifying target demographics

After you've nailed down your concept and done some initial research, consider what you've learned about your potential players. Identifying your target audience is helpful because knowing who your game is for allows you to tailor the gameplay experience to meet their specific needs and expectations. It also helps you find those players when your game is ready to play!

The information you'll want to know about includes basic demographic data and an understanding of player behaviors, preferences, and habits. For example, for our game *Chief Emoji Officer*, we targeted young professionals ages 18 to 40, who had used office messaging software before. We didn't target a specific gender, just folks who liked satire and understood corporate politics and emojis. We knew that people in this group may be working and not have a lot of time to play games, so we made the game chapter based, so that you can save your play at each stage. The game also runs on the shorter side of gameplay time to be respectful of players' time.

So back to your game! Start writing out some key items you'll want to know about your ideal players:

>> **Basic characteristics of your ideal players:** How old are they, what gender do they identify with, where are they located, and what do they do for a living? For example, are you targeting teenagers who may live in a hot climate and spend time with their friends online to beat the heat, or are you aiming for adults who work all the time, have kids, and don't have much spare time for gaming?

>> **The kinds of games your audience likes to play:** Are they into text adventures with nostalgic themes, or do they prefer fast-paced games with detailed graphics?

>> **Their motivations:** Is your ideal player looking to relax from a hard day at work, or are they looking to compete with other players online?

>> **Similar games:** Understanding similar games can provide insights into potential gaps or opportunities for your game. You can even get inspiration from the features and content from those other games.

It can be enough to simply write these into your game design document, but you may also consider creating a player persona. A player persona is a representation of your ideal player and helps guide game design, marketing strategies, and user experience decisions. A well-crafted persona can also enhance communication within your team, providing a shared reference point that keeps everyone focused on the same player goals. I cover how to craft a persona in Chapter 10. Now that you're working on your own game concept, it's time to put it into practice!

By understanding your target demographics, including their gameplay behaviors, time availability, and preferences, you can design a game that not only meets players expectations, but could even stand out in this saturated market! Doing the work to prepare and develop an understanding of players will prove helpful in fine-tuning the game as you progress and refining a marketing strategy when it's ready to go. With all this preparation, you'll have a much better chance of your game finding its players.

Reaching your players

The gaming market is incredibly saturated right now, with many aspiring developers dreaming of creating an interactive experience that takes the world by storm. The effort you put into crafting your game's design and understanding your audience contributes to reaching players and getting your game into the hands of those who will appreciate it. In this market, having a solid strategy to connect with your audience is just as vital as the game itself.

For me, preparing a marketing strategy goes hand in hand with goals and deadlines I've set for the project. Your early players will be the champions of your game, help you refine it, and be a voice that can help promote it to other players. I've also learned to start this process early so that I have an early community of players to tap into for feedback as soon as possible.

Many indie developers have used their early communities to create a following for their game, growing it through development so that they aren't starting with zero at launch. I've seen communities spawn from Reddit, Discord, a Steam page, and / or a website/landing page. You can use a variety of different platforms, but the most important piece is to keep everything in a central location. Players need a place to land so they can see all the info about the game, and so you can get in touch with them when you need to.

TIP

Building in public is often a great way to build a community and establish a player base. This means showing your work as you make progress — as simple as posting a work-in-progress level on Reddit for feedback or something a little more time-intensive like streaming 3-D model creation on Twitch. Doing this builds trust, invites early advocates of the game, and gets you necessary early feedback to improve your game.

IN THIS CHAPTER

» **Reviewing what each phase of development entails**

» **Defining your game**

» **Launching your game**

» **Iterating on your designs**

» **Testing your game to make improvements**

Chapter **14**

Following a Step-by-Step Game Design Process

L aunching a game today is more challenging than ever. The market is not only super competitive, but players' expectations also are high, and the algorithms and curator's guidelines are often changing. You'll have to keep in the know about them.

I highly recommend solo developers and teams alike to have a solid plan ready for each stage of development and to always be learning about what's happening in the industry. Each stage should have its own goals and priorities, and knowing about what other game developers are doing will help you see opportunities when they arise.

This chapter takes you step by step through the game design process that I overview in Chapter 3.

Designing from Concept to Launch

Game development has various stages, even when you're developing by yourself. The fun part is that you will never be done with design! Design in the beginning stages may look more like planning, and in the middle and end stages your game will require a lot of iteration and adaption from your original designs and plans. The stages for your development plan might look like what's shown in Figure 14-1.

FIGURE 14-1: The various stages of game development.

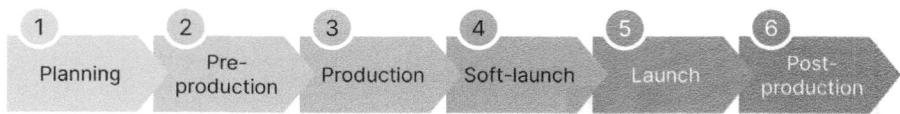

1	2	3	4	5	6
Planning	Pre-production	Production	Soft-launch	Launch	Post-production

What you do in each stage may differ from project to project, but overall, I've encountered the same tasks in each stage in the projects I've worked on. I go over those tasks in the following sections.

REMEMBER

The various phases of game development are guides to help you develop a language among your team and yourself. They've been helpful for me working on a two- to five-person team to help us figure out what's acceptable for each phase and timing when the game is ready to roll out to players at each phase.

Defining a gate for each phase of development will help you know when you're ready to move forward. A *gate* is a set of criteria or goals that you define that signals when you can exit one phase and move onto the next. For instance, a gate for the planning/concepting phase may be that you've fully documented your game with visuals for what you plan it to look like. For the next phases, your gates may be the completion of assets; a complete, playable vertical slice; or even hitting a certain numerical value of testing hours.

Planning

For planning, you'll spend time concepting and collecting references, studying, sketching on paper, making spreadsheets, and maybe even prototyping.

Determining a few foundational elements

Before you start developing your game, you need to answer a few fundamental questions:

>> What genre will your game be?

>> Will it be 2-D or 3-D?

>> What art style will you use?

>> What gameplay mechanics do you want to include?

>> Are there any main characters?

>> What's the story if there is one?

>> Which game engine will you use?

You also may need to make decisions around the following:

>> How your game will be monetized

>> How long the game will take to make

>> If you need to hire extra talent

>> What platforms you'll publish it on

Concepting

You're sketching out the vision, deciding on the core mechanics, and dreaming up what makes your game stand out. It's time to brainstorm, wireframe, and whiteboard galore. Even at this early stage, thinking about your audience and market can steer your creative choices in the right direction.

Some of the tasks you'll be completing in the concept stage include

>> Brainstorming what you want your game to be

>> Identifying the audience

>> Setting goals, like what you want players to feel or experience

>> Researching other games like yours

>> Defining the story or theme

>> Defining the genre

>> Collecting art references

>> Sketching mechanics or even prototyping

>> Getting feedback on your initial concept from a close circle of peers or friends

Pre-production

For pre-production, you'll want to start prototyping to test your ideas quickly, testing out art styles (see Chapter 9), and writing dialogue, characters, and the world (see Chapter 8). *Prototyping* means creating something quick and dirty to validate or invalidate your ideas, before committing to the idea and writing production code for it. You may be prototyping in Unity, Godot, Unreal, on paper, in a spreadsheet, or in another game engine of your choice. Prototyping is an experiment to see if your core gameplay is a viable option or not, and it's an integral part of pre-production.

Prototyping in a spreadsheet

I like to prototype in a spreadsheet because playtesting systems and levels for systems-heavy games goes super quickly. My business partner, Bo Boghosian, and I once made an entire turn-based game inside a spreadsheet, as shown in Figure 14-2. We played once through and made a ton of adjustments for the next playthrough in another tab in the worksheet.

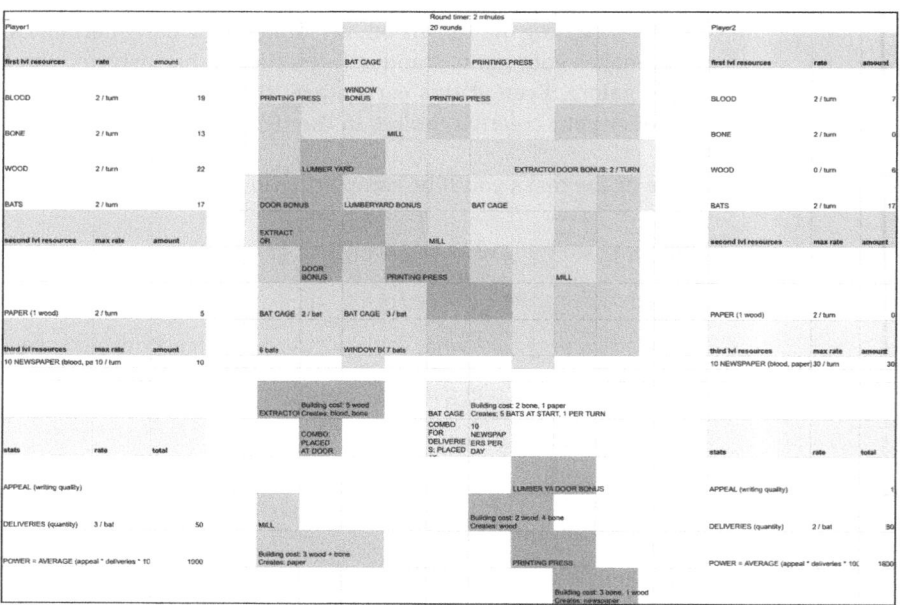

FIGURE 14-2:
An entire playthrough of a game we made in Google Sheets.

This prototype was for a two-player strategy game, in which players placed machines in a room to manufacture new resources every turn. To make this prototype, we set up the level from a top-down perspective and mapped out the important elements of the room, like doors and windows. These were important because we wanted them to allow machines to manufacture resources more plentifully than machines that weren't placed next to them.

We then created the shapes of the machines in the spreadsheet cells and took turns placing them where they fit in the level. We defined which resources we wanted machines to produce in cells, and we manually tallied up resources each turn and compared how we did once there was no longer any space on the spreadsheet board.

This was a quick way to prove out our concept by seeing how the turn-to-turn gameplay felt and whether we developed our own strategies as players. We were also able to see which resources we needed to add, and what numbers we needed to amend so that the gameplay felt balanced. This prototype took only a few hours to make, and it had just enough fidelity to help us understand whether we wanted to move forward with the concept or not.

TIP

Try prototyping your game systems in a spreadsheet before committing to an idea! It'll help you understand the data and systems that go into your game.

Making decisions

Here's where the groundwork happens. Prototypes are built, tested, and tossed aside or refined. This phase is about locking down your art style, tech stack, and game systems. Pre-production is also when you start forming a testing strategy because, trust me, you'll need it sooner than you think.

Some of the tasks you'll be completing in the pre-production stage include

>> Defining the core game loop, what makes the game fun, and what the player will spend their time doing

>> Documenting your work and ideas in a game design document

>> Defining roles and responsibilities if you're working on a team of people

>> Prototyping core features and systems

>> Making concept art

>> Defining the story outline, character arcs, and world-building

>> Choosing the tools and technology like game engine, art software, and version control

>> Creating early marketing plans

>> Creating schedules and budgets

>> Testing early prototypes and defining how and when you'll test with players

Chances are if you're new to making games, pre-production and the next production stage will be a bit blurred together. Delineations exist between tasks for each, but you'll probably find that you need to revisit a plan and keep making changes to it or go back into planning. It happens!

Production

Production requires a lot of time developing your plans and iterating on what you've envisioned for the game. Production is very fun because your ideas come to life, but it can also be tedious and a slog as you fix bugs and solve problems and change what you had initially envisioned for the game.

Testing and more testing

You'll need to test most changes you make in ways you may have not even realized. My partner and I were watching Summer Games Done Quick when I was creating *Watchmakers.* He was really into speedrunning games, so every time he'd go to playtest my game, he'd try to run up a wall and get out of the level's boundings. He'd find holes in the walls and places he could escape into the outer bounds of the level. So, I spent some time adding colliders (boxes that the player character can't move through) to the outer edges of the level to make sure players wouldn't get out and have a bad experience because the rest of the area wasn't ready to play or access.

When games are in production, you need to complete these tasks:

>> Build the game's world, coding dynamic environments and defining rulesets that complement the story, art direction, and gameplay mechanics.

>> Create, render, and animate models of main characters and non-playable characters (NPCs).

>> Record soundtracks and in-game effects, from bleeps and bloops to ambient effects like a creaky floorboard.

>> Write dialogue or in-game text, like naming NPCs and writing item descriptions.

>> Create other art assets (like user interface) and bring them in-engine.

>> Test your environments, performance, crashes, difficulty, and any other scripting errors.

Grinding to get things done

This is the implementation phase — assets get made, levels designed, and bugs born and squashed. This phase is less about new ideas and concepts, and more about producing, testing, and iterating so that the entire experience feels right.

You'll be in the thick of it, and external testing becomes your best friend. Start testing early and often to reduce the risk of a rocky launch. During production, various stages are used for milestone planning and to help define who is testing and when. These stages have various names depending on the platform you're launching on. For instance, Google Play has tracks called "Open Beta" and "Closed Beta" but Steam calls it "Early Access."

If you talk to a console developer or someone who used to publish physical copies, you may get various other stage names. I've generalized these in the following list:

>> **Internal testing:** This stage is perfect for rapid feedback loops with internal teams and quality assurance (QA). Plus, you get to test out all your platform tools, like private branches for internal testers to test key features like cloud saves, controller support, or mobile platform features like in-app purchases and device compatibility. You'll be able to test how the game feels on a variety of devices, from budget Android phones to high-end models.

>> **Alpha:** This track gives you a controlled environment to test with a select community of users. You can use email lists to bring in your trusted testers, who'll provide feedback that stays private. You may want to distribute and test with your friends, family, and peers here or playtest locally if you're not ready to distribute a build.

>> **Beta:** Beta is where things get real! You'll want to upload it to your platform of choice like Steam or Google Play. You'll be able to distribute and test but without the pressure of public ratings and reviews. This stage is for testing tech performance, engagement, and monetization.

>> **Soft launch:** This is totally optional for a solo developer, but it's a great way to do a dress rehearsal for your big debut. Soft launch is typically done in a specific market to test out organic potential, K-factor, and monetization insights. Players in your chosen market will treat it like a real launch, giving you genuine feedback. When we soft launched *Peridot,* we launched it in Malaysia first, because many folks there speak English and had the devices we were targeting. The country is small enough to not burn a bunch of players if something went wrong.

>> **Pre-registration:** Pre-registration on platforms like Google Play lets you build launch hype and capture demand before your game even drops. Users can sign up early and get a nice push notification (or even auto-install) when your game goes live. You may even sweeten the deal with exclusive rewards to make them feel like VIPs.

REMEMBER

The stages for your first game may look like build and launch, and that's it! Your process doesn't have to include all these stages. If you're getting your game out there, you've made progress. Fail fast, iterate faster, and come out stronger.

Soft launch / launch

The soft launch phase is for testing out your game with a subset of players and testing out marketing the game. Doing this ensures that your beta doesn't have any game-breaking bugs, so you can judge whether the game is ready for global distribution on the devices you plan it to be on. It's a test run before launching it out to the entire world and can save you embarrassment. Imagine if a step of your game's tutorial kept players from moving forward in your game — wouldn't you want to figure that out for a small subset of players instead of the entire world? Yeah, me, too.

For a solo developer or even a small team, it's not necessary to do a soft launch (also called *pre-launch* on some teams). For a soft launch to work, you need to have a marketing budget for user acquisition (like ads or social media) to get people into the game. For a smaller team and a small budget, I wouldn't recommend the extra effort, and instead I would put all the effort into a single launch.

On the larger teams I've worked on, a soft launch was necessary because we were still testing global distribution for a lot of the tech stack. It helped us understand any issues at scale and get a sense of how players retained, churned, and where they experience issues.

On mobile for iOS and Android, you can launch it in certain countries, and on Steam you can do Early Access to let players know the game is still in development. For Bodeville, we launched one of our games as a soft launch in New Zealand. New Zealand, Singapore, and Malaysia are good places to launch first for mobile games from the United States because people in those countries speak English and have a wide variety of mobile devices. You can launch your game without translating it to another language, and a good majority of people will be able to run the game on their devices (at least for mobile).

REMEMBER

Launch day is an important time, and even though you only get one, you can continue building your community over time (see Chapter 16). Steam allows many different types of events and announcements. Remember that not every successful game was a hit at launch. Games like *Rocket League* and *Among Us* took some time to become super popular.

Post-production

You only get one launch! You want to make it count. Every phase, every track, every decision builds toward this moment. Post-production, you'll be launching the game into the wild with the marketing plan you planned far before launch. And once you've launched, it's not over! Post-launch, you're facing tougher competition, pickier players, and skyrocketing marketing costs. This is where your retention strategies and live ops come into play.

Some of the tasks you'll be completing in post-launch include

>> Getting reviews! You should be getting as many reviews as possible on day one. For *Chief Emoji Officer,* we got 15 reviews on Steam on day one, and we were launched into the discovery queue.

>> Testing your K-factor, testing and optimizing your ad campaigns, and making sure your tech stack is solid

>> Running ads if you have the budget and it's in your plan

>> Working with influencers and players

>> Talking to press and anyone who will play or share your game

>> Promoting your game on social media

This list shows some of the most helpful things we prepared for post-production:

>> **A list of people we wanted to contact:** We sent out information on our game launches to a variety of people. We spent quite a bit of time collecting many press outlets and emails in spreadsheets.

>> **A press kit:** A few press people reached out and told us that having a press kit (logo, summary, GIFs, screenshots) was very helpful for them to post information about our game.

>> **Ads and ad experiments:** We spent less than 100 dollars to start testing ads on various platforms to see what worked for us. As an indie team with no marketing budget and no experience in ads, doing this helped a lot so that we knew how to optimize our small budget when we needed to make it matter the most at launch.

TIP

Try to get at least ten reviews for your game on day one. This is widely mentioned as a metric to affect algorithms for various platforms. It may not be the same on all the platforms like Google Play, the App Store, and Steam, but it's a good goal to hit.

Your reviews must come from paying customers! People who received a promo or key for free as a tester and review your game don't count toward your ten reviews.

Acquiring the Skills Needed to Launch

Launching something into the wild takes a lot of bravery and guts. Every single time I've gone to launch, a doubt played in my mind: *Are we ready? Is the game ready? Is the game even good?* Once you reach that point, these questions will inevitably surface.

Launching games these days takes much more than it used to. The competition is fierce, and players have countless options to choose from. Games need to stand out with something excellent: the art, gameplay, tech, content, or even the level of player choice. Acquiring the skills to make a game that stands out takes practice and a curiosity to learn more about other skillsets outside of what you're used to doing. I've been able to acquire a variety of skills by accepting positions at different types of companies, trying out new roles, doing hobby projects, and being open to helping others with their work.

You'll face many challenges when it comes to finishing the game. The old saying, *"the last 10 percent of the work is the hardest part,"* couldn't be more accurate. Even after nailing down gameplay and the game's design, there's a bunch of additional tasks to tackle:

>> **Testing and polishing the game:** You'll be fixing newly found bugs, adding new art, and maybe adding in extra elements to make the game feel more alive.

>> **Contacting press:** If you want your game to get seen, you'll need to contact press and start cold calling. Cold calling is where you find the target audience and contact them to let them know about your game. It's necessary in all businesses; games are no exception.

>> **Creating trailers and store assets:** I'm no expert artist, but I did all the store assets for many of our games by myself, and it took me a few weeks to have something that we were happy with. You'll have to export many different sized assets and read through asset documentation to figure out what compositions are best (see Figure 14-3).

>> **Optimizing your store page for visibility:** You'll have to spend time optimizing your storefront. There's even an acronym for this in software, called App Store Optimization (ASO).

Steam Store Assets

Steam Library Assets

FIGURE 14-3:
Just a few of the assets we had to create for the Steam storefront for the demo of our game, *Watchmakers*.

TECHNICAL STUFF

I use Figma for all of the user interface and formatting needs for the storefront assets for our games. If you go this route, you can find useful templates for Steam, iOS, and Google Play. Having those will get you a head start on formatting the assets for your game's storefront.

At the launch stage of development, the skills that have served me best are

>> **Dedication:** Staying committed, even when the finish line feels distant. Set small, manageable goals that you'll stick to and reward yourself for completing them.

>> **Perseverance:** Push through setbacks and roadblocks by creating a routine that includes consistent work on your goals. Having a support system like peers, mentors, or a community can prop you up and keep you motivated to continue.

>> **Flexibility:** You'll be completing a variety of tasks at this stage that don't have much to do with game development and incorporate a wide skillset. You may be doing graphic design or writing copy for the store, contacting press or making press kits, or making trailers and editing videos and music.

The best ways to develop these skills are by

>> **Participating in game jams:** I only have this dedication because I've done around 15 game jams, which are small hackathons that take place usually

over a weekend. They teach you to complete something in a short amount of time.

>> **Seeing projects through to completion:** Starting projects is easy; finishing them is hard. You won't necessarily enjoy doing the hard work but know it has to get done. The feeling of accomplishment will be worth it — trust me!

>> **Learning new skills to expand your toolkit:** I don't love monotonous testing, but I know it's necessary for a good game. Working with testers in larger organizations has helped me learn more about efficient processes and some automations so that I can lessen the burden on myself when I'm doing it alone. It makes it easier to do!

>> **Staying curious and being open to new ideas:** It's important to be open-minded about learning more about topics you may not be interested in right now. I don't ever remember being interested in marketing when I was first starting out in game development, but nowadays I'm very interested in it. The more knowledge I get, the more I'm able to make marketing tasks really fun and engaging for myself. Doing marketing makes me feel like a sleuth trying to find the audience!

Be open to learning new skills and different ways to approach development. Dedication is showing up, and perseverance is not giving up. Focus on progress, not perfection, and embrace challenges as steps toward future growth. All of these are the top skills you'll need to make it in such a project-based field like games.

REMEMBER

Do one thing on your game a day. This practice will help you keep progress and consistency. It can be as small as changing a font or the color of an asset.

Accepting the Final Release (Versus What You Envisioned)

Designing a game involves solving lots of problems you figure out along the way. The first idea you have may morph into something completely different. You may find out the size of the idea was too big or too small, or you may find something much more fun while you're developing. Sometimes even an unintended thing like a bug or glitch in your work can turn into a delightful experience.

When you start developing your idea, each decision, from core mechanics to aesthetic choices, builds on the last. There's no one-size-fits-all approach to design, and that's why various design philosophies exist to help navigate the challenges you face, as shown in Figure 14-4. There are a couple ways to approach further developing your initial idea:

» **Additive design:** You can begin with a simple mechanic, idea, or theme and then add features, content, or complexity as you go. This approach focuses on expanding the game by identifying opportunities for improvement or enhancement during development.

» **Subtractive design:** Subtractive design involves starting with a larger concept or more ambitious scope and then refining it by removing elements that don't add value or align with the core experience.

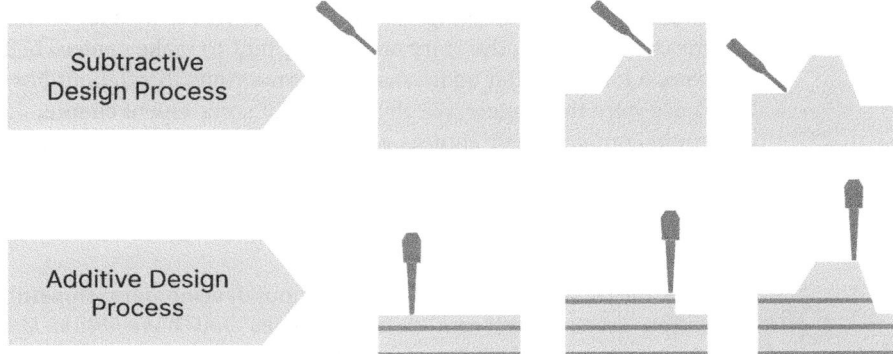

FIGURE 14-4:
An illustrative example of each design process, the additive method and the subtractive method.

TIP

Personally, I favor an additive approach, though you'll probably do a bit of both throughout development. I've typically worked on teams with a large idea and a bunch of prototypes. But starting with a small, manageable idea allows for incremental growth, which not only keeps the scope under control but also provides flexibility. Plus, as the project grows, you can bring in additional talent to address specific problem areas.

In game development, where you're juggling diverse disciplines like art, programming, and audio design, the workload can quickly balloon. Unlike designing a board game, which may focus primarily on rules and balance, video game development demands a much broader skillset. By starting small, you can focus on refining core mechanics or fleshing out a fun theme.

For example, additive design could begin with a simple mechanic, such as a unique movement or combat system, and expand as you discover new ways to engage the player. Alternatively, you may start with a rich theme or world and allow the mechanics to evolve organically, shaped by the rules and logic of that world.

In *Chief Emoji Officer*, we knew the main game loop was going to be something like "make choices by selecting an emoji to progress the story and unlock new emojis" when we started, and we knew we wanted the game to resemble a chat interface. Some of the problems we had to solve included

>> Choices didn't feel meaningful to players.

>> The story didn't have enough progression.

We didn't initially intend to have a performance review at the end of every chapter when we started planning our idea, and we had to do a lot of work on the patterns for choices within the story and the content to make choices feel impactful. There were a lot of smaller additions and subtractions throughout our development, but those were the biggest. We also had to cut some end of chapter data (where players could compare their choices with other players' choices) because it was going to require too much engineering work. Our game didn't turn out like how we originally envisioned, but it was close enough, and we were happy with how players were reacting to it.

REMEMBER

Your initial vision will change throughout development. Hopefully you take inspiration from your team or experiences you have while you're working on your game that inspire some different ideas and approaches. Depending on your approach to design, the end result will almost never look exactly like the original plans.

Iterating on Your Designs

Design is never finished. Designing something is a process of constant refinement until it's at a quality bar that you're happy with or one you and your team have aligned on. My preferred style of iteration goes something like this:

1. Get a first pass on paper.

It doesn't matter how ugly it is. The purpose of this phase is just to put your thoughts down so they can be sculpted into something better through feedback and your own reflections.

2. Create a rough prototype.

Use this to figure out any early problems and lean into the fun parts of the prototype.

3. **Get early feedback.**

   Share the prototype with a small, trusted group (team members, collaborators, or friends).

4. **Refine and iterate.**

   Take the feedback you've received and refine your design, looking for patterns in the feedback to help prioritize.

5. **Test with a broader audience.**

   Once you've improved the design, share it with a larger group, such as playtesters or your target audience.

6. **Polish the design.**

   Pay attention to small details that enhance the overall experience, like visual polish or intuitive controls.

7. **Repeat as needed.**

   Iteration doesn't mean that you're starting over. It means you're building upon something you previously made to address problems you've found and making continuous improvements.

TIP

Keeping a log of your iterations can provide motivation and show how far you've progressed. Figure 14-5 shows my initial iterations of some of the characters in *Chief Emoji Officer* and then two more iterations of them as we progressed. After the first pass, I learned how to improve the art style in its cohesiveness across the game, which helped me scale it to 30+ characters in the game.

FIGURE 14-5:
Character
iteration, from
the initial quick
draft to the
final version.

Improving through Player Feedback

Players will see your game in ways you never did. Each and every person comes from a different background with varied experiences, and their feedback is the way to discover new problems to improve your work. When you seek feedback, keep an open mind for the following:

>> What's working

>> What's not working

>> How players feel

It can be easy to focus on negative feedback, but positive feedback can be even more valuable. It feels good to hear (who doesn't love a little praise?), but it's more than that; positive feedback can help you lean into the fun. This problem-solving approach zeroes in on what's already working and encourages you to do more of it, instead of hunting for problems to fix. Solutions to problems may work, or they may flop. But if something's already working? Well, you know it works.

When we were testing *Chief Emoji Officer,* we had lots of problems to solve. But we also spent time on the things that were working. We heard what players found fun and leaned into these things the best we could:

>> The characters all felt different and had their own personalities.

>> Players liked that the story was based on current events.

>> The emojis gave a sense of agency and interpretation. Players were interested in seeing how the story went based on their choices.

REMEMBER You can approach iteration in multiple ways, including solving problems for what's not working or leaning into the best parts of the game and where players are having fun. See Chapter 12 for more about playtesting and how to incorporate feedback.

Chapter **15**

Finishing Your Game

G ame design and development is chaotic in nature. It combines a wide range of skills and tasks, requiring constant juggling and organization. The creative process also can be a bit, well, creative and messy, taking you down paths you never expected to go.

Making games has taught me to embrace the unpredictable, go with the flow, and let go of the need to control everything — otherwise, you'll never get your game finished. This is especially true with working in user-generated content and games tooling. You will always encounter emergent behavior, and players will surprise you and do things you never anticipated. This can be a good thing!

For example, while I was working on a VR platform, a group of users took their world-space user interface shaped like a tablet and threw them all into a fiery pile to burn them as a protest against the interface's design. This is just one of the many moments in my career that's reminded me that some things are simply out of my control. Sometimes the best approach is to lean into that to maintain sanity: Be open to feedback in its many forms and be open to change. What you envisioned for your game or maybe even a single feature may change once it ends up in the player's hands.

The key to thriving in the creative environment of game design is to accept a bit of disorder. Not everything will be perfect, and some things won't go as planned. But that's also part of the fun! If everything always ran smoothly, we wouldn't have any surprises or excitement in our lives.

This chapter provides a way to help you navigate the chaos and maintain order — and your mental health — by showing you ways to keep your game on schedule, avoid pitfalls that can prevent you from publishing your game, and ensuring that all members of the team remain productive.

Avoiding the Top Reasons Games Don't Finish

It is difficult to finish a game. It's difficult to produce a finished product. It takes dedication, resourcefulness, and some blind faith to really see something through. As a regular Reddit user, I've seen at least 25 posts in the last year from people talking about how they're struggling to complete their game. It's such a common theme that it inspired me to write this book!

REMEMBER

If you're struggling, just know you're not alone. There are ways to stay on track and see your project through. I've got about 30+ unfinished projects sitting in my folders but only around three that I still pick up and work on every now and then.

Here's why finishing a game can be so tough:

>> **Scope creep:** It's easy for the project to grow too big. You start adding more features or ideas, and suddenly, it feels unmanageable. You can avoid this by simplifying your ideas as much as possible and overestimating how long something will take to make. You can read more about scope creep in Chapter 3.

>> **Burnout:** Game development is intense. Working long hours without a break can drain your energy, and before you know it, you've lost the motivation to keep going. Taking breaks benefits the creative process, because you'll have time to reflect on your learnings. Make sure to go on walks outside and step away from the computer a day or two a week.

>> **Perfectionism:** Sometimes, developers feel their game isn't "good enough" yet, so they keep tweaking it endlessly, never feeling like it's ready to launch. Perfect is the enemy of finished! Playtest as soon as possible and get outside opinions on your game as you develop it.

>> **Loss of interest:** After working on something for awhile, the excitement can fade. New ideas start looking more fun, and it's tempting to leave the old project behind. If you're losing interest, try to analyze why that is. Is it because you're stuck on something, or because you've learned that another project

may be better? Again, breaks are good here, so that you can reflect and reprioritize as needed.

>> **Technical challenges:** Running into bugs or hitting limits in your knowledge can be overwhelming. Connect with others in the industry on Reddit, in Facebook Groups, or on LinkedIn so you have a community to lean on.

>> **Lack of feedback:** Without feedback from players or peers, it's easy to start doubting the project. You may feel like it's not worth finishing if no one's excited about it. Posting your progress on Reddit may get you some good feedback to help motivate you to keep going.

>> **Life happens:** Sometimes, external things like financial pressures or life changes can get in the way, and the game has to take a back seat. It's okay to take a break and revisit your project at a later time (even a much later time). I've been working on a puzzle book for two years, on and off. It's still an important project to me, but I give myself grace because life happens.

>> **Team issues:** In group projects, disagreements or poor communication can cause frustration and stall progress. It may be that you and your business partner don't agree on a path forward, but the most important thing is that you move forward. Make sure to pick your battles, which means that sometimes you may need to disagree and commit. Sometimes, it's better to move forward than be right.

>> **Market doubts:** As trends change, you may start questioning whether your game will be relevant or successful, leading to a loss of confidence in finishing it. Again, take a moment to analyze the market to figure out if the project is something you want to continue.

REMEMBER

It can feel a little guilty to let a project go. But knowing these reasons are completely valid can help you give yourself permission to call it off when needed, so you can move on to bigger and better things.

Making Decisions for Your Game

For me, making decisions is the most important part of making games and making it through life in general. Decisions are risky. You may spend time on something that closes doors to certain paths, or a decision may lead you down a path you didn't intend. Decisions affect how your game will turn out and how your work is perceived.

I'll share some of my fears about making decisions in the hopes you may relate:

>> What if I make the wrong decision?

>> What if others think my decision is dumb?

>> What if that decision makes the game worse?

>> What if I can't come back from the path a decision takes me down?

Sometimes I even feel like my creative integrity may be at stake when I'm making a decision. But the reality is, no one else thinks about my creative integrity, and it's more important to choose a path than to deliberate on a specific path.

It can be easy to get caught up in decision paralysis when you have many different options or paths to go down. My philosophy is that most decisions were good ones in hindsight, and there is never a right or a wrong. You'll never truly know what could have been, and it's futile to try and figure that out. You must do your best in the moment to assess what the risks are with making a specific decision, considering points like these:

>> The best fit for the situation

>> How big the impact of the decision is

>> Whether you can live with the consequences (because there are always pros and cons to any decision)

A decision I'm frequently faced with is "Should we build it, or should we buy it?" This decision pertains to building tools for a project or buying tools for a project. I've designed a lot of features and content in games, but often this requires designing new tools to test those features or simulate how the content will play out. For the past two years I've been working on many projects that are narrative-based or branching stories. Often throughout these projects my team and I have discussed what tools to use to write the story or content.

I worked on the questing system and the content in *Peridot* at Niantic, and we built our tools and systems from scratch. At the time, I researched what was on the market and games that were using the narrative tools that were available. I felt that there was a gap in the market for a simple tool that worked well with Unity and had the ability to organize information visually.

That experience is what really sparked my interest in branching out into using narrative tooling and specifically led me to using Twine throughout my subsequent games instead of building from scratch (see Figure 15-1). It can pay to not re-invent the wheel, especially when you're not a huge company with a lot of resources.

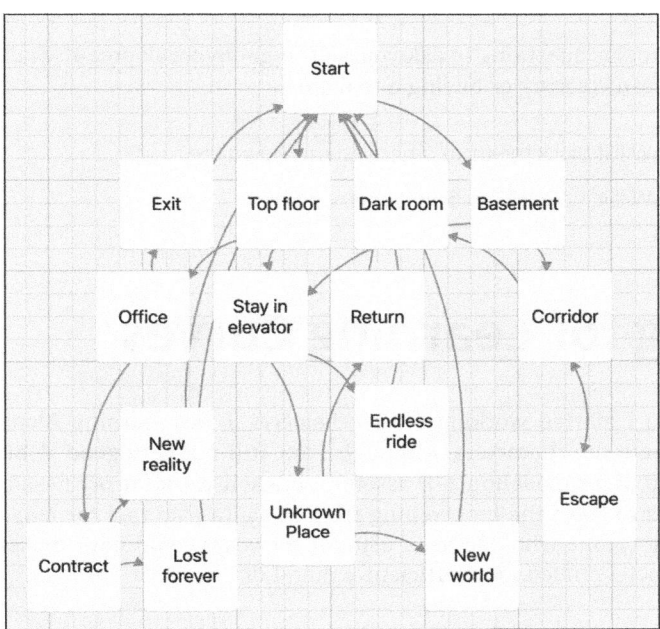

Here's an example for how I made the decision to use Twine in some of my projects instead of building from scratch:

1. I first identified the problem I was having, which was that it was difficult to write stories with choices in a linear format, like a spreadsheet.

2. I researched dialogue tooling currently available. This led to me quite a few different ones like these:

   - Yarn Spinner, `https://www.yarnspinner.dev/`

   - Obsidian, `https://obsidian.md/`

   - Twine, `https://twinery.org/`

3. I outlined my needs: low-cost, a visual editor, good resources and examples, and easy to get started.

4. I discovered Twine is free and open-source. Meaning that it costs nothing, and I could build upon Twine to my liking and contribute to the tool if I needed to improve it for my own use.

5. I also wanted to make sure that using Twine wouldn't block me from utilizing other tools down the way. The scripting parts of Twine could prevent me from integrating with other tools, but I wouldn't need to use the scripting parts of the Twine editor.

The major questions to ask yourself in game development when you're choosing between creating or buying a tool are

>> Will it block me from other systems down the road?

>> Will it increase my development time?

Estimating for Learning Curves

When I started working on *Watchmakers*, I was learning Blender to model and animate the characters. Although I am still not very good at Blender (which is a free tool for modeling 3-D assets), I made it work for my needs. It took me many hours to learn the tool coming from Maya (a paid tool for modeling 3-D assets), but someone who had been using it for years could have modeled and animated characters much more efficiently than I did.

It's quite difficult to estimate time for something you know very little about, so I tend to *timebox* it instead. This means I limit myself to working on a task for a set amount of time. For instance, for creating the first character, model, animation, and all, I gave myself two weeks for the first draft and then moved onto other tasks. Conversely, my friend, an experienced 3-D modeler, modeled and animated a character in one day at a game jam we attended.

After you make the first of something it becomes much easier to make the rest. You know how to complete it at its simplest; you can reuse work you've already done; and you know where you can cut corners to achieve what you want.

Keeping Your Game in Budget

When you're working solo or on a small team, you probably won't need a big budget. You may be working on this after school or after work and not getting funding at all. Or maybe you're using funds from your day job to hire contractors to help you with art and sounds. Either way, you'll probably want to keep costs low to free. You can do this by learning new skills and using as many free assets as possible.

Figuring out what to hire for depends on your own skills and areas where you are less practiced. For instance, sometimes I need a more practiced artist to create better artwork or in a different style. Depending on your strengths and weaknesses, you may consider the time you'd take to learn something, and instead hire out for it. Then you can spend your time on other things that need to get done.

The cost of hiring can vary widely based on the person's experience, location, and role. You may need to shop around and see who's available in your budget if you have one. Here are some places where you can start your search:

>> **r/INAT:** A subreddit dedicated to bringing together creatives for the purpose of collaboration, networking, and gaining experience in team-based development

>> **r/gamedevclassifieds:** A subreddit where people can post their game industry-related services or available positions

>> **Indie Games Developer group on LinkedIn:** A group dedicated to sharing game development progress and a place where you can post to hire services or find collaborators

The items I've often paid for in my own work are

>> **Character art:** I'm not a practiced artist, and someone else will be able to accomplish better artifacts more quickly than I can.

>> **Social media content:** Understanding trends and making fun content to suit the audience takes a lot of work. You could dedicate an hour a day to it, but it's easy to get sucked into social media and spend a lot of time there.

>> **Store art:** Your store or the front page of your game is going to attract players and sell the game. Your gameplay will keep people coming back.

>> **Playtesters:** It can be difficult to source playtesters, especially after you've asked all your family and friends more than once. Or you may not have access to the game's target audience. Sometimes it can really increase the speed at which you iterate.

Designing a Routine: A Survival Guide

Producing a game is no easy feat, so you'll need to develop a routine and good habits to finish it. There's a saying that "the last 10 percent takes 90 percent of the time" — meaning that the final stretch is the most difficult and time-consuming part of the process. Just know that putting in that last effort to finish the game is completely worth the feeling you get once you've accomplished it.

The endorphins and the pride aren't the only good part of making games. You're expressing yourself, possibly inspiring others to do the same, and even creating opportunities for yourself because people can connect you to your work once it's published (and maybe even want more).

When I pushed the publish button on *Chief Emoji Officer*, it was a huge celebration! We got to post out to our networks that we had accomplished something, something that we had hoped would make a statement, and there was a feeling of relief that we had finished the game. And it was the best we could make it at the time. People started playing it. We started getting feedback about it, from positive feedback to "I have a bug to report" to "this could be better." All of which was welcome because people were invested in it! They related to it and were delighted that something like this was made.

REMEMBER

Surviving the lifecycle of a game's development means you'll need to be intentional about your working habits by developing routines and being consistent in the way you show up to the work on your project. Routines develop a muscle for dedication.

The best routines I created when I was developing solo were

>> **Do one thing every day.** It can be something like changing a font or a color, to animating an entire character. One thing everyday amounts to a lot.

>> **Work at the same time every day.** When I was working on our games at Bodeville, we worked four days a week, about 10 a.m. to 4 a.m.

>> **Schedule a playtest at the same time every week.** Playtesting once a week on a set day and time keeps you accountable to that meeting to get what you need to get done, done. Even better if you can schedule outside playtesters for these times.

Managing Your Time

I'm going to tell you right now, it's best to get started as soon as possible and work toward a date. The reality is it can be easy to procrastinate and wait until the last minute to get things done. If you do that, I suggest starting early to be able to think through what you may do in your downtime. Then when you come back to it, you'll have more of an idea in your mind about the path forward.

TIP

Some people work best under pressure. Limit the time you work on items that could take a long time. If you get stuck, move onto something else. That break may help you come up with a new approach to finishing the previous task, and the pressure of time may help you focus on the end goal.

Staying Consistent

Do one task a day, no matter how small it is. The completion of tasks and checking of the box will keep you motivated to continue. Seeing progress can be very motivating.

I also like to keep a *developer log* to see where I started on something and where it's at in my current progress. A developer log is essentially a diary of the work you've completed on your project. Seeing how much the project has improved over time is hyper-motivating and can be a great reminder that the hard work you're putting in is paying off. Figure 15-2 shows a sample from my developer log for *Watchmakers,* where I compiled tutorials and resources I used, as well as thoughts and next steps to remind me about where I've left off in my work.

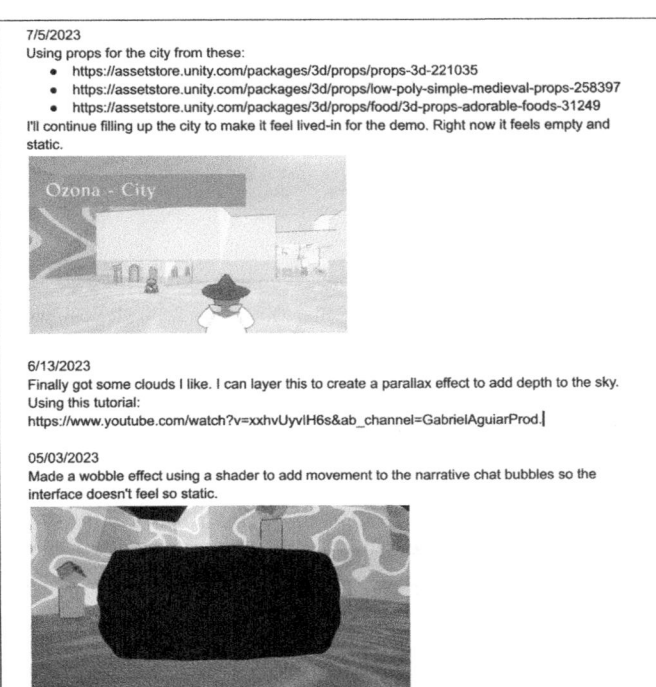

FIGURE 15-2:
A sample from my developer log for *Watchmakers*.

Here's what I recommend including in a developer log:

>> **Things you learned, either through the work or from testing with players:** This way you can point back to when you learned something and possibly even remind yourself why it was important to learn.

>> **Resources you used in the game (links to tutorials, fonts, or assets):** You may need to reuse these in the future, or you may need to review the licenses when you go to publish your game.

Make sure any assets you use in your game are free to use or that a license to use has been paid for.

>> **Things you want to focus on next and why:** This helps remind me where I am in my project, especially if I take a break for awhile.

>> **Screenshots of your progress:** These come in handy when you are stuck in a project and feeling like you're not making progress. You can look back and remind yourself how far you've come and boost your own morale.

Assessing the progress and improvements I've accomplished over a span of time, like between the two images shown in Figure 15-3, is also helpful to me. Seeing progress can be very motivating. It's a great way to look at how far you've come on something, especially if it feels like you haven't made any progress!

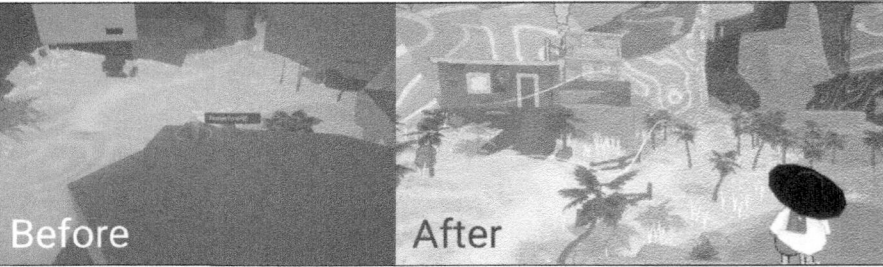

FIGURE 15-3: Seeing progress you've made can be a great motivator to keep going.

Improving Your Productivity

Productivity comes and goes in waves. Sometimes I find myself having a lot of motivation for extended periods of time, and sometimes I must become a lot more structured to make sure I get something — anything! — accomplished. It can feel like a slog at times.

TIP

The creative process looks different for everyone, but thinking about it in terms of stages can help you understand what you do best at each step of the process, and it may even help you value the downtime you have.

According to Graham Wallas in the *Art of Thought* (1926), the creative process has four stages:

>> **Preparation:** This stage involves gathering information, defining the problem, and exploring various possibilities. It's the stage where you may collect references, research about your game, play other games, and generally gather information and ideas to help you design.

>> **Incubation:** After the preparation stage, you'll want to give your mind a break from active processing to incubate the newly found information. During this stage, you can shift your attention to other things, take a walk, exercise, or come back to your ideas in a week's time. Or maybe you think best in the shower.

>> **Illumination:** This is the "aha" moment when the solution or a breakthrough idea suddenly emerges into consciousness. You may suddenly decide that two pieces of information you dug up on two completely different games connects in a very interesting way. This stage is difficult to control or intentionally cause to happen, and rest or distraction is often necessary to find an interesting answer.

>> **Verification:** In this final stage, you'll evaluate and test your idea or solution to ensure that it's feasible and effective. You may want to talk about your idea with others to get more input, make a paper prototype, or develop a spreadsheet to poke holes in the idea.

TAKING TIME TO REST AND REFLECT

Taking breaks allows you to reflect on what you've experienced in life. As I'm writing this book, I reflect upon the last few years of my life in which I've been working on large teams or starting my own endeavors. I haven't taken enough time to reflect on what I've accomplished and understand where I want to go next. These past few months I've been taking a break after starting a game studio and leaving larger teams to deeply think about the things I've learned from my craft and the people I've met. It's helped me solidify my values and where I excel, like understanding that my happy place is working on a small, agile team and with others who are open to working outside the bounds of their titled role. Some people like to manage other people, but I like to know how things work by being involved. Breaks help you develop your own opinions and are generally important in life . . . it's easy to forget.

For me, the incubation phase has been easy to overlook. You have to give yourself space to just think, for an "aha" moment to occur, which can be hard in this day and age in which our attention is constantly grabbed by work, school, friends, family, and screens or phones. This means we must make sure to practice giving space and being intentional about meditation, walking, or in general just being seemingly "unproductive."

Here's a list of some of the best ways I have found to increase productivity:

- » **Make a list of tasks and check them off.** The act of doing this will give you a burst of dopamine that will help you keep going. Plus, the list keeps you organized.

- » **Find an accountability buddy.** Having someone to report your progress to can help you keep your own promises.

- » **Do one thing to make progress every day.** I have written this a few times in this chapter, but that's because it's so important! Just doing one thing a day moves you forward, and after accomplishing that one thing, you may be motivated to do a second thing.

- » **Create a schedule and stick to it.** A routine is helpful to establish a practice in work — and in relaxation. Remember the incubation stage of the creative process? Take breaks to recharge your batteries and allow your mind to wander.

- » **Focus on one thing for a certain period of time.** Multitasking is a skill, but it also takes away from being able to finish one thing well, and it can increase the risk of making mistakes.

- » **Avoid social media!** Enough said.

- » **Make a dev log (refer to Figure 15-2).** Tracking your progress can help motivate you. It can be easy to forget all the progress you've made.

- » **Schedule a demo each month.** To be clear, this demo is for an external party, such as your best friend, an investor, a teacher, or maybe even your mom. By committing to an external party, hopefully you'll be motivated enough to make steady progress each month so that each demo highlights how the game is coming along. You don't want to let your mom down!

REMEMBER

Start your day by writing a list of the things you want to accomplish. You'll soon figure out how much you can realistically accomplish in just a matter of a couple of weeks. Checking off the boxes gives you that dopamine rush and can get you motivated for more.

5

Publishing and Marketing Your Game

Learn how to get your game noticed by players and how to distribute on popular game platforms. You also discover some practical steps for approaching marketing and why marketing your game is important.

Discover the various ways you can publish your game, from self-publishing to finding a publisher, and what each means for your game.

IN THIS CHAPTER

» Defining what marketing is

» Understanding why marketing is important

» Building a marketing plan

» Optimizing your game's storefronts

» Managing your community and their feedback

» Preparing for launch day and beyond

Chapter **16**

Getting Your Game Noticed

Marketing, in the context of game development, is the process of understanding your audience, building interest in your game, and convincing players to play your game. Marketing is more than just promotion and advertising; it starts with your product (your game in this case). A well-designed game is the foundation of any successful marketing strategy, and this only happens when you understand your audience. Good trailers and screenshots to show off your game don't hurt, either!

Marketing Games in This Market Is Hard

Getting your game noticed in this market is hard. You can't just build a housing development with no road and expect people to move in, no matter how cool the houses are. This section isn't meant to scare you; it's just meant to show you that if you want people to play your game, you'll have to put in effort to get them to notice it. I picked up this rule of thumb somewhere: You should spend one hour on marketing for every hour of development you do. That was mostly true for the indie games I've made with my business partner.

As relatively no-name people who were affiliated with some bigger names, we spent much of our marketing time and budget on the following activities:

>> Promoting the games on socials

>> Optimizing the storefront

>> Making trailers and assets

>> Making a press kit

>> Sending information to press

>> Networking and building community

Why is marketing hard right now? Look at how many games have been released by year in the last ten years on Steam, a popular distribution platform for video games (data from SteamDB; `https://steamdb.info/`):

>> **2,826** games were released in **2015.**

>> **4,664** games were released in **2016.**

>> **6,938** games were released in **2017.**

>> **8,885** games were released in **2018.**

>> **8,099** games were released in **2019.**

>> **9,689** games were released in **2020.**

>> **11,314** games were released in **2021.**

>> **12,392** games were released in **2022.**

>> **14,338** games were released in **2023.**

>> **17,309** games were released in **2024.**

The number of games released on Steam in 2024 is almost six times the amount published ten years ago! These numbers don't show just quality games, though. Many lower-effort games are being published, but many more higher quality games also are being published. Game development has become a lot more accessible in recent years, and self-publishing is as easy as ever. It just takes dedication and artistic and technical skills to complete something worth playing around with. And the good news is a lot more people are playing games these days, too!

REMEMBER

It would have been a very nice time to publish a game on Steam in 2006; only 70 games were published back then! The more saturated content gets, the harder it becomes to get your creations noticed. Though I'm sure other difficulties were to be had back then, like a much less optimized publishing process on Steam, and fewer players on the platform.

Understanding Marketing and Its Importance

Marketing shouldn't be an ambiguous term, but I find it often is! I didn't know what marketing truly entailed until I ventured out to build and promote my own products. Before that, I had worked in large companies with established brands, where marketing efforts were already in motion, or at companies where the business model wasn't business-to-consumer (B2C). As a result, I wasn't directly exposed to the full scope of what marketing involves.

Marketing in games, especially for indie developers, solo creators, or small teams, is often business to consumer (B2C). You're selling directly to the customer, which means catering to an entire community of people and their varied interests, rather than focusing on a handful of stakeholders. It's about understanding what makes your audience tick, figuring out what excites them, and managing their expectations while carving out your space in a crowded industry.

For businesses that rely on B2C marketing, success comes from observing trends closely, researching customer behavior, and monitoring competitors' strategies. You'll have to know the challenges and understand how to break through all the noise to find success with your game. You'll have to connect with potential players on a personal level, speaking their language and offering something that stands out.

Marketing in this context is a multifaceted effort, requiring you to do the following:

>> **Create a better game!** A good product will always be the cornerstone of any effective marketing strategy. You can make a better game by honing your game design skills and knowing what a player wants out of a game.

>> **Understand what players are and aren't interested in.** This involves gathering feedback, conducting surveys, observing behavior on social media, and genuinely listening to your audience. Chapters 10 and 12 have details about finding out who your audience is and getting them to give you feedback.

>> **Create visual content for the community.** Eye-catching trailers, GIFs, screenshots, or character art can help showcase your game in ways that grab attention and build interest. If you don't know what assets to create, check out Chapter 14 for some ideas.

>> **Optimize content and repurpose it for the community.** Share your content across platforms, tailoring it for each channel. A trailer may work for YouTube, a GIF may thrive on Twitter, and a behind-the-scenes post could resonate on Instagram. See "Optimizing for Discoverability," later in this chapter, to find out more about this important topic.

Marketing follows the classic framework of interest, desire, and action. First, you capture interest through a teaser, a viral tweet, or even a unique game mechanic that people want to talk about. Then you build desire by showing why your game is worth their time. You can offer demos, reveal interesting features, or share player testimonials. Finally, there's the call to action (CTA). This can be an ask to wish-list your game on Steam, join your newsletter, or buy the game on launch day.

REMEMBER

Marketing is about getting to know your audience, connecting with them, and showing them why your game is worth their time. For indie developers, it's about sharing your game's story, building a community around it, and using eye-catching content to grab attention and stand out.

TIP

Marketing is not just promotion. Promotion is when you post about your game on social media, and just focusing on promotion can lead to a spammy feeling. Marketing is promotion but it also includes reaching out to press, developing relationships with people who can promote your game, making and running ads, and making a good trailer and storefront, on top of a few other things I cover in the following sections.

You may think, "If my game is good, people will naturally find it!" But in today's market, that's rarely the case. Marketing is the bridge between your hard work as a developer and your audience. It's what ensures that your game doesn't get lost in the flood of new releases.

As a smaller team, here are some obstacles you'll face:

>> **Oversaturation:** Thousands of games launch every year, so it's easy to get buried.

>> **Limited resources:** Indie teams often don't have huge budgets or a dedicated marketing team, so they have to do more with less. My business partner and I had a lot to do without a dedicated marketing manager.

>> **Trust:** Players need to feel confident that your game is worth their time and money, especially in a world full of unfinished or low-effort projects.

Investing in marketing can help

>> **Build hype:** Early teasers, trailers, or dev blogs can generate interest and anticipation. Some games built a large following by using simple GIFs of their gameplay. *Ooblets* is a great example of this. They posted a GIF of the player character with a bunch of cute little creatures following in tow as the player ran around a town.

>> **Create a community:** Engaging with players through social media, Discord, or newsletters can help you build a loyal fan base.

>> **Improve your game:** Feedback from marketing efforts, like surveys or playtests, can help refine your game before launching it.

Building a Marketing Plan

Building a marketing plan during production or right before is most helpful for me. At that stage, I'm able to set goals and understand what success may look like for my game. Success can look like a variety of things:

>> Selling a specific number of copies of the game (or having a certain amount of people play it)

>> Getting featured on a platform

>> Building a strong community before launching

After you've defined your goals, your marketing plan details can start to take shape, including dates and milestones you want to hit, where you want to promote your game, your budget (which includes not only just money but the time you put into marketing), and how you'll promote it to players.

Planning your marketing

Having a clear, actionable plan to get your game noticed by the right people at the right time will help a lot. It'll help you stay organized, maximize your impact, and make sure your efforts don't go to waste. Some of the things you'll need to define for your plan are

>> **Your audience:** Who are you making this game for? Narrowing this down will help you choose where and how to market.

>> **The timeline:** Map out key milestones, like teaser trailers, early access launches, or pre-registration campaigns.

>> **Your channels:** Decide where you'll market your game. This can be on social media, streaming platforms, influencers, gaming conventions, or all of the above.

>> **Your playtest milestones:** These will get feedback on your product and help you shape it for the audience.

Try to define your goals before laying out your plan. This helps you understand the steps to reach those goals. For instance, getting featured means you'll need to be under a certain crash rate on some platforms, and you'll need to have all of your art optimized on your storefront for different views. Having a goal of reaching a certain number of players may not require those same steps (though getting featured can help you achieve that goal). Here are some of the goals we had for *Chief Emoji Officer*:

>> Get 10 reviews on day 1 launch on Steam and iOS/Android.

>> Get featured on day 1 on Google Play.

>> Get featured on day 1 on App Store.

Some of the tasks that'll go into your marketing plan include

>> Posting on social media for feedback and input

>> Playtesting

>> Visuals and branding

>> Trailers, key art, logos, and store assets

>> Press kit

>> Advertising

>> Developing a list of streamers, influencers, and partnerships

>> Developing a list of hashtags, tags, and keywords

TIP

As a smaller team, you may want to include your own personality in your game's community. That human touch can make a difference for indie games. Play to your game's strengths and find the channels where it naturally shines.

Budgeting time and money for marketing

Although marketing is a necessary thing you'll have to do for your game (which you may grow tired of me saying), there's no one-size-fits-all approach to crafting the perfect viral campaign. A lot of marketing success boils down to three key factors:

» **Having a great game or product, which may or may not be done when you start marketing the game:** Actually, a lot of games start marketing while the game is in production.

» **Good timing:** I discuss the timing of your game's release into the world later, in the aptly named "Timing your launch" section.

» **Putting consistent effort into product, promotion, and community to get your game noticed:** You'll need to test your product (the game) with the audience, promote to them and to new players, and keep your community engaged and interested.

TIP

You can start doing this early on in production; that way you have a pool of dedicated testers before launching your game.

A TALE OF TWO GAMES

Rocket League is a hugely popular game that launched in 2014. But many people don't realize that its developers had already released a very similar game in 2008, called *Supersonic Acrobatic Rocket-Powered Battle-Cars* (SARPBC). Quite a mouthful, right? Although the core gameplay and even the level designs were nearly identical, there were notable improvements in controls, platform compatibility, and multiplayer functionality.

However, the biggest difference between the two was branding! The developers learned from their first launch, iterated on their product, and rebranded it as *Rocket League*. That combination of lessons learned and stronger branding contributed massively to the game's success.

The second example is *Among Us*. This game was out for about two years before it became super popular in 2020. It's a great game, but it hadn't found it's place until the pandemic hit. Although *Among Us* was released in 2018, it wasn't until mid-2020 that it saw a surge of popularity Twitch streamers, and YouTubers began playing it en masse, turning it into a cultural phenomenon. Not to detract from this game's fun factor, but timing had something to do with the success of Among Us.

(continued)

(continued)

These examples highlight an important point: Budgeting time and money for marketing is something you have to do, especially for indie developers. Big AAA studios spend millions of dollars and countless hours on marketing. For smaller teams, you may not have the same resources, but every effort counts when it comes to getting your game noticed.

In the larger studios, a lot of the budget goes into

>> **Trailers, art, and promotional material:** These can get pricey if you outsource them but may take a few iterations and time from you if you do them yourself.

>> **Playtesting and focus groups:** Playtesting is an ongoing process, that largely takes up time, not so much money.

>> **Experiments and store optimization:** Do this in soft-launch or after launch; luckily these tools are built into Google Play so it's easy enough to accomplish. You may need to test two different versions of your game on other distribution platforms.

>> **Influencers and partnerships:** Finding partnerships takes time, and often many influencers are looking for a chunk of change. This all depends on how many followers an influencer or streamer has.

WARNING

Beware of fake followings! Lots of people buy their followers.

>> **Advertisements:** You may spend some time testing out different ad formats and content, but ultimately this is all monetary budget.

For a smaller developer, everything you can do to get your game out there counts. Although there was never any one thing that contributed to our games selling, it was a variety of efforts that weaved our game into the internet and got people's eyes on it. I'm going to take a moment to rank the things that worked best for our small team of two:

>> **Search engine optimization:** We got quite a bit of traffic to our stores and website by using *backlinks* (a link from one web page to another, in this case, from news sites to our website) and getting other influencers and streamers posting on our behalf. No money spent here, just our own time spent finding and emailing news outlets about our game.

>> **Store optimization:** We spent time testing out different images, in terms of content and composition, to see which images got better clicks. We didn't spend anything on this except for our testing time.

>> **Advertisements:** I credit us getting featured by Apple for Game of the Day from the few hundred dollars we spent on ads for launch. We tried ads on various platforms and optimized for the ones that converted best.

>> **Playtesting:** We didn't spend anything on this. We were able to recruit a few hundred people to playtest over the course of our developments by working with students, our friends, and people on Reddit.

TIP

Allocate at least one hour of marketing work for every one hour spent on development. This includes creating assets, engaging with your audience, and running campaigns.

REMEMBER

Marketing is a reality of game development. A polished trailer, an intriguing storefront, and consistent outreach can make a big difference. Even if you don't have a big budget, focusing on these smaller, actionable efforts can help get your game out into the world.

Looking at example marketing campaigns for games

Sometimes the best way to figure out your own marketing strategy is by seeing what worked for others. Here are a few examples of campaigns that worked:

>> **Among Us:** This game was around for two years before it became huge in 2020, all thanks to Twitch and YouTube influencers. One influential streamer started playing it during the pandemic lockdown and it became a viral hit from there. Watching streamers have fun with friends made it impossible not to want in on the chaos.

>> **Hades:** Supergiant Games used the free Early Access feature on Steam not only to get feedback but to build excitement. Early Access is a category label on Steam that signals that your game is ready to test, but maybe not quite ready for launch. Regular updates and sneak peeks kept players hooked even before the game's official launch.

>> **Stardew Valley:** A one-person project that gained massive traction through word of mouth and an incredibly supportive community on Reddit. The game's developer, ConcernedApe, interacted directly with fans on Discord, and the game's cozy farming vibe naturally drew in streamers and YouTubers who loved sharing their gameplay.

Optimizing for Discoverability

Store and website optimization is an art in itself, like the art of being found. This means making your store page and website as effective as possible to draw in visitors and get them to play your game. It may not directly impact your game design, but it's one of the most important factors in how successful your game becomes. If players can't find your game, or if your storefront doesn't grab their attention, they'll never hit that "Download" or "Buy" button.

Optimizing for discoverability means that for every storefront you have for your game you're trying to find the best

>> Images and trailers

>> Application icon

>> Keywords and tags for the genre

>> Descriptions

TIP

Market research should be your first step when making your game, and your research here will impact how you define your game and how players discover it. You'll need to understand what mood, art, and gameplay gamers expect in the genre of your game. A great place to start for this type of research is a platform like data.ai.

REMEMBER

Certain genres/subgenres can be more saturated than others. Getting your game noticed in saturated genres can be more difficult!

Using tags and keywords

Tags and keywords vary by platform, with each having unique requirements. But at a high level, games have specific genres, themes, or gameplay mechanics that users search for. Keywords are your way of ensuring that your game shows up when players are looking for something similar.

For example, relevant terms like "puzzle game," "RPG," or "multiplayer shooter" may help players discover your game. Think of tags and keywords as a breadcrumb trail that leads your audience to your game.

Here's a brief list of what you'll want to know to start developing your list of keywords:

>> Check successful games in your category to see which terms they use.

>> Prioritize keywords that resonate with your target audience and align with your game's unique features.

>> Consider both broad keywords (to capture a wide audience) and specific ones (to target niche players).

The App Store has specific rules for App Store Optimization (ASO; see the following section) that you'll need to follow. Here are some tips:

>> **Character Limits:** Keywords are limited to 100 characters, so make every letter count. Combine terms creatively to maximize space like "puzzle, logic, brain" instead of repeating "puzzle game" and "logic puzzle".

>> **Don't use spaces:** Commas separate keywords, so avoid wasting characters on spaces. Write keywords like this: adventure, action, exploration.

>> **Skip duplicate words:** Don't repeat terms already in your app's title or subtitle; they don't count twice.

>> **Localize keywords:** If your game is available in multiple regions, include localized keywords for each market.

For *Grift*, we developed a list of the following keywords:

idle, dressup, dollmaker, sim, indie, tycoon, management, incremental, casual, free, picrew, story, dating, life

First, I wrote down a list of all the words associated with our game and the words players who are interested in our game may use to search. Then, I removed duplicate words and compared it to our descriptions to check for duplicates there. Then, I prioritized them in order by looking at similar games, and putting the *longtail keywords* (phrases containing three to five words that can enable you to be more specific with your keywords) toward the bottom of the list.

TIP

Longtail keywords are your friend! Phrases like "family-friendly puzzle game" or "open-world exploration RPG" have less competition and may attract players who are more likely to play your game.

App Store Optimization (ASO)

App store optimization (ASO) is a process to improve the visibility and ranking of a mobile app or game across various app stores. You can do ASO on Steam, the App Store (Apple), and Google Play. This part is important because the first impression of your game's page will affect who buys it.

Some best practices for each platform include

>> **Feature art or app icon:** Keep it simple and eye-catching. Your icon can make or break whether someone clicks on your game. People are more likely to click on a striking icon, and studies show it influences 60 to 80% of installs.

>> **Screenshots:** Highlight the best parts of your game with clean, exciting visuals. Good screenshots can boost downloads by 30%.

>> **A/B Testing:** Don't guess what works. Make sure to test it! Test different icons, screenshots, and layouts to see what resonates most with your audience. Many platforms offer free tools (like Google Play's A/B testing feature) to help you figure out what works.

Here are some guidelines and tips for each platform:

>> **App store:** Add keywords to your title the best you can within the small limit. Add translation for different languages. Ask for reviews in the game to get players to leave reviews.

>> **Steam:** Start by using Steam's Tag Wizard to select tags that reflect your game's genre and mechanics. Your capsule image should be bold and eye-catching, acting as the poster for your game. Make sure your description is short and impactful and quickly conveys what makes your game fun. In the extended description, you can add GIFs and list important features. Your trailer should show gameplay within the first few seconds, and include four or five screenshots of the gameplay.

>> **Google Play:** Use the longer character allowance in descriptions to tell a compelling story about your game. Optimize your app name with searchable keywords without making it sound clunky. You may even format it like "Grift: Scam Tycoon" to include keywords in your name. Again, asking for reviews in the game here can help a lot.

TIP

Don't forget to use tools like Google Play's dev console A/B testing to test out changes to your store. It's free and doesn't take much time to test. It could make a huge impact on what eyes get on your game!

Search engine optimization

Search engine optimization (SEO) is when you improve your website's visibility on search engines like Google (or even ChatGPT these days). It often involves writing key words into your web page, getting other sites to link to yours to increase credibility, and making sure that your site loads quickly for visitors. Spending time on SEO will help players find your game outside of the app stores, rank your game higher in search results, and help you develop a history on the internet.

After launch, your game's presence will live on. Spending time getting an imprint on the internet will keep your game relevant for longer and enable people to find it even years from now. Here are some of reasons to invest in SEO:

>> **Ranking:** A higher ranking on search engine results pages (SERPs) means more visibility for your game. Players are more likely to click on links that appear on the first page of results.

>> **Build authority:** Optimized content helps position your game or studio as trustworthy and credible. Backlinks from reputable sources (like game reviewers or industry blogs) can significantly boost your authority.

>> **Organic traffic:** SEO brings in organic (free!) traffic, meaning you don't have to rely solely on paid ads. The right keywords can bring consistent visitors to your site long after you've published content.

>> **Attracting an audience:** By targeting specific keywords, you can attract people who are already searching for games like yours. It's a direct line to players who are more likely to convert into customers.

TIP

Most businesses of all types will benefit from spending time on SEO so their customers can find them today, tomorrow, and five years from now. Just make sure to revisit your SEO every few years as search engine algorithms can change.

Now that you know what SEO is, how do you improve it? Here are some ways to improve the imprint of your game on the internet:

>> **Research keywords:** Use tools like Google Keyword Planner or free alternatives to find the phrases your potential players are searching for. Think like your audience: What would you type into Google to find a game like yours?

>> **Optimize your website:** Include keywords in key areas like your page titles, headers, and meta descriptions.

>> **Create quality content:** Blog posts, press kits, and dev diaries can all bring in traffic while giving players information about your game. We kept a blog for Bodeville (`https://bodeville.com/blog.html`) during development, which is a great way to create a history, get a variety of traffic, and have something to post to social media.

>> **Work with influencers and media:** Reviews, articles, and gameplay videos that link back to your site can drive traffic and improve your search rankings. This is called backlinking and it contributes to ranking.

>> **Track your progress:** Use analytics tools to see what's working and what isn't. Adjust your strategy based on the results.

SEO may not show results overnight, but with some patience and consistency, it can become a powerful tool to help players discover your game!

Preparing to Launch a Game

A smooth launch requires planning and preparation. This can be as simple as a task list in a document or in project management software to make sure you don't get swept up with the launch and forget to complete some things. Here's what you can do to set yourself up for success:

» **Build hype in the month or so before launch.** You can share sneak peeks, trailers, and behind-the-scenes updates to get people excited. Having your social media active will get more player's eyes on it and show that you're readying for something. See the later section, "Getting on social media," for more details.

» **Talk about release date in your communities.** It's good to get people prepared early so they know when to expect to play. If you don't have a community yet, or it's only your family and friends (a great place to start!), head to the later section "Building a community."

» **Apply launch discounts on Steam if you need to.** Your standard price may not be what you want to launch with. Steam's launch discounts can only be set up prior to the product's release date, not after. When a launch discount ends, the product can't run any other discounts for 30 days.

» **Review your store page and have your friends or your game's playtesters review the page.** Check for spelling or grammatical errors, and places where you can be more concise about the gameplay or features. Make sure your best gameplay footage and images are the first images potential players see when they visit your page.

» **Reach out to influencers who may want to play your game and send them early access codes.** On Steam, these early access codes (or promo codes) are called Steam keys and need to be requested by you and have a review time, so make sure to request them in advance. It typically takes three business days to receive your Steam keys. You can request lots if you need to, but I typically start with an amount based on the length of my press/influencer list, plus some extras.

» **Prepare all your social media posts in advance.** I format all my social media posts differently according to the platform and include trailers or GIFs. Figure 16-1 shows an example post from when we launched *Grift* in New Zealand. See Chapter 14 for a list of assets you may want to create for your game's launch.

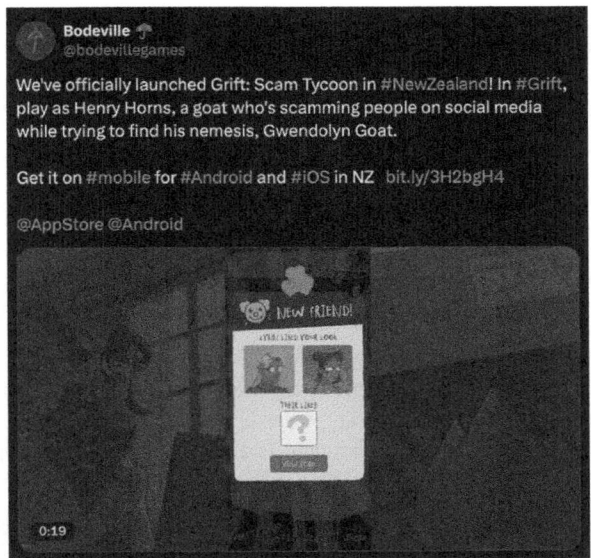

FIGURE 16-1:
A social media
post from when
we launched our
game, *Grift*, in
New Zealand.

The rest of this section covers the important pieces for you to consider and to ensure that your game gets the best send-off into the world that you can give it.

Timing your launch

Before launching, consider what day you want to release your game.

TIP

Your game will have to go through a review process for each platform. The official process can usually take about a week for review, but you can find the specific timing on each platform's developer documentation. Make sure to go through this process to have your game ready for launch day. You can let the build sit as approved until you're ready to release it.

Each time and day of the week offers different benefits or drawbacks. Here are some considerations:

>> Launching on a Friday may mean you'll have to fix bugs over the weekend. But it could also mean that more people are available to play your game over the weekend and get early reviews. I know a successful solo indie who typically launches on a Friday. On larger teams, this is typically frowned upon because you'd need the entire team to be available over the weekend.

>> Launch on a day when there's another big event in the industry and your launch could get drowned out. We launched *Chief Emoji Officer* when the industry was pretty quiet and nothing big was happening that day. It can be

hard to plan this as we don't always know what big companies have planned, but keeping up-to-date on what's happening in the industry can help. Make sure to check gaming news websites:

- Kotaku, `https://kotaku.com/`
- GameDeveloper.com, `https://www.gamedeveloper.com/`

» If you're preparing for something like Steam's Next Fest, you have to launch at a specific time determined by the event. We had to have our *Watchmakers* demo approved and released for mid-morning Pacific time.

Steam Next Fest is a multi-day event on Steam where developers showcase their upcoming games through free playable demos, live streams, and Q&A sessions. It's a great opportunity to generate buzz, get feedback, and build hype before a game's official launch. The nice thing is that it happens several times a year.

» If you launch earlier in the day, you have more time to get eyes on your game and get reviews that day. I typically try to launch and post out right when people are getting ready for their day, or potentially looking at their phone on the toilet in the morning (everyone does that, right?). I've typically planned for the time zone my players are in.

Building a community

If you followed my advice throughout this book and put in the time and effort into creating a game that people will want to play, congratulations! You've actually taken the first step toward building a community. Unfortunately, in today's world, if you don't have a marketable game, you may struggle to find an audience. But once you've created that audience, even if it's just one or two people (you have to start somewhere), then building a community from there requires that you engage with them. Engaging with your community is as simple as

» **Responding to feedback.** Be friendly and invite feedback and make people feel heard so that they'll continue being a part of the process.

» **Being humble and showing appreciation.** If you're only one developer or a small team, you don't have to go overboard. Just make it verbally known that you appreciate that folks are willing to contribute.

» **Responding to reviews after launch.** This affects whether or not your game will get featured. If you respond to reviews, you'll have a better chance of getting featured on the platform. This only applies to mobile games, though.

» **Curating and structuring platforms like Discord, Reddit, and Twitter.**

>> **Posting updates about the game to show you're listening.**

>> **Encouraging content like fan art, memes, and gameplay clips.** These are gold for spreading the word and building loyalty.

REMEMBER

Your game's community is its hype squad! They will not only promote your game, but they'll help you fix bugs and improve the product. The earlier you start building it, the better.

Besides that, you can find people to play in a few ways:

>> There are public relations/marketing agencies that provide groups of playtesters or otherwise help you find communities who will play your game.

>> Advertising is a great way to lead people to your game from their own communities.

>> Attending events and conventions is not only a great way to network, but you'll meet other developers and players and be able to watch them play your game.

Getting on social media

Social media may be a necessity for promoting your game as a solo developer with a small budget. You could potentially focus on your storefront on Steam or another platform instead of spending any time on social media. But social media isn't just a place to promote the game, it's also a good place to get feedback — from your community — which you can use to improve your product.

I'm a big proponent of *building in public,* which, to me, means that I'm posting my work on the internet for everyone to see and comment on. This requires that you put yourself out there and allow others to see your work in progress.

That can be difficult to do, and it can even be a bit scary to show early work, but this strategy has a few benefits:

>> **Receive feedback fast:** You get quick feedback and sentiment about your work.

>> **Build a community of fans:** You develop a following of "super fans." You may not develop a huge following, but those super fans will stick with you and be willing to help you along the way

>> **Foster motivation:** The quick feedback loop gives you immediate feedback that can help motivate you to keep improving and moving forward.

At the same time, this strategy has a few drawbacks:

- >> **It requires a thick skin.** You may get negative feedback. Ignore the haters and keep going!

- >> **Someone else may steal your idea.** I don't see this as a big risk because if you're already gaining momentum enough for someone to steal your idea, then that's a good thing, but it is a risk. I see it as a bigger risk for larger studios because they are putting lots of funding into the projects.

- >> **It takes time.** This time could be spent on development, but the benefits outweigh the cons historically.

TIP

As you're working on your game, you may find people on forums or on social media who are interested in a game like yours. Keep these links in a document so that you can comment and promote your project when it's ready to play. This is a great way to find places on the internet where your players hang out.

Social media moves quickly right now. Communities are shifting; social media companies are being purchased; and laws are or may be going into effect. Instead of listing out various platforms, I focus here on Reddit because that is where I've had the most value come from for our games.

Here's a list of subreddits you'll want to investigate, where you can either post for feedback or promote your game:

- >> r/gaming
- >> r/rpg_gamers
- >> r/iosgaming
- >> r/DestroyMyGame
- >> r/Playmygame
- >> r/TheMakingOfGames/
- >> r/AndroidGaming
- >> r/adventuregames
- >> r/devblogs
- >> r/indiedev
- >> r/Unity3D
- >> r/interactivefiction

>> r/choiceofgames

>> r/pcgaming

WARNING

Each group has a lot of rules to read, and they all differ widely. I got banned from r/scams (whoops!) when I posted about *Grift*. I posted a link to our game and some information about how it related to the subreddit, but self-promotion was against the rules. Being respectful of the community is important but sometimes going against the grain and taking a risk can pay off. I got hundreds of eyes on one of our games from that subreddit before I was banned from posting.

REMEMBER

No matter what platform you pick, it's best to focus on one at a time but still experiment and learn about others. This way you can learn about the algorithm, community, and what content is best for each platform.

Managing launch day

Launch day will be hectic, and you'll probably be so wrapped up that you may completely forget your plan. This is why I like to make a documented plan and have all the tasks split up between the team members. This way, you have just one thing to remember on launch day: Read your plan!

Here are some of the things you'll want to do on launch day:

>> **Hit the release button on your reviewed and approved game.** Remember, each platform has a process to review your game ahead of launch day. That process can take a week, so plan ahead.

>> **Post your prepared social media posts.** You'll want to prepare these prior to launch day so you're ready to copy and paste them into social media. I write and format these for each platform like LinkedIn, X, Reddit, etc.

>> **Enlist help from your friends.** Ask your friends to help promote your game by posting or sharing on social media.

Also ask your friends to write and post reviews. You want to get as many reviews as you can for your game.

TIP

>> **Send out a newsletter to your mailing list (if you have one) about your game's availability.** We created a mailing list for our game because many folks don't use social media and some don't check their Discord server but still use email. We automated our mailing list with MailChimp, a free mailing list tool, and it was as simple as pasting our social media posts into the email format and sending it off.

Managing player feedback

When you have a larger amount of people giving feedback, it can become a lot of information to deal with. Larger teams may have *community managers* who are the go-to for sentiment reports of all the information. *Sentiment reports* in community management analyze how players feel about a game. The information usually comes from social media, reviews, forums, support tickets, and surveys. But as a small team or solo developer, you'll have to synthesize the information by yourself.

The things that have worked for me include

>> **Using surveys to scale up feedback collection and keeping it in one place.**
Having it in one spreadsheet from a survey created in Google Forms will make it easy for you to take all the feedback and summarize or sort it using something like ChatGPT.

>> **Making sure all the player feedback is in one spot.** So, if you're using Discord, get all the feedback into one channel. Then you can use a bot to scrape it from the channel and summarize it.

>> **Preparing canned responses and keeping those in a document for future use.** For example, if someone reports a bug, you can use the same "Thanks for reporting this bug. We've triaged it and will start our investigations."

>> **Creating a system for bug collection.** In our Discord server, we used emojis to signal if something was in progress or fixed. There are also bots you can use to triage fixes and tasks publicly, so your team and players know when the issue is fixed.

TIP

Always respond to feedback. It helps people feel like they are contributing and ensures that players will continue to provide input. It can be very hard to get people to give feedback, so make it known that you value it!

Giving Your Game Life after Launch

After your game goes live, keeping it alive and thriving requires ongoing effort, even if it's not a live service game. Just because the game is out doesn't mean it's the end of the road for development and community engagement.

For example, with *Peridot* at Niantic, we initially planned events and content for six months post-launch. Because the game was designed to be a "forever" game, we knew we'd have to create more content down the road, but this was a solid starting point. For *Chief Emoji Officer*, we had no plans for additional content after the launch. However, a year later, we were inspired by industry events and decided to add a new chapter. Headlines were buzzing about a new round of layoffs at a large gaming studio, right after the CEO reportedly purchased millions of dollars' worth of vintage cars. It was too good not to make satire out of. This showed that even when you think your post-launch content is wrapped up, inspiration can strike unexpectedly, especially as the community and industry evolve.

You'll also need to address bug fixes, performance issues, and player feedback after launch. Many players will report bugs, and maintaining communication with your community about fixes and updates will show them you're dedicated to improving their experience.

Here are some of the things to expect after launch at the very least:

>> Providing bug fixes or improvements based on feedback.

>> Responding to feedback, sharing upcoming plans, and encouraging fan content.

>> Processing returns — if your game is premium (sold for a cost) and you have no in-app purchases, this can all be handled by the platform and you won't need to intervene.

>> Providing updates or change logs.

>> If you've launched on multiple platforms, cross-promoting content or updates across them — For example, we can promote the new chapter of *Chief Emoji Officer* on social media or through newsletters to help re-engage players who might have lost interest.

>> Adding new content, creating events, or adding new Steam achievements

REMEMBER

Launching a game is just the beginning. Keeping your game alive post-launch is a balance of creating fresh content, engaging with your community, and consistently improving the player experience. If you keep the lines of communication open and show that you're invested in your game's future, players will keep coming back for more.

Chapter **17**

Publishing Your Game

Congrats, you made a game! Now comes the fun part: figuring out how to get it out into the world. Do you self-publish and handle everything yourself, or team up with a publisher to help with marketing and distribution? Where do you release it? On Steam, mobile, your own website? There's no one-size-fits-all answer, but this chapter walks you through your options, so you can figure out what makes the most sense for your game, your goals, and your budget.

Deciding How to Publish a Game

You have so many different options for publishing your game. Once upon a time, game developers had to have a publisher who could print and distribute a disk to get a game in players' hands. Today, it's as simple as making a build in a game engine and uploading your build to a website!

Publishing a game means making it available to players. This can be through a major digital storefront, a mobile app store, or your personal website. Publishing can also involve distributing updates, marketing the game, and maintaining a community after launch. Publishing has many levels, from self-publishing, where you manage everything yourself, to working with a publishing partner. Each path comes with its own pros and cons.

A publishing partner can help you with many different aspects of the publishing process like

>> **Marketing:** This includes advertising, managing storefront listings, creating trailers, running promotional campaigns, and reaching out to press or influencers.

>> **Distribution:** Publishers handle the logistics of getting your game onto digital storefronts like Steam, the Epic Games Store, or console marketplaces and can even help with keeping APIs and legal documents up-to-date.

>> **Funds:** Publishers often provide funding to cover development costs, marketing expenses, or other financial needs. In exchange, they may take a share of the revenue or ownership rights, so be sure to weigh the trade-offs.

>> **Quality assurance:** Publishers usually have dedicated QA teams to test your game for bugs, glitches, and overall playability across platforms.

>> **Localization:** Publishers often have resources to translate and adapt your game for different languages and cultural contexts, making it accessible to more players worldwide.

>> **Porting:** Publishers may have teams or connections to help port your game to other platforms, like consoles or mobile devices.

At Bodeville, we chose to self-publish our games because we wanted to focus on creating smaller projects that we could launch quickly. We each had prior experience in distributing games, particularly on mobile, so we felt confident managing the process ourselves. Additionally, we had the financial runway from saving up from our day jobs to sustain a couple of years of development and a modest budget to hire help as needed. We considered looking for funding in a grant or taking investors, but we wanted creative freedom and full control of our products and business.

Looking back, I would approach it similarly if I were to do it again, but with the following key adjustments:

>> Create a deeper, more complex game funded entirely from my own resources.

>> Partner with a publisher for quality assurance and bug testing to ensure a polished experience.

>> Collaborate with a publisher to port the game to multiple platforms, expanding its reach.

Although I'd consider working with a publisher for store optimization and trailer creation, various excellent third-party services are available that can handle those tasks. These assets can also be developed much earlier in production to help build an audience from the start.

You also need to consider how much money you'll expect to make for the amount of effort you're putting in. For us, the cost of working with a publisher for a small game that we only expected to make a few grand on wasn't worth it. Consider the following example of net revenue after store fees, publishing fees, and taxes:

Entity	Revenue Percentage
Store (Steam)	30%
Engine (Unity, under 200k revenue)	0%
Value Added Tax (VAT), US	5%
Refunds	5%
Publisher	10%
Developer	50%

Your actual fees will change based on the following factors:

>> The store you publish on

>> The engine you're working in

>> The revenue threshold your game hits

>> Where you are located

>> What you negotiate with your publisher (if you choose to go with one)

As you can see, you have a lot to think about when choosing a platform and engine, and working with a publisher. A publisher may help you navigate these taxes and expenses, but your best bet is to hire an accountant who is informed on your locale's taxes and e-commerce for small businesses.

You can see the current tax rates for your country on Steam's developer documentation: `https://partner.steamgames.com/doc/finance/taxfaq`

Just a note for all you folks who may be employed in technology or games reading this. Make sure to check the employment agreement you signed when you started your job to make sure that your employer does not prohibit you from publishing your work in your off time, whatever publishing route you may choose. You may encounter legal or employment issues if your employer prohibits this, and the more successful the project is, the higher the risk.

Choosing whether to self-publish or enlist a publisher depends on many factors, and the right decision often varies based on your goals, resources, and experience.

Learning self-publishing basics

Going through the self-publishing process can provide you with a wealth of experience and reward you in full (after you pay the store's fees and taxes) for your efforts. One of the biggest advantages of self-publishing is having full creative control over your project. You decide the scope, timing, and direction of your game without external interference. Working with a publisher can come with constraints, as they often have a say in design choices, timelines, or marketing strategies.

Self-publishing requires you to handle all costs upfront, including development, marketing, and distribution. If you have the financial runway to sustain your project or another place you get your resources from, this may be the way to go.

Here are some options for where you can self-publish your game:

>> **Itch.io:** Particularly popular for experimental, niche, and creative projects, with a strong community of developers and players supporting unique and innovative games. Free and easy to publish and has an optional revenue cut if you choose to monetize.

>> **Kongregate:** A platform that started as a hub for browser-based games and now supports downloadable games on PC and mobile. It also provides publishing support for developers looking to expand their reach.

>> **Steam:** The largest digital distribution platform for PC games. Steam offers tools like Steamworks for implementing achievements, cloud saves, and other features, though it requires a $100 submission fee per game. Your game has to go through a review process to get published, but it doesn't take too long and it's not very difficult to get it approved.

>> **Your website:** Publishing on your own website gives you complete control over your game's distribution and branding. This option is ideal if you already have a strong following or want to offer direct downloads, newsletters, or unique promotions.

- >> **Epic Games Store:** A PC and Mac distribution platform with a favorable revenue split for developers (88/12). Epic Games Store can also provide financial incentives for exclusivity, and its curated storefront helps games stand out.

- >> **Apple App Store:** The go-to marketplace for iOS games. With strict quality guidelines and a large user base, the App Store is an excellent choice for polished mobile games. A developer account costs $99 annually, and Apple takes a 30% cut of the revenue. Your game goes through a rigorous review process to get published, which may take a few days to a week.

- >> **Google Play:** The primary platform for Android games, offering access to a massive global audience. Google Play has a one-time $25 registration fee for developers, allows frequent updates to your game, and developers who enroll in the 15% service fee tier pay 15% on the first $1 million of revenue they earn each year. After that, the fee increases to 30%. Your game goes through a review process to get published, but it doesn't take too long and it's not very difficult to get it approved.

- >> **Samsung Galaxy Store:** A secondary Android marketplace that specifically targets Samsung device users. This store provides an opportunity to stand out in a less crowded environment.

- >> **Nintendo eShop:** Nintendo's digital marketplace for Switch games. Publishing on the eShop is ideal for developers with polished, family-friendly, or unique gameplay experiences that align with Nintendo's audience.

- >> **Xbox Marketplace:** A platform for publishing on Xbox consoles. Through programs like ID@Xbox, independent developers can self-publish games with access to Xbox tools and services, including Game Pass opportunities.

- >> **Poki:** A browser-based game platform with a strong focus on casual and HTML5 games. Poki provides opportunities for monetization and visibility to players looking for quick, accessible gameplay.

- >> **Newgrounds:** One of the oldest platforms for hosting browser-based games, animations, and creative projects. Great for small, experimental games or prototypes.

- >> **Game jams**: Publishing through game jams like Ludum Dare or showcasing at events like Indiecade or PAX can help build an audience.

- >> **SideQuest:** An alternative store for Oculus/Meta VR games. SideQuest allows developers to publish VR projects without going through the official Meta App Lab approval process, making it a popular choice for early builds or experimental games. SideQuest does not typically take a percentage cut of sales directly from developers.

- >> **Meta App Store:** The official marketplace for Meta's virtual reality (VR) platforms, including Quest devices. The Meta App Store is highly curated, requiring developers to meet specific quality standards and pass a review process before their apps or games are approved.

- >> **Meta App Lab:** A more accessible alternative to the main Meta App Store, App Lab allows developers to distribute their VR games and apps without the strict curation process.

- >> **User-generated content platforms:** You may even try your hand at making games within a company's platform, like Roblox, Minecraft, or Rec Room. They each have their own store fees and algorithms.

TECHNICAL
STUFF

To publish on some of these platforms, you may need a business LLC. Platforms like Steam require this because you need a business bank account hooked up to Steamworks (the developer side of Steam).

TIP

After you start making it known that you're developing a game, you may notice a wave of publishers reaching out to you. Beware of scams that may include self-proclaimed publishers that take your money but provide no real support, and others that may deal in *shovelware* (favoring quantity over quality), flooding storefronts with low-quality games and fake reviews to deceive players into making purchases. Always do your research, check their track record, and ensure that their values align with your vision before entering into any agreements.

Getting someone to publish your game

A small or solo team may struggle to handle every aspect of publishing, from QA to localization to marketing. A publisher can fill those gaps and let the team focus on development. Self-publishing often requires juggling multiple roles, which can take time away from development. A publisher can streamline the process, allowing you to focus more on creating the game while they handle distribution, marketing, and other logistics.

Maybe you've already nailed down a fun concept or even have a playable version ready to share. After you've got that, it's a great time to start looking for a publisher. Keep in mind, publishers are all different, but most will want to see your game in a playable state to feel confident that you have what it takes to bring the project to life. I've even heard of some publishers wanting a Steam page already live with proof of wish lists and a community. It all depends on what the publisher has to offer.

You may want to get someone else to publish your game because publishers often have relationships with platform holders, media outlets, and influencers. This can give your game a better chance to stand out. If your goal is to reach a large or global audience, a publisher's network can be super useful.

Here are some things that you'll need to pitch your game to a publisher:

>> A playable prototype of your game

>> Some visuals or clips to show the highlights of the gameplay

>> A rough timeline of how long it will take you to complete the game

>> An understanding of the support you'll need throughout development. This could be funding, marketing, new talent, or experience and advice.

>> A budget of how much it will take to make the game, including any new hires you may need to complete the project

>> A deck or document featuring all these items to show to potential partners

WARNING

Every publisher will have a different business agreement for your needs. To protect yourself, have your own lawyer review the paperwork before making a deal. Video game business lawyers are quite niche, but you should be able to find a start-up lawyer to review your paperwork. These services may carry a medium to high upfront cost, but they're well worth it, and I recommend them before you enter into a long-term partnership.

REMEMBER

Self-publishing can be a great learning experience, building your skills and reputation as an independent developer. Working with a publisher, however, may lead to new opportunities, collaborations, or expanded resources for future projects.

Publishing on Different Platforms

When it comes to publishing a game, the platform you choose can have a big impact on how you reach players and how your game is experienced. This is because each platform

>> **Has a different discovery algorithm.** This can greatly affect how and when your game gets seen and what you have to do to get an audience for your game.

>> **Caters to different devices.** Some may allow players to play on PC, Linux, web, in a headset, or on a phone.

>> **Caters to different audiences.** Someone looking for a mobile game to play is likely a more casual gamer looking to fill their time while completing another task, but players on Steam are looking for more complex, longer, and more dedicated gameplay sessions.

When you're just starting out, pick one platform and stick to it. It takes a lot of time to learn the features of the storefront and then further analyze and tweak things to make a game show up for players. Publishing on multiple platforms can split your focus.

Fortunately, it has become very easy to make builds for different platforms (mobile, PC, VR) in game engines like Unity. But there's a world of changes you'll need to make to account for the renderers, interactions, and features available on those platforms for every game.

Throughout the rest of this section, I explain several platforms where you can self-publish your game directly to your players.

Steam

Steam has a huge audience. An estimated 120 million active users are on Steam. The largest age group on Steam is 20 to 29, representing 37 percent of the user-base, and the second-largest age group is 30 to 39, representing 32 percent of the userbase. All of these folks go to Steam to play games, so it's likely that if you publish an interesting game on Steam, you may get some eyes on it!

Some of the major pros to using Steam on top of that large audience are

>> The Steamworks developer platform (the back end of Steam) can handle things like achievements, cloud saves, and community features.

>> The built-in tools for beta testing and early access make it easier to get feedback before a full release.

>> The tagging system helps people find your game and games like yours.

>> Community events help drive people to certain types of games. They have four major seasonal sales events per year and a few themed ones sprinkled throughout the year.

Itch.io

Itch.io is perfect for indie developers looking to share experimental or small-scale games with a creative and supportive community. Although I can't find any details on the audience, the most recent public report in 2019 revealed that Itch.io hosted more than 200,000 games.

Some of the major pros to publishing on Itch.io are

>> Itch.io lets you set your own pricing, run sales, or even offer your game for free with an optional donation.

>> It lets you publish games in the browser, making them accessible for anyone to play.

>> It has a community forum where players and developers can chat, and game jams are hosted often to bring new games to the platform.

Consoles

Publishing on consoles like PlayStation, Xbox, and Nintendo Switch can give your game a premium feel, but it requires a more formal submission process. Each console has its own developer program like Sony's Partner Program, Microsoft's ID@Xbox, and Nintendo Developer Portal. Each provides tools for certification, development kits, and platform-specific features. Although more complex and resource-intensive, console publishing often comes with a strong audience looking for polished experiences.

Mobile app stores

Mobile platforms like the Apple App Store and Google Play Store offer huge audiences for casual and free-to-play games; anyone with a mobile device can be a player. Publishing on mobile involves making sure your game meets platform guidelines, which cover everything from in-app purchases to design standards.

Some of the major pros to publishing on mobile are

>> You potentially have a massive audience.

>> The scope and development timelines of mobile games typically move quicker than more complex PC games.

>> These stores have built-in tools for beta testing and early access, making it easier to get feedback before a full release.

User generated content platforms

User generated content (UGC) platforms like Roblox, Fortnite Creative, and Minecraft Marketplace let you publish games or interactive experiences within larger ecosystems.

Some of the major pros to publishing on UGC platforms are

>> You already have a large audience on the platform.

>> Many UGC platforms also have monetization programs where you can start generating revenue early once you've made something.

>> Features may be readily available to you out of the box, like character controllers, achievement systems, leaderboards, or other game systems or interactions.

Virtual reality platforms

Virtual Reality (VR) platforms like the Meta App Store, App Lab, and SteamVR cater to the growing VR gaming audience. Publishing for VR often means designing games specifically for immersive interaction, which requires testing to meet hardware requirements and to avoid player discomfort.

Augmented reality platforms

Publishing augmented reality (AR) games often involves platforms like the App Store, Google Play, or specialized AR ecosystems such as Niantic's Lightship platform. AR games are best suited for mobile devices and wearable tech like headsets. If you plan to publish a game using AR, focus on blending gameplay with real-world environments. Games that stand out often showcase innovative use of the camera passthrough, image detection like grass or sand, or digital objects in physical space.

6

The Part of Tens

Discover the different paths various designers took when it comes to their career and the games they've worked on.

Discover resources for learning more about game development and design and the terms we use in the game industry.

Chapter **18**

Ten Game Designers You Should Know

A wide variety of people are out there making games: those who are indie, those who are part of a large AAA company, and those who fall somewhere in between, carving their own niche in the game industry. No matter their path, each game designer brings something unique to the table, shaping the way we play, think, and feel about games.

This chapter celebrates ten game designers and the work they've brought to the world. These are by no means the only game designers out there, and I didn't stick with the most famous ones either. Their paths are accessible to anyone reading this book. I've chosen individuals whose contributions I think you should be familiar with because these designers have great potential to do even greater things. They have already started making an impact on the industry's growing body of work over the last ten years and will continue to do so.

I chose game designers who followed different paths to their success. Some have an extensive portfolio of titles, and others are newer voices who have burst onto the scene with innovative ideas. Each one has their own style, approach, and philosophy about what makes a game not only fun but meaningful. Their stories remind us that there's no single way to succeed in game design.

This chapter offers a glimpse into the journeys of these remarkable creators. I hope their accomplishments inspire you to find your own way, as they have inspired me.

Ah Young Joo

Occupations: Game designer, technical artist, 3-D technical character artist

Notable industry credits:

>> *Stay: Forever Home* (Windup Minds)

>> *Peridot* (Niantic)

>> *Dreamland Confectionery* (Wondersea Studio)

>> *Beasts of Maravilla Island* (Banana Bird Studios, LLC)

Ah Young Joo is an up-and-coming game designer with a background in tools, vfx, and feature prototypes. She studied at the University of Southern California's Games program, where she led and designed multiple projects. Her most notable professional experience includes working on *Peridot*, Niantic's first AR pet simulation game. In addition to her work on AR/VR/MR projects, she's passionate about creating games that enrich players' lives through both systemic depth and engaging mechanics.

Ian MacLarty

Occupations: Video game developer

Notable industry credits:

>> *Mars First Logistics* (Shape Shop)

>> *Dissembler* (Shape Shop)

>> *The Catacombs of Solaris Revisited* (Shape Shop)

>> *Jumpgrid* (Shape Shop)

>> *Action Painting Pro*

Ian MacLarty is an Australian indie game developer known for his experimental approach to game design. He has released more than 40 small non-commercial works, alongside several acclaimed commercial titles like *Mars First Logistics* and *The Catacombs of Solaris*. With a background in computer science, Ian often incorporates generative techniques and self-made tools in his games, which blend technical craft with artistic expression. His work explores a wide variety of themes, from abstract first-person experiences to more structured simulation-based titles, showing his broad versatility in the field of game development.

Action Painting Pro was a big inspiration in my work when I played it as an undergrad. For a deeper dive into Ian MacLarty's work, you can check out his collection of games on itch.io, where he shares both of his projects.

Grace Bruxner

Occupations: World's most amazing game developer (from her site)

Notable industry credits:

>> *Frog Detective 1: The Haunted Island*

>> *Frog Detective 2: Corruption at Cowboy County*

>> *Frog Detective 3: The Case of the Invisible Wizard*

Grace Bruxner is an Australian game developer, best known as the Creative Director of Worm Club, a studio recognized for its whimsical, low-key adventures. She is particularly celebrated for her work on *Frog Detective*, a series of quirky, low-poly mystery games. The first of these, *The Haunted Island: A Frog Detective Game*, mixes gentle humor with charming, simple puzzles. This game embraces a unique style. Players interact with eccentric characters to help solve a mystery, with all puzzles serving the story rather than complicating it. Bruxner's approach prioritizes sweet, unpretentious humor and quirky animation, creating a delightful, warm atmosphere. She is really fun to follow on social media, too.

Bruxner is also passionate about making games that resonate personally with her, as she once explained that she created her games because she couldn't find titles that matched her specific tastes. She's shared her journey in talks and frequently advises for WINGS (https://www.wingsfund.me/), a fund supporting diverse leadership in the gaming industry.

Tim FitzRandolph

Occupations: Vice President of Creative, producer, Senior Game Designer, Game Design Director, game designer

Notable industry credits:

- *Parking Garage Rally Circuit* (Walaber Entertainment)
- *JellyCar Series* (Disney, Walaber Entertainment)
- *Very Very Valet* (Toyful Games)
- *Pro Gymnast Simulator* (Walaber Entertainment)
- *Disney Epic Mickey* (Disney)
- *Jurassic World Alive* (Ludia)
- *Toy Story 3* (Disney)
- *Spectrobe Series* (Disney)

Tim FitzRandolph is a well-known game designer going by the alias Walaber at one of his game studios, Walaber Entertainment. He's especially recognized for his work on *Where's My Water?* and the *JellyCar* series. He has a significant background in both indie and large-scale game development. FitzRandolph's career includes roles at major studios like Disney, where he contributed to various titles, including *Disney Epic Mickey*, *Funko Pop! Blitz*, and *Jurassic World Alive*. He also teaches game programming and development at ArtCenter.

Along with his professional work at Disney, he's part of Toyful Games, collaborating with Chad Cable on accessible and creative gameplay, like *Very Very Valet*. FitzRandolph has a passion for creating engaging and fun games with a focus on game physics.

Timothy Staton-Davis

Occupations: Game designer, producer, community manager, game developer

Notable industry credits:

- *God of War: Ragnarok* (Santa Monica Studio)
- *Marvel's Avengers* (Crystal Dynamics)

>> *Halo Infinite* (343 Industries)

>> *Middle-Earth: Shadow of War* (Monolith Productions)

>> *Crumble Party* (Melanated Game Kitchen)

Timothy Staton-Davis is an experienced game designer and community manager with a rich background in both AAA titles and indie projects. He's contributed to the *God of War* series and *Middle-Earth: Shadow of War*. In addition to his work at Brass Lion, he plays an active role in the Melanated Game Kitchen, co-leading the team behind *Crumble Party*.

Beyond his game development work, Timothy is also known for his leadership in the Black in Gaming community, where he manages the organization's Discord server.

Staton-Davis has a strong educational background with a bachelor's in computer science from howard university and a master's in entertainment technology from Carnegie Mellon University.

Anton Hand

Occupations: Game designer, community manager, game developer, YouTuber

Notable industry credits:

>> *Hot Dogs, Horseshoes & Hand Grenades* (H3VR) (Rondomedia)

>> *Museum of the Microstar* (Rondomedia)

Anton Hand is a highly regarded game designer and co-founder of RUST Ltd., a creative studio based in Los Angeles, Michigan, and New York. He specializes in designing and prototyping for video games, virtual reality (VR) experiences, and other creative projects like board and card games. He is particularly well known for his work on *Hot Dogs, Horseshoes & Hand Grenades* (H3VR), a VR sandbox game that has garnered lots of attention for its immersive and sometimes absurd gameplay.

In addition to his work at RUST Ltd., Hand has made significant contributions to several other projects. He was a key figure in the development of Museum of the Microstar, a tech demo showcasing advanced DirectX 11 features. His diverse skill set includes expertise in tools, technical design, and VR interactions.

Austin Grossman

Occupations: Game designer, creative director, writer/novelist, Director of Game Design and Interactive Storytelling

Notable industry credits:

- » *YOU* (novel by Austin Grossman)
- » *Stay: Forever Home* (Windup Minds)
- » *Dishonored* (Arkane Studios)
- » *Epic Mickey* (Junction Point Studios)
- » *Deus Ex* (Ion Storm)
- » *System Shock* (Looking Glass Studios)

Austin Grossman is a seasoned game designer and novelist, known for his work on titles like *System Shock, Deus Ex, Dishonored,* and *Epic Mickey*. He began his career at Looking Glass Studios, where he contributed to the groundbreaking *System Shock*. Later, he worked with DreamWorks Interactive, Ion Storm, and Crystal Dynamics on various major projects, including Tomb Raider: Legend.

In addition to his game design career, Grossman is an accomplished author, with novels such as *Soon I Will Be Invincible, YOU,* and *Crooked*. His writing has been featured in notable publications like *Granta* and *The Wall Street Journal*. Grossman has also worked as the Director of Game Design and Interactive Storytelling at Magic Leap, shaping immersive experiences for augmented reality. I particularly like Grossman's background because it shows narrative contributions and a different path than pure game design.

He holds an M.A. in performance studies from New York University and has pursued further graduate work in English literature at UC Berkeley.

V Buckenham

Occupations: Game designer, creative developer, curator

Notable industry credits:

- » *Downpour* (Independent, mobile app for game creation)
- » *Beasts of Balance* (Sensible Object)

- ›› *Mutazione* (Die Gute Fabrik)

- ›› Cheap Bots Done Quick (Independent, tool for making Twitter bots)

- ›› Curator for Now Play This (Event)

- ›› Curator for Wild Rumpus (Event)

V Buckenham is a creative game developer and designer, well known for her work on titles like *Beasts of Balance* and *Mutazione*. She is the creator of Downpour, a mobile app that lets users easily make their own games by taking photos and linking them together, making it accessible to a wide audience. Additionally, she developed Cheap Bots Done Quick, a website for creating Twitter bots. V has also curated events like Now Play This and Wild Rumpus. Her focus is on creating playful, accessible experiences for a diverse audience, and she's an advocate for simplifying the game creation process to allow anyone to participate.

I worked with V at Niantic, and her work there was experimental with a hint of alternate reality game (ARG). It's a truly interesting genre and path to check out in the industry.

Elaine Gómez

Occupations: Game designer, creative director, co-founder and president (Latinx in Gaming)

Notable industry credits:

- ›› *Blink Land* (Midnight Hour Games, developed in collaboration with the American Optometric Association)

- ›› *Beyond Blue* (E-Line Media)

- ›› *When Rivers Were Trails* (Indian Land Tenure Foundation and Michigan State University's Games for Entertainment and Learning Lab)

- ›› Co-founder and President of Latinx in Gaming, supporting the Latinx community in the gaming industry.

Elaine Gómez is a seasoned game designer with experience in narrative-driven and impactful games. She is the founder of Midnight Hour Games, which developed *Blink Land*, a health-focused game developed in collaboration with the American Optometric Association. As a co-founder and president of Latinx in Gaming, she's dedicated to supporting and uplifting the Latinx community in the gaming industry. Her work combines creative design with a commitment to inclusivity and meaningful experiences.

John Bernhelm

Occupations: Game designer, VR prototyper, and interactive storyteller

Notable industry credits:

>> *Supernatural* (Supernatural/Meta)

>> *Tales from the Borderlands* (Telltale Games)

>> *Gnomes & Goblins Preview* (Wevr, collaborated with Jon Favreau)

>> *Massive Chalice* (Double Fine Productions)

>> *Uncharted 4: A Thief's End* (Naughty Dog)

>> *Uncharted 3: Drake's Deception* (Naughty Dog)

John Bernhelm is a seasoned game and VR designer with a focus on interactive storytelling and prototyping. He has contributed to high-profile projects at companies such as Meta, Naughty Dog, Double Fine, and Telltale Games. Known for his work on VR experiences like *Supernatural*, *The Blu: Deep Rescue*, and *Gnomes & Goblins*, as well as his role in developing fan-favorite narrative-driven games like *Tales from the Borderlands*, Bernhelm is a leader in both traditional and immersive game design. He has been involved in several indie game juries and leadership roles, including as a juror for IndieCade and a mentor at Gameheads. Aside from being immersed in other digital and physical games, he's most inspired by the animal kingdom, musical jam sessions, and the playful inventiveness of his mother.

Chapter **19**

Ten Free Resources for Game Designers

G ame development and design is an evolving art form. As new generations make new games, you will see new stories from diverse perspectives and people using whatever new technology there is to make new mechanics. Games have changed so much since I was a kid playing cartridges on a console that so I'm excited to see what's to come!

For now, I'm sharing some free resources to help you continue learning, answer some questions, and help you stay in the know of what's new in the gaming industry. This chapter is a collection of community websites, tools and assets, game jams, and YouTube videos that I find incredibly useful.

GameDeveloper.com

https://www.gamedeveloper.com/

Game Developer is a website dedicated to all things game development. I read through this site often as a student, and it helped me become exposed to deeper topics and other resources. Many different game developers post in the blogs section, so it's nice to get a variety of perspectives. It's a great place to stay updated on industry trends, learn from seasoned pros, and connect with the game dev community.

How to Market a Game Blog

https://howtomarketagame.com/

How to Market a Game is an absolute gem of a blog, especially if you're trying to figure out how to promote your indie game. Written by Chris Zukowski, a video game marketing consultant and indie game maker, it's packed with practical advice, research, and strategies tailored for indie developers.

The blog dives deep into topics like boosting your Steam wishlists, crafting effective social media campaigns, and building a loyal player base. What makes it stand out is how Chris breaks down complex marketing concepts into simple, actionable tips.

SteamDB

https://steamdb.info/

SteamDB is a great resource for finding information on other games published on Steam. I've used it to check out stats for other games in the genre and see what people are playing. I found a related and amazing spreadsheet — Steam Trends 2023 by @evlko and @Sadari — packed with detailed game store data, making it a gold mine for analyzing trends, understanding market behavior, and refining your game's tags. If you're trying to navigate Steam's ecosystem, both resources are absolutely worth checking out!

Assets by Kenney

https://docs.google.com/spreadsheets/d/1D5MErWbFJ2Gsde9QxJ_HNMltKfF6fHCYdv4OQpXdnZ4/edit?gid=1714749788#gid=1714749788

Assets by Kenney is a treasure for game developers, offering thousands of free and affordable 2-D, 3-D, and audio assets for your projects. Kenney is a prolific asset creator and indie game maker, and he publishes assets for a variety of genres that are great for prototyping new concepts. The assets come with liberal licensing, so you can focus on creating without worrying about legal headaches.

Mixamo

https://www.mixamo.com/

Mixamo is a total lifesaver if you need character animations but aren't an animation expert, and it's free! You can upload a 3-D character, and Mixamo will rig it for you automatically. It's a great tool for animating humanoid characters quickly. You can browse through tons of pre-made animations and apply them with just a few clicks. Perfect for adding that extra flair to your game or project without getting buried in animation work.

Game Accessibility Guidelines

https://gameaccessibilityguidelines.com/basic/

Game Accessibility Guidelines is an awesome resource if you want to make sure that your game can be played by as many people as possible. Designing with accessibility in mind will allow many folks to play your game no matter what their ability. This resource is like a checklist of tips and best practices for improving accessibility, from basic features like readable text and simple controls to more advanced options like remappable buttons and colorblind modes.

Global Game Jam (GGJ)

https://globalgamejam.org/

TIP

Global Game Jam is like a hackathon, but for making games! This is an annual virtual and in-person event where game developers, artists, writers, and anyone interested in making games come together to create something over a single weekend. I'd highly recommend trying a game jam at least once, and Global Game Jam (GGJ) has been a really great experience every time I've gone to one. Since 2021 GGJ has also supported hybrid and online-only sites as well. If you join, you'll have a chance to experiment, collaborate, and have fun building a game from scratch. Every event has a unique surprise theme.

Ludum Dare

https://ludumdare.com/

Ludum Dare is one of the longest-running and most popular online game jams. Every event has a unique theme that's announced right as the jam begins. Themes are suggested and chosen by the community. Ludum Dare is a great way to flex your skills, experiment with ideas, and connect with the game dev community. I did one completely online with a remote team one time, so I know this event is possible remotely.

Game Maker's Toolkit

https://www.youtube.com/@GMTK

Game Maker's Toolkit is a great YouTube channel created by Mark Brown, a British games journalist, which dives deep into game design and development. It's full of insightful, well-researched videos in which Mark breaks down the mechanics, storytelling, and design choices behind various games. It's all presented in a casual, engaging style that makes complex design concepts easy to grasp.

Game Developers Conference (GDC)

https://www.youtube.com/channel/UC0JB7TSe491g56u6qH8y_MQ

Game Developers Conference is probably the largest conference for game developers and is hosted in San Francisco, California, every year. If you don't have the funds to fork up a couple grand on tickets to the main event, I recommend getting an expo pass (which is a few hundred dollars) to be able to check out the expo to discover new tools and games and chat with other game developers in the community. You can pay for access to a larger vault of videos, but a lot of videos are on YouTube to view for free.

Glossary

Here, for handy reference, are definitions of dozens of the most common terms we use in games and in the video game industry:

accessibility: Making sure everyone can play your game, including people with disabilities. This covers things like colorblind options, subtitles, and remappable controls.

app store optimization (ASO): Making changes to your mobile game's app store page so more people find and download it.

art style: The overall look of your game, from colors and shapes to textures and themes.

balance: Making sure the game isn't too easy or too hard and that no one strategy or mechanic is overpowered.

brainstorming: Coming up with ideas, a sometimes chaotic process, or a more methodical one, using brainwrite or mind map tools.

churn rate: The number of players who stop playing your game.

concepting: The early phase of game development in which you figure out the big idea and core elements.

core loop: The main cycle of gameplay that players keep doing over and over, like fighting enemies, getting loot, and upgrading gear.

core mechanic: The main action players do repeatedly, like jumping, shooting, or crafting.

daily active users (DAU): The number of unique players who play your game each day.

design constraints: The limits you have to work within, like time, budget, or technology.

design pillars: The core ideas that define your game and help guide development.

difficulty curve: How the game's challenge increases over time. Ideally, it should be smooth and not feel like hitting a wall.

discoverability: How easy it is for people to find your game in stores, search engines, or social media.

feature: A specific part of your game, like a crafting system, multiplayer mode, or skill tree.

feedback: The info you get from playtests or players about what works and what doesn't.

feedback systems: Ways the game gives players information about their progress, like sound effects, animations, and UI cues.

first-time user experience (FTUE): The experience of a player the first time they enter the game, including onboarding and tutorials. Also called NUX (new user experience).

flowchart: A visual way to map out how players move through the game, like a decision tree.

flow state: The feeling when players are totally absorbed in the game, with just the right balance of challenge and reward.

free-to-play: A game that's free to download but may have in-app purchases or ads.

fun: The thing that makes people want to keep playing. This can be challenge, story, social interaction, or just messing around.

game design: The overall process of designing how a game works, from mechanics to story to player experience.

game feel: How satisfying the game is to play, like how jumping, shooting, or movement feels responsive and fun.

game mechanic: A rule or system that defines how players interact with the game.

game system: The set of rules, data, and calculations that make the game work.

hard currency: The premium currency in a game that players usually buy with real money or earn through special events.

immersion: When a game is so engaging that players forget they're playing and feel like they're really in the world.

in-app purchases (IAP): Things players can buy inside the game, like skins, power-ups, or extra lives.

interactions: Any input from the player, like making a choice or pressing a button.

iteration: The cycle of making changes, testing, and improving a game.

launch: The official release of a game.

live-service game: A game that keeps getting updates and events over time instead of just being a one-time release.

long-term goal: A big goal that keeps players engaged over weeks or months, like hitting max level or unlocking all achievements.

lore: The backstory and world-building details that give a game depth.

luck: Random elements in a game, like dice rolls or loot drops.

milestone: A deadline with a specific goal, like finishing a prototype or launching a beta.

monetization: The process of generating revenue from a game. This can be done through in-game purchases, ads, subscriptions, or even donations.

monthly active users (MAU): The number of unique players who engage with the game over a month.

new user experience (NUX): The experience of a player the first time they enter the game, including onboarding and tutorials. Also called FTUE (first time user experience).

player persona: A made-up profile that represents a typical player, including their motivations and habits.

playtesting: Letting people try your game before release to find bugs and see what works.

porting: Making a game work on different platforms, like bringing a PC game to consoles.

premium game: A game that players buy upfront with no free-to-play mechanics.

production: The main phase of game development during which most of the content is built.

progression: How a player moves forward in the game, like leveling up or unlocking new areas.

prototype: A rough early version of a game to test ideas quickly.

publishing: Making a game available to players, whether self-published or through a publisher.

quality assurance: The process of testing a game to find bugs and make sure everything works.

razor statement: A short, sharp summary of what makes your game unique.

release: When a game officially goes live for the public. (Also called launch or publish.)

resources: Items or currencies in a game that players use to progress, like wood for crafting or coins for buying upgrades.

retention: How long players keep coming back to your game, often measured in days (like day 1, day 7, and day 30 retention).

scope: The size of the game you're making, including how much content and how many features you can realistically finish.

scope creep: When a game's scope keeps expanding beyond the original plan, usually leading to delays and stress.

search engine optimization (SEO): Making a website or game page rank higher on Google or other search engines.

sentiment reports: Reports that summarize how players feel about your game, often using categories like positive, neutral, or negative.

short-term goal: A small, immediate goal in a game, like completing a level or upgrading a weapon.

skill: How much a player's ability (rather than luck) determines success.

soft currency: In-game money that players earn by playing, like coins or XP.

soft launch: A trial for launch, usually done in a subset of countries or markets instead of globally.

storyboard: A step-by-step visual map of a player's journey through a game.

supporting mechanics: Extra mechanics that add depth to the core gameplay, like crafting or side quests.

tutorial: A section of a game that teaches players how to play.

user experience (UX): How enjoyable and easy the game is to navigate and play.

user generated content (UGC): Content created by players, like custom levels, skins, or mods.

user journey: The steps a player goes through while interacting with your game, from discovery to long-term engagement.

virtual economy: The system of currencies and resources in a game, including how players earn and spend them.

wireframe: A rough sketch of a game's interface or layout, used in early design stages.

worldbuilding: Creating the lore, setting, and details that make a game's world feel real.

Index

B

backlinks, 268
balance. *See* game balance
Bernhelm, John (game designer), 302
beta, 223, 237
BigQuery, 195
Bitbucket, 80–81
Blender, 9, 72, 73, 75–76, 140, 252
blind playtesting, 199
blockchain-based assets, 113
bools, 189
brainstorming, 213–214, 307
Brotato, 135
Bruxner, Grace (game designer), 297
Buckenham, V (game designer), 300–301
budgeting
  for art style, 150–151
  finishing and, 252–253
  time and money for marketing, 267–269
building in public, 230, 277–279
burnout, 248

C

call to action (CTA), 264
camera, in art style guide (ASG), 141
Capcom, 143
captioning tools, 175
cardboard, 57
Cards Against Humanity (game), 10
Celeste, 179
challenge systems, 108
challenges, balancing, 26
channels, marketing plan and, 266
character guides, 122
characters
  archetypes, 123
  in art style guide (ASG), 141, 142
  designing, 135
  developing, 121–123
ChatGPT, 67
chats, 111
Cheat Sheet (website), 3
Chess, 185

Chief Emoji Officer, 13, 281
chroma (saturation), 144
churn rate, 221, 307
clans, 112
clarity, in UI design, 173
class progression, 108
climax, 124
Clip Studio Paint, 72
cold calling, 240
collaboration
  project management tools, 80–81
  with team, 54–55
  wirth artists and designers, 151–152
collectible systems, 108
color accessibiity tools, 175
Color Oracle, 175
color palette, 134, 142
color theory, 144–145
Color Wheel, 144
communication, as a skill of game designers, 48
community, 110–112, 265, 276–277
complementary color schemes, 145
Computer Entertainment Rating Organization (CERO), 154
conceit, 120–121
concept art, 34, 137
concepting phase, of game design, 34–35, 233, 307
consistency
  art style and, 150
  in artwork, 137–138
  audio and, 147
  finishing and, 255–256
  in UI design, 173
  in world design, 131–132
consoles, 291
constraints, designing around, 27–28
Construct 2, 27–28
constructing your first game, 14–16
content, quality of, 273
contributions, in portfolios, 64
cooldowns, 103
cooperative gameplay, 109
copyright law, 29–31
core gameplay charts, 38

positive punishments, 22

post-production phase, of game design, 36, 223, 239–240

Power BI, 194

PowerPoint, 56

practicing, 66–67

premium game, 309

pre-production phase, of game design, 35, 223, 234–236

pre-registration, 238

prestige systems, 107

principles, 103–104, 173–174

prioritization, as a skill of game designers, 48

process

  about, 231–232

  accepting final release, 242–244

  acquiring skills needed to launch, 240–242

  improving through player feedback, 246

  iterating, 244–245

  planning, 232–233

  in portfolios, 64

  post-production, 239–240

  pre-production, 234–236

  production, 236–238

  soft launch/launch, 237, 238

Procreate, 9, 72, 73, 76–77, 140

production, 34, 309

production phase, of game design, 35, 236–238

productivity, improving, 256–258

progress tracking, 273

progression, 86, 101, 309

progression curves, 105

progression systems

  about, 104–105

  creating, 89–90

  creating rewards structures, 106–107

  examples of, 107–108

  structuring leveling systems, 105–106

project management, 72, 78–81

project planning, 219–220

promotional material, 268

props, in art style guide (ASG), 142

Protospiel, 201

prototypes, 34, 35, 38, 223, 309

prototyping

  about, 60–63

  as a skill of game designers, 48

  in spreadsheets, 234–235

  tools for, 72

PS4, 9–10

psychological aspects, of gaming, 21–22

publishing

  about, 283

  defined, 309

  methods for, 283–289

  platforms for, 289–292

  self-, 286–288

punishment, as player motivation, 21

putting pen to paper, 73

puzzle game designers, 45

PvP arenas/battlegrounds, 112

Python, 194

Q

quality assurance

  defined, 309

  publishing partners for, 284

quests, 85

Quixel Suite, 141

R

R, 194

ranking, 273

razor statements, 38, 226–227, 309

Rec Room, 111

Reddit, 110, 111, 163, 200

references, in art style guide (ASG), 141

registering work, 30

release, 223, 309

release date, 274

Remember icon, 3

renderer, 152

replayability, 84

representation, in art style, 155–156

reputation systems, 108

researching, 212–213, 273

resolution, 124

About the Author

Alexia Mandeville is a co-founder and game designer at Bodeville, an independent studio creating narrative games. She's an assistant professor of game design at ArtCenter College of Design in Pasadena, California. She's also a former Game Designer at Niantic and Meta.

Author's Acknowledgments

I have far too many people to thank in this section. I've had the privilege of working with countless individuals throughout my career. I've been fortunate to learn from so many talented and hardworking people who love making games and products.

First and foremost, however, I want to thank my editors: Jennifer Yee for giving me this opportunity with Wiley; Nicole Sholly for being an exceptional editor; and Dino Ignacio — an incredible designer, mentor, and my first manager at Facebook — who served as the technical editor.

I'm also grateful to my partner, Joseph, for always being my go-to playtester; and my friend Kat, for reading my blogs and offering feedback on my writing; and my friend Bo, who took a leap into the games business with me.

To everyone else who has influenced, supported, or inspired me along the way . . . thank you!

Publisher's Acknowledgments

Acquisitions Editor: Jennifer Yee

Project Manager/Development Editor:
Nicole Sholly

Copy Editor: Kelly Henthorne

Technical Editor: Dino Ignacio

Managing Editor: Sofia Malik

Cover Image: © Gorodenkoff/Shutterstock

Printed and bound by CPI Group (UK) Ltd, Croydon, CR0 4YY

24/11/2025

14777866-0001